"... The world overcomes us, not merely by appealing to our reason, or by exciting our passions, but by imposing on our imagination."

JOHN HENRY NEWMAN,
Fifteen Sermons Preached before the University of Oxford, Sermon VII.2

"Give me a lover, and he feels what I say. Give me one that longs, that hungers, one that is traveling in this wilderness, and thirsting and panting after the fountain of his eternal home, give such and he knows what I am saying."

AUGUSTINE,
Tractatus in Evangelium Ioannis 26.4

"... He who loved her beauty, knew her to be also beautiful within. What are those inward charms? Those of conscience. It is there Christ sees her; it is there that Christ loves her; it is there He addresses her, there punishes, there crowns."

AUGUSTINE,
Enarrationes in Psalmos 45.27

THE ACT OF FAITH

Christian Faith and the Moral Self

ERIC O. SPRINGSTED

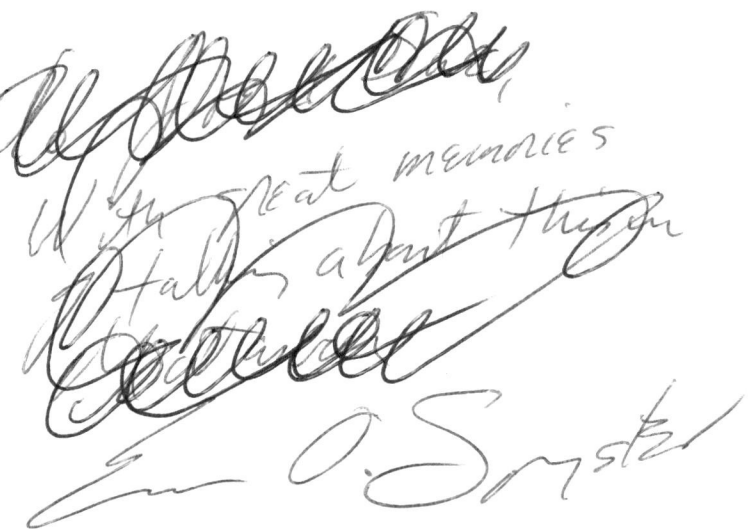

William B. Eerdmans Publishing Company
Grand Rapids, Michigan / Cambridge, U.K.

© 2002 Wm. B. Eerdmans Publishing Co.
All rights reserved

Wm. B. Eerdmans Publishing Co.
255 Jefferson Ave. S.E., Grand Rapids, Michigan 49503 /
P.O. Box 163, Cambridge CB3 9PU U.K.

Printed in the United States of America

07 06 05 04 03 02   7 6 5 4 3 2 1

Library of Congress Cataloging-in-Publication Data

Springsted, Eric O.
    The act of faith: Christian faith and the moral self / Eric O. Springsted.
       p.   cm.
    Includes bibliographical references.
    ISBN 0-8028-4888-5 (pbk.: alk. paper)
    1. Faith. 2. Christian ethics. 3. Faith — History of doctrines.
    4. Christian ethics — History. I. Title.

BT771.3.S67 2002
234'.23 — dc21
                                    2001053853

www.eerdmans.com

CONTENTS

Abbreviations of Classical and Frequently Cited Sources   vii

Preface   ix

I. Reason and the Reasons of the Heart   1
    1. Introduction: The Heart Has Its Reasons   1
    2. The Lockean-Humean Picture   7
    3. The Spectator's View   24
    4. Shattering the Mirror of Nature   33

II. Moral Space   45
    1. The Notion of Moral Space   45
    2. The Center of Value   48

III. The Concept of Faith in the New Testament   69
    1. Faith and Faith in Christ   71
    2. Paul   79
    3. John   94
    4. The Letter to the Hebrews   100

CONTENTS

IV. Augustine   105

    1. *Will and Order: The Moral Self in Augustine's De Libero Arbitrio*   107

    2. *Faith, Understanding, and the Moral Self: Authority*   119

    3. *The Word and the Inner Word*   133

V. Aquinas and Calvin   149

    1. *Catholics and Protestants: Ancient and Modern*   149

    2. *Aquinas on Faith*   157

    3. *Calvin and "Reformed Epistemology"*   175

    4. *Summary*   190

VI. Attention and the Embodied Self   193

    1. *Nussbaum's Enriched Liberalism*   196

    2. *Simone Weil and the Formation of Attention*   203

    3. *Conclusion*   211

VII. Conscience, Faith, and the Knowledge of God   215

    1. *Souls and Life in the Good*   215

    2. *Thinking with Assent: The "Inner" Act of Faith*   223

    3. *Faith in God*   242

    4. *Conclusion*   251

    Bibliography   254

    Index   266

ABBREVIATIONS OF CLASSICAL AND FREQUENTLY CITED SOURCES

Augustine

Ad.S	*De Diversibus Quaestionibus ad Simplicianum* (To Simplician — On Various Questions)
C. Ep. Man.	*Contra Epistulam Manichaei Quam Vocant Fundamenti* (Against the Epistle of Manichaeus Called Fundamental)
Civ. Dei	*De Civitate Dei* (The City of God)
Conf.	*Confessiones* (Confessions)
De Doct.	*De Doctrina Christiana* (Christian Teaching)
De Gen. ad Litt.	*De Genesi ad Litteram*
De Lib.	*De Libero Arbitrio* (On Free Choice of the Will)
De. Mor.	*De Moribus Ecclesiae Catholicae* (On the Morals of the Catholic Church)
De Mor. Man.	*De Moribus Manichaeorum* (On the Morals of the Manichaeans)
De Praed.	*De Praedestinatione Sanctorum* (On the Predestination of the Saints)
De Trin.	*De Trinitate* (The Trinity)
De Util.	*De Utilitate Credendi* (The Usefulness of Belief)
De Ver.	*De Vera Religione* (Of True Religion)
En. in Ps.	*Enarrationes in Psalmos* (Expositions on the Book of Psalms)
Retract.	*Retractationes* (Retractions)

ABBREVIATIONS OF CLASSICAL AND FREQUENTLY CITED SOURCES

Sol. *Soliloquia* (Soliloquies)
Tr. in Io. *Tractatus in Evangelium Ioannis* (Sermons on the Gospel of John)

Thomas Aquinas
ST *Summa Theologiae*
De Ver. *De Veritate* (Truth)

John Calvin
Instit. *The Institutes of the Christian Religion*

John Locke
Essay *An Essay concerning Human Understanding*

John Henry Newman
GA *Grammar of Assent*
US *Fifteen Sermons Preached before the University of Oxford between A.D. 1825 and 1843*
PP *Parochial and Plain Sermons*

Charles Taylor
Sources *Sources of the Self*

Simone Weil
SW *Simone Weil: Writings Selected with an Introduction by Eric O. Springsted*

PREFACE

When I first began teaching, a good share of my instructional duties involved courses that fulfilled the school's two-course Religion requirement. At the beginning of each course I informally quizzed students about their religious knowledge. Repeated inquiries over a number of years yielded the consistent result that fully 80 percent did not know who the Trinity is. This was in a school in which 90 percent of the students were self-reported Christians. Even the Catholic students who came from parochial schools and found the requirement onerous because they had taken "Religion" for the last several years knew no better than their Protestant classmates. Reasoning that if it were not a moral outrage for somebody who believed in the existence of matter to teach physics, then it would not be one for me to teach theology, I did so with a course titled "Basic Questions of the Christian Faith." The course began with an examination of the notion of faith itself. Another informal survey at the beginning of this course gave no cause for surprise. The vast majority thought faith was "believing something without proof." The surprise came after.

In the first years of the course the students read Tillich's *Dynamics of Faith* in order to come to grips with what faith is. For my generation and the generations before us, that book had opened our eyes widely, and as quickly as the snapping on of a light in a dark room. But they found it very tough going, nearly incomprehensible. This was the 1980s, and the great causes that had fixed my generation's attention, and that made the idea of an "ultimate concern" so very obvious, were gone. So apparently was any pervading

PREFACE

sense of a centered personality. "Virtual" personality had replaced it, as one could be thought to be one thing in one context and somebody quite different in another, neither of which was the real person; one simply projected images. Students would attend significant events in their lives, such as a graduation ball, and worry about "making memories" — looking at how they looked, not actually doing anything. Well, so much for Tillich's view that everybody has an ultimate concern. A practical paganism of several different goods without unity now held the day, something a booming economy and technology could aid and abet. But at the end of the course what truly puzzled me was that no matter whom we read, the number of those who still thought faith was belief without proof and that was all it was, even if they were sincere believers themselves, was little changed.

Over the course of the next several years my own philosophical and theological interests came to include more and more matters of social and moral philosophy, especially what it means to think *within* a personal and social context. Doing so makes many, many philosophical and theological problems look very different, particularly those that touch on the good. They are not *just* intellectual problems as we normally define "intellectual"; they are, as thought by somebody, self-involving, and that affects how we think about them. Moreover, how we think about ourselves affects how we think about these kinds of problems. But how we have thought about who we are as selves has varied. It was then that I began to see what had been going on with my students when they tried to think about faith. The inability to see faith consistently as "trust," "ultimate concern," or any similar thing was linked to a sense of the liberal, autonomous self that sets the horizons of political and moral choices, and only much more shallowly to any supposed conflict between science and religion, or faith and philosophy. Faith was a "personal" choice (albeit in a shallow sense of "personal"), the choice of a person who chose from the outside, and did so habitually. If they didn't know who the Trinity is, they did know to a person how society came to be. Without ever having read a word of Locke, they could reproduce his notion of the social contract without a doubt in the world. The idea of faith as knowledge gained by interpersonal dealings, or as a matter of being linked to a tradition, a history, or a community, didn't make sense because traditions, history, and communities didn't make sense at any deep level. All those things, all those relations were accidental, and largely free choices. How different that is, say, from Calvin who saw us as naturally related to each other because of a common parentage! Here then lies the concern that looms over this book. As John Henry Newman suggested, the world overcomes us not by appealing to our passions or our reason, but by imposing on our imaginations. Our imaginations have been severely imposed upon since the Enlightenment, for we imagine that we can observe the world from the vantage point of God himself, as if our descriptions and choices did not give us away.

That sense of distance, of radical reflexivity about the goods most important to us, was not how the Christian world before the Enlightenment saw things, although they knew well the need to distance oneself from the immediacy of the passions that distort rather than enhance our standing as persons. The self for that world was a "moral self": it was defined by character; questions of good were personal questions, and personal questions were questions of a good that surrounded human life and knit it together, and knit humanity to itself. Their understanding of Christian faith dwelt within that space. That is what I intend to argue is the case with some of the most important contributors to the concept of faith in the Christian tradition: Paul, John, the author of the Letter to the Hebrews, Augustine, Aquinas, and Calvin. There are, of course, differences in how these figures describe the concept of faith. Calvin was a humanist — sometimes; Aquinas depends on a highly complex theory of the virtues; Augustine uses the concept of an "inner word." They varied also in how they treated the related issue of grace and the free will. But despite the differences there are certain vital important characteristics that they variously share, namely:

1. Some sense of an inner aspiration to a perfect good, a sense of some kind of *fides humana*, although they do differ in how sharply they distinguish that from divine faith. All do distinguish it in some sense from *fides divina*, and none try to build Christian faith out of it. If anything, it is quite the opposite; the sense of having found the will's perfect good, or more accurately, the way to that good in Christian faith, causes them to describe *fides humana* the way they do.
2. The revelation of Christ as opening up a new "space" for imagination, thought, and the will. The perfect good that God offers in Christ is not a simple development of conscience, but a specific act of revelation that opens up the fulfillment of conscience and gives what conscience only hopes for on its own. Faith is then a matter not only of trusting, but also of waiting, and a radical openness to being taught. Theology is a matter of being a student, not a teacher.

PREFACE

3. Faith is personal especially in the sense that faith is *participation* in God. This means at least that the role of the will in faith is less to will propositions as such and more to fix one's focus on God, to identify with God. Life is then continual interaction with God, fed by God. It is a matter of the will and self identifying with God in order to be taught by God. We are to become what we think.
4. This participation in God is also a matter of participation with other human beings in a historical community. Indeed, God is chiefly known through life in this community, and the concept of faith cannot be divorced from this space opened by God. All therefore link faith to crucial communal practices — moral, sacramental — as well as to doctrinal traditions.

The understanding of the nature of faith that I am urging is one that can be called Augustinian. Augustine, of course, did not *invent* it. What he wrote is deeply indebted to the Scriptures, especially Paul and John. He also was, as were most serious thinkers of his age, a Platonist. Perhaps the Platonism at times did create an odd bastard when mated with the Scriptures, but much less so than many contemporary would-be liberators from Greek thinking would have us think. Especially with respect to how they understood the self, Isaiah, Paul, and John may well have had more in common with Plato — and Augustine — than they have with us, and it is a presumptive conceit to think otherwise. Certainly many of the brightest lights in the generations that followed them thought so. (They may also have understood what Plato was getting at far more clearly than we do.) It may very well have been the mix that allowed Augustine to think clearly about what Paul had said about faith being "Christ in me," or what John had said about the Word and what it means to believe *in* it. What Augustine was after was not the beginning of Western thinking's unholy individualism, but his articulation of what Eastern theologians were already calling *theiosis* — "divinization," the formation of the self in the image of God within the living communal embodiment of Christ, the Church. So Augustine did not invent this notion of faith on this account, either. But he did focus it for the West, and provided for the West the framework by which to understand the gospel call for faith. Augustine was serious when he said already in the *Soliloquies* that all he wanted to know was God and the soul. That runs throughout all his thinking, even if he matured in how he approached the issue. But that is not only all that he wanted to know; the very issue of what it is as a soul to know God occupies him continually also. These are his chief issues, and it is on these issues that the modern world began to lose the concept of faith as something that is personal and a matter of participation. Not only are these Augustine's issues, they are Aquinas's and Calvin's, and Pascal's, too. If some of the other chief figures of this book — Newman, Kierkegaard, Simone Weil — are not the conscious readers of Augustine that Aquinas and Calvin were, nevertheless, they too are participants in the Augustinian tradition, for they put the heart's thirst for good at the center of their understanding of faith. And perhaps because they were not conscious students of Augustine, their own distinctive contributions make Augustinianism, at least with respect to the concept of faith, that much more accessible.

I owe many thanks to many for their support, questions, and advice. The first draft of this book was written while I was a resident member of the Center of Theological Inquiry in Princeton. One cannot imagine a better place to work, a more supportive staff, or better colleagues. The discussions at the Center were immensely helpful. Portions of this work were also presented during the 1998 Institute of Theology at Princeton Theological Seminary, and as a series of lectures for a Lenten Studies series at Madison Avenue Presbyterian Church in 1999. I thank Fred Anderson of "MAPC" for the kind invitation to give the series. Dan Migliore, Sandy McKelway, and Diogenes Allen read portions of the manuscript and made helpful suggestions. I owe Allen particular thanks for work that he did many years ago on conscience, which I have obviously made use of. Alan Padgett, Ellen Charry, and Larry Schmidt read early versions of the full manuscript, for which I am extremely grateful since their suggestions were vital to reducing the blooming confusion it tended toward. Portions of this book have appeared in different form as: "Spirituality and Theology: Why Theology Is Not Critical Reflection on Religious Experience" in *Spirituality and Theology: Essays in Honor of Diogenes Allen* (Louisville: Westminster/John Knox, 1998); "Loving Neighbor: Having a Soul and Being a Moral Self" in *Arob@se: Journal des lettres et sciences humaines* 4.3; "La politique de la perception" in *Cahiers Simone Weil* XXII.2; "Will and Order: The Moral Self in Augustine's *De Libero Arbitrio*" in *Augustinian Studies* 29.2; and a review from *Philosophical Investigations,* 22.2.

I owe greatest thanks and gratitude to my wife Brenda, and to our daughters Simone, Leidy, and Elspeth for their support and encouragement, patience and interest, which made the effort worth the candle.

CHAPTER I

Reason and the Reasons of the Heart

1. INTRODUCTION:
   THE HEART HAS ITS REASONS

Blaise Pascal in his *Pensées* in an imaginary scenario tells a story that illustrates the nature of faith. Ironically, few stories in their subsequent retellings have illustrated so well the modern world's *misunderstandings* about the nature of faith, misunderstandings that range from the title given it by textbooks — "The Wager *Argument*," suggesting that it is an argument to make belief in God rational — to the various points that are commonly taken away from it.

Pascal's story is that of a gambler who is confronted with the option of Christian faith. He is not inclined to exercise it. He is then presented with an argument that suggests, in a way that appeals to where a gambler's treasure is, that faith is a good bet. If there *is* an eternity, then he should believe, for by giving up all he personally owns to, which is a finite matter after all, he stands to reap an infinite reward. On the other hand, if there is no eternity, whatever he might lose by believing is simply finite. Thus the expected return on this bet outweighs any possible loss he might incur. As the story continues — and this is its point — the gambler despite seeing the virtues of the wager, despite seeing its reasonableness, simply cannot make the bet. Pascal then suggests a way out for him. He tells him to follow the example of many before him. He says: "Follow the way by which they

THE ACT OF FAITH

began. They behaved just as if they did believe, taking holy water, having masses said, and so on."[1]

Pascal's point in this story is that faith cannot be exercised simply by reasoning ourselves into it. There are other aspects of our lives, such as our baser passions, that war against our reason, and that keep us from making commitments we know we should make. This does not mean that faith is a matter for the passions, though. Rather faith is a matter of the heart. As he says in a well-known phrase, "the heart has its reasons that the reason does not know." But until the passions are quieted, the heart's deeper desires cannot be fulfilled. So neither intellect itself nor the passions are the key to faith. It is the gambler's passions that keep him from making the bet and living out the reasons of the heart. It is his life's commitments that keep him from it. That is why Pascal recommends acting as if he believed, for the gambler's problem is not one of reason (he understands the nature of the bet); it is one of the heart and of action. It is only by bringing his life into conformity with what he bets on that he will be able to commit himself.[2]

That, however, is rarely the way the story is taken. Frequently the wager itself is taken as the point of the story, as if Pascal thought that we could argue ourselves into faith. Just as often Pascal is taken to be suggesting that we can simply will faith. Thus with respect to the advice that the gambler "act as if he believed," Pascal has been taken to recommend everything from making faith into a matter of fraudulent auto-suggestion to inviting dishonesty and superstition. Just why approaching faith as Pascal seems to in this story is appalling to many people can be seen in another story, this one told by the American philosopher W. K. Clifford:[3] A ship

---

1. Blaise Pascal, *Pensées*, trans. A. J. Krailsheimer (London: Penguin Books, 1995), p. 125.

2. On this point cf. Diogenes Allen, *Three Outsiders: Pascal, Kierkegaard, and Simone Weil* (Cambridge, Mass.: Cowley Publications, 1983), pp. 39-40: "The Wager Argument is thus used to show a particular kind of person who does not believe that it is his passions, not intellectual reasons, which hinder his belief, and Pascal offers him a way to overcome this particular barrier to belief. So the Wager Argument belongs to the level of the 'flesh,' which is below the level of the mind." I would add one point to Allen's observation: not only is there an issue here of overcoming the passions; by directing the gambler to partake of religious life, Pascal is also in effect recommending that the gambler make *contact*. His approach has to be concrete, not abstract and distant.

3. "The Ethics of Belief" from *Lectures and Essays* (1879).

2

owner was about to put a ship to sea filled with many emigrants hoping to go to a new land. He had many reasons to doubt the seaworthiness of the ship, however, and that caused him many doubts about whether he should let it sail. Nevertheless, in time, he was able to overcome these doubts, reasoning that in years past when it was young the ship had weathered many storms, and also reasoning that Providence could not fail to protect all these worthy emigrants. Thus he let it sail, and in time collected his insurance money when it went down in mid-ocean. This man, Clifford contended, was guilty of the death of all those people, for he had no reason to believe on such evidence as was before him. He did not earn his faith in Providence by examining Providence; he simply stifled his doubts. Such would also seem to be the case with Pascal's gambler and others who have religious faith without having first examined the evidence.

Clifford's appeal appears to be common sense not only in things worldly, but also things religious. That is to say, we assume as a matter of course that belief — e.g., belief that God exists, that God is good, that God is capable of doing the things that religious people claim God is capable of doing — must be established, at least with some probability, before we can put our trust, our faith, in God. The thought seems obvious at first blush. If we did not first believe that God exists, if we did not already believe that God is good, we could not trust God. And yet for all the apparent obviousness of this approach to thinking about faith and belief, it is wrong. Pascal thought it was wrong, as well as any number of Christian thinkers from St. Paul to Augustine to Aquinas to Calvin, Newman, and Kierkegaard.

Why Pascal and Clifford differ is important to understand, for their disagreement lies chiefly in their characterization and understanding of the nature of faith. For Pascal, faith is a matter of the heart, and understanding that God is — and what God is — can be severely limited if the heart is not engaged. Indeed, there is no *real* knowledge of God without it, only the knowledge of the philosophers. But consider the sort of air that talk like that of Clifford has. It gives a sense that one first stands apart from what might be committed to, apart from what one might have faith in, and from that distance one simply surveys the landscape of possibilities. It is only from that vantage point and after such a survey that one can legitimately decide whether or not to commit oneself. Now, this process works fine when trying to determine whether or not a ship should sail. Indeed, as Clifford saw, such judgment is ethically demanded. And it works fine for anything we can survey and have knowledge about from a distant stand-

THE ACT OF FAITH

point. It works fine in cases where engineering decisions have to be made; it works fine when arrangements for travel are undertaken; it works fine when one cooks dinner.

But this method does not work with everything. It does not work very well with things that we do not have control over or with things that we can only know by committing ourselves to them — things that we do not know all about ahead of time, things that we have to work with in order to know them. It particularly does not work very well with persons. When we want to get to know somebody better, usually the only way of finding out what she is really like is by dealing with her. We can't send out a private detective to give us all the evidence ahead of time. Indeed, if someone knew that we had ever done such a thing, we would fail to get to know most things about her, including her telephone number. The man who tries to decide whether the institution of marriage is meaningful or not, may or may not reach an answer, but is not likely to get a wife for having done so, for such a person fails to understand that what counts in marriage is nothing less than a full-fledged commitment to another person.

This method also does not work very well with God. For God is not a possibility we can survey; God is not even the sum of possibilities. God is not even the meaning of our lives; He is the creator of them and the Word that upholds every thought we have, including thoughts about God and meaning. For that reason we can never stand back and survey the evidence, for whatever evidence there is, and whatever surveying might be done, is nothing more than what God has created and what God is at the very heart of. As the psalmist sang: "O Lord, Thou hast searched me and known me. Thou knowest when I sit down and when I rise up; Thou discernest my thoughts from afar. Thou . . . art acquainted with all my ways. Even before a word is on my lips Thou knowest it altogether" (Ps. 139:1-2). Because, as the psalmist understood, God is at the very heart of our being, creating whatever being we might have, there is no standing apart from God and surveying the possibilities. There is with God, as with human beings, only responding to their presence. For their very existence addresses us and demands a response. What we then come to know of their existence very much depends upon how we respond to that address.

Throughout his writings St. Augustine frequently quotes a passage from Isaiah that he translates this way: "Unless you have faith, you will not understand." What he meant was that understanding, which is something much deeper and more profound than mere knowledge, comes only when we respond with ourselves, with our hearts and minds and bodies to that by which we are addressed. It only comes when we respond with our commitment and trust. For Augustine, God's Word, the Word by which all things are created, addresses itself continually to the human heart. Our response to that Word, our faith in that Word, is the very beginning of our coming to understand; not understanding simply either the world or ourselves, but of understanding at all, for what is understanding but the acceptance and love of all that is created? We can know many things and reason about many things without loving them; we can reason about them and know them from great distances. But *understanding* means accepting and loving them as God created them. It is only when we understand things in this way that we will ever know what we believe about them.

Thus there is a stark contrast between the way that Pascal and Augustine approach faith and the way Clifford does. For Pascal faith is a matter of the heart, something more than mere belief. It is a matter of responding to a personal demand. For Clifford, for faith to be at all morally acceptable it must involve a neutral survey of possibilities before we commit ourselves to them. This contrast, however, is not simply a difference between two philosophers' views of the world. In the difference lie embedded crucial differences in the way entire ages have looked at faith. The late Wilfred Cantwell Smith argued that the very idea of religion as "belief" as we now use it is a modern invention whose grammar and usage differs markedly from what historically had been understood by the term "faith."[4] Not only does it differ, it is simply *other* than what "faith" and an older usage of "believe" conveyed.

For the ancient and medieval world, faith was primarily a commitment of the person, and was construed within personal categories. The Latin *credo* has as its root the word *cor* (heart). To say "*credo*" meant to set one's heart. Similarly the medieval English "believe" derived from the German *belieben* — "to hold dear" or "to prize," with its root in *Liebe* — "love." When used as a verb, its object was generally a person; even when it was a statement that was believed, it was believed on the credit of a person. The subject of the verb most frequently was "I" or "you." To believe then was to commit oneself, and "I believe" was chiefly a performative statement. To believe in God and God's goodness was self-involving; it was not

---

4. Wilfred Cantwell Smith, *Belief and History* (Charlottesville, Va.: University of Virginia Press, 1977).

THE ACT OF FAITH

a report on a fact to which we can be indifferent.[5] To believe in God in this way therefore entailed an entire life — to renounce the Devil and all his works, etc. — and its meaning derived from that life. It was a question of self-engagement, as Pascal saw. In its relation to "truth" it was a positive affirmation and commitment to truth.

"Belief" in the modern sense moves in quite the opposite direction. Whereas earlier faith was in persons and was the self-involving commitment of a person, "belief" came over time to become directed more and more at ahistorical propositions as such. It also came to be a matter of third-person descriptions — of what *somebody* believes, of religion as a "belief system," and a state of mind.[6] These two changes show a "growing impersonalism both of the object and of the subject of our verb; and the growing abstraction. . . . 'Believe' is a word that used to conceptualize something solid in the realm of interpersonal relations. . . . Today, on the other hand, it has come by a slow steady process to designate something else, in quite another realm, for all but a small minority."[7] Finally, "believing" has come to be severed from its link with truth, and is frequently sharply *contrasted* with knowledge. In the modern world Mark Twain could get a laugh by claiming in the mouth of a schoolboy that "faith is believing what you know ain't true."[8] A medieval would not have gotten the joke.

Pascal's and Clifford's positions illustrate a radical shift in the understanding of "faith" or religious belief. Pascal, on the one hand, represents a traditional Augustinian view. Faith is a matter of the heart, an engagement of the whole person. Clifford, on the other hand, represents the modern view in which faith is put on a continuum with intellectual positions that we can be initially indifferent to. What was it that caused the shift? How did faith come to be seen as something that had to be justified in a neutral epistemological court? The investigation is not an idle one for the simple reason that we very much stand under the modern view. Everything is af-

---

5. On this point also cf. Donald D. Evans, *The Logic of Self-Involvement: A Philosophical Study of Everyday Language with Special Reference to the Christian Use of Language about God as Creator* (London: SCM Press, 1963).

6. On belief as a state of mind, cf. H. H. Price, *Belief* (London: George Allen & Unwin, 1969).

7. Smith, *Belief and History*, p. 58.

8. Smith, *Belief and History*, p. 66.

fected: our understanding of faith, of course, but also of God, of persons, of theology, of the conceptual relations between science and religion.

2. THE LOCKEAN-HUMEAN PICTURE

2.1. Hume's Dismissal of Religion

We may first consider the nature of the shift by looking at how faith's relation to reason has been discussed philosophically in the modern world. The *locus classicus* is found in one of the undisputedly most important texts in modern philosophy of religion, David Hume's *Dialogues Concerning Natural Religion*. The *Dialogues* crystallize a discussion that had been going on for a hundred years; in the next two hundred they will have provided in that crystallization not only many of the chief issues concerning the relation of faith and reason but also the distinctive *approach* of the modern world to the concept of faith.

The *Dialogues* have three discussants: first, Demea, a believer of classical but much outdated stripe, who thinks God is a mystery and that reason is inappropriately applied to knowledge of God, particularly the way his conversational partners apply it. Second is Cleanthes, a Deist who reflects his age's concern with reason, and who believes in a God he refuses to make any claims for that he does not think are based in obvious analogies and evident chains of inference. Specifically, he believes that since the world is so obviously like a machine (he, like his age, is under the influence of a Newtonian metaphor) and machines have makers, that the world has a maker. That is where reason takes him, and he refuses to go any further, denying claims of God's ultimacy and omnipotence. His claims are therefore for a God that is quite limited in relation to the one Demea claims to worship. The third conversational partner is Philo, the skeptic. The upshot of their discussion is, first, but almost as a sidelight, the dismissal of Demea as foolish and having little to say. Philo's reaction to his claims is the key here. Like Demea, Philo is willing to say that if there is a God, God is a mystery. But for the ironical Philo this means that the less a reasonable person says about God, the more reasonable he will be. It takes the naïve Demea some time to realize that he has been toyed with throughout the discussion. Cleanthes, who claims to stand on reason alone, is given much more of a hearing. But in the course of the argument, it becomes clear that

THE ACT OF FAITH

even he can't say very much. Even if his basic intuition has plausibility, other analogies do too, Philo suggests. For example, the world may be seen as being like a vegetable; it is also just as plausible to think that it is an accident. And, Philo keeps repeating, surely it goes beyond the realm of possible experience to infer from a slim analogy between the world and a machine that there *has* to be a world maker, much less to infer any positive qualities of the maker.

The point to be taken home from reading Hume's *Dialogues* is not Hume's apparent dismissal of religion. Instead it is the sort of problem he recognizes in discussions before him and that he sets for future discussion. That problem is that religious claims need to be justified, and justified in terms that answer to the question, "How do you know that?" Demea is treated as a fool because he refuses even to engage the question. Cleanthes, already the inheritor of a philosophical tradition that believes one ought to answer this question, is given a hearing because he is willing to provide reasons and to assent to no more than reasoning will allow. But alas, the conclusion of that tradition is Philo's skepticism, for, as it turns out, Cleanthes doesn't have very good reasons after all. Thus, we learn, for faith to be reasonable it has to have some kind of reasons for asserting that there is a God to believe in, and for asserting any particular qualities about that God.

The positions of Philo and Cleanthes are the ones that have commanded the most attention. But it is perhaps instructive to ask why Demea is *not* taken seriously. He is not as much of a straw man as first appears. His views on faith and reason, and the nature of faith and its object, are well drawn and they fairly represent important views of an earlier day, views that at one time commanded, in one form or another, a great deal of respect. Why, then, can Hume brush him off so easily now? What has happened so that Cleanthes thinks for his part that he *has* to water down the divinity he worships, saying no more about God than a faddish analogy and inference will allow? Why does Cleanthes thereby in portraying the reasonable man of faith make "reasonable faith" so vulnerable to Philo's even more reasonable skepticism? Clearly a change has taken place here.

2.2. Locke's Evidentiary Faith

What that change involves can be seen in Hume's English predecessor, John Locke. Locke is a pivotal figure in this story, both for what he says as

8

an original thinker and also insofar as he reflects and articulates important religious and intellectual changes about the nature of faith, reason, and the human person in Western culture. He provides a dominating picture that continues to exercise great influence even to the present. Locke was one of those rare thinkers who was not only original, but who could also draw together important threads of the fermenting intellectual and cultural life of his age. His authority and interest for us thus is not so much as a dominating intellect, but the sense he shows of an age and the creativity he used in giving it coherent, although perhaps mythical, shape. Historically, Locke reflects changes that were both broad and deep in his own day. But they are not necessarily things *we* recognize now as being changes. They now tend to be nearly bedrock assumptions in our thinking about these matters. For that reason they need to be brought to the light.

In his *Essay Concerning Human Understanding* of 1690, Locke proposes to discover the nature of human understanding. Following an ancient principle of Aristotle (and Aquinas), he asserts that there is nothing in the understanding that was not first in the senses. Knowledge cannot be had by mere ideas alone; ideas must be rooted in sense experience. How we understand comes about by the association of our empirically rooted ideas, their combination and mixing. These explanations of understanding need not detain us. What is of more interest to us is his concluding discussion of knowledge in Book IV.[9] According to Locke, knowledge can be of only three kinds. *Intuition* is when "the mind perceives the agreement or disagreement of two ideas immediately by themselves, without the intervention of any other" (Essay IV.2). *Demonstrative knowledge,* which is not so easy or clear as intuitive knowledge, is when this immediacy of agreement or disagreement does not strike the mind, so the mind has to rely on proofs. Each step in the proof must be intuitive, though; together these small intuitive steps allow us to discover the truth of complicated propositions. A complicated mathematical proof is a good example of demonstration, but demonstrative knowledge is not limited to mathematics.[10] Finally, there is *sensitive knowledge,* wherein we have intuitive knowledge "about the particular existence of finite beings without (i.e., external to)

---

9. For an extensive discussion of Locke on the problems here presented cf. Nicholas Wolterstorff, *John Locke and the Ethics of Belief* (Cambridge: Cambridge University Press, 1996).

10. Essay IV.2, pp. 262-65.

us" (Essay IV.2). Further knowledge of particulars, e.g., quality, category, etc., depends on bringing additional ideas into play. For Locke, any *knowledge* has to be rooted in one of these three; "whatever comes short of one of these, with what assurance so embraced, is but *faith* or *opinion*, but not knowledge" (Essay IV.2), lacking the certainty and "assurance" of knowledge.

To understand Locke's overall picture, there are three further points to keep in mind. First, Locke's standards for knowledge are rather elevated. Thus knowledge as knowledge is actually rather rarely gotten for Locke.[11] Even in the course of well-directed human understanding there are simply not many instances when it can be found. What we usually are dealing with in the understanding is therefore probable relations of ideas. Second, because knowledge is an association of ideas, knowledge is always of propositions, "verbal or mental." Third, because of the gap between knowledge and probable propositions, and for reasons that shall become clearer in a moment, one has a moral duty not to put more credence in any proposition than the evidence for that proposition warrants. Because we cannot *know* most propositions, the degree of assurance we can take in them therefore has limits. A proper use of the understanding involves recognizing those limits and tailoring our assent proportionally. That recognition is dictated by the evidence that can be afforded them.[12]

What does all this mean for belief in God? Surprisingly (to us) Locke is really quite optimistic about the rationality of such belief. Following his own insistence that the object of the understanding is propositions, particularly propositions about empirical fact, he considers faith in God to

---

11. Wolterstorff, *John Locke and the Ethics of Belief*, p. 37.

12. This gives rise to what is called "evidentialism," which philosophically requires us to provide evidence for whatever proposition we assert. Evidentialism is currently enjoying much less favor than it did in the past. It is important to keep in mind, though, the overall picture in which it plays a role, for the concern for finding evidence is tightly tied in that picture to what is called "the ethics of belief," the view that one has a *moral* duty not to assent to any belief that is not rational. The classic text in the ethics of belief debate is W. K. Clifford's "The Ethics of Belief," in *Lectures and Essays* (1879; reprinted in B. Brody, ed., *Readings in the Philosophy of Religion: An Analytic Approach* [Englewood Cliffs, N.J.: Prentice Hall, 1974]). Louis Pojman's *Religious Belief and the Will* (London: Routledge & Kegan Paul, 1986) and David Wisdo's *The Life of Irony and the Ethics of Belief* (Albany: State University of New York Press, 1993) present recent opposing views in the discussion and a thorough review of the debate.

Reason and the Reasons of the Heart

be belief in propositions that God has revealed. Since many of those propositions are anything but obvious, and since he also asserts that "revelation cannot be admitted against the clear evidence of reason" (Essay IV.18), it is surprising that he would be optimistic. However, Locke does believe that God's existence can be demonstrated,[13] and since faith is "the assent to any proposition, not thus made out by the deductions of reason, but upon the credit of the proposer" (Essay IV.18.2), a first important step can be taken toward faith by that demonstration. Because we can know that God exists, we can have faith in what God reveals. But how can we be sure that what is revealed is actually revealed by *God*? Evidence would appear to be needed for believing that. For Locke the evidence is provided by miracles.[14] Thus, in the end, faith in God is rational because we can know that God exists and we have evidence for what God has revealed by the testimony of miracles.

The picture that has dominated much modern philosophy of religion and even less sophisticated, popular understandings of the nature of faith now begins to come into view. Faith is a belief in matters of fact that we don't find at all obvious. If faith is at all rational, it is because (1) the existence of God is rationally defensible and we have rational grounds for assuming it, and (2) there is reason (in Locke's evidence) to have faith in what God has revealed. Conversely, of course, if faith is irrational it is because the existence of God cannot be rationally established and/or there is not good evidence to believe what it is said that God reveals. Between these two poles much of the modern field of philosophy of religion operates, arguing for and against such as things as demonstrations of God's existence, including discussions of whether the concept of God is coherent or not and thus whether it is even a possible candidate for demonstration, and arguing out topics such as the rationality of belief in miracles and the evidence for the claims of faith. Modern philosophy of religion is assuredly not simply a set of footnotes to Locke; there are profound objections to his conclusions, and Hume quickly provides many of them. Nevertheless, a picture like this has tended to encompass a great deal of what has been discussed within the field for the last three hundred years.

The details of the picture that emerges from Locke are, of course, not utterly novel. Ancient and medieval Christian philosophers certainly un-

---

13. Essay IV.10, pp. 310-12.
14. Essay IV.19.15.

11

THE ACT OF FAITH

derstood that faith believes things that cannot be rationally proved or grasped. Miracles, too, were often seen as providing evidence for supernatural claims. Indeed, in numerous biblical stories a miraculous occurrence engenders faith.[15] But it is novel in one particular way that can be seen by invoking an ancient formula for defining faith that Aquinas quotes from Augustine. According to this formula the act of faith can be distinguished in a threefold way. Christian faith for Augustine and Aquinas is a matter of "believing God" *(credere Deo)*, which is a matter of believing what God has said because God has said it. An example would be believing doctrine, which is revealed. Second, it is also a matter of "believing about God" *(credere Deum)* (or as it is also translated, "believing in a God"), which is a matter of believing certain things about God — e.g., that God exists, is omnipotent, is a Trinity, etc. Third, it is also "believing in God" *(credere in Deum)*, which is a matter of trusting and loving God, a matter of thinking "God" with assent. Locke's rational understanding of faith certainly involves the first two elements; it does not involve the third, however. But it is the third that was in prior Christian theologies of faith the most important. Christian faith as it was understood traditionally actually is driven by this third element. Without it, faith would amount to no more than the cognitive information that demons possess.[16] For Augustine and Aquinas and many others, the reason one has faith that God is a certain way, or even

---

15. E.g., Luke 5:1-11. Peter after fruitlessly fishing all night is told by Jesus to let out his nets again. When his nets are filled to the bursting point and he sees it, he falls on his knees and for the first time calls Jesus "Lord." Aquinas, too, thinks miracles provide evidence. Yet: "Aquinas emphasizes the value of miracles as confirming the supernatural origin of a revelation. Miracles, he thought, provide the best evidence that a revelation was genuine. However, even in Aquinas, this emphasis on what might be called objective, public evidence is not the whole story. In addition to the evidence of miracles, Aquinas mentions that the one who believes in the revelation is moved to believe by 'an inward impulse towards God, who invites him.' Such an 'inner impulse' does not look much like evidence in the normal sense" (C. Stephen Evans, *Faith Beyond Reason* [Grand Rapids: Eerdmans, 1998], p. 139).

16. Avery Dulles suggests how this formula operates in Aquinas: "Faith, for St. Thomas, is a dynamic perception. The mind, impelled by desire for union with the divine, cannot find its rest in propositions or created realities, but only in God himself. . . . For this reason, faith is not simply a belief in the authority of God *(credere Deo)*, or a belief in the existence and providence of God *(credere Deum)*, but also a belief that tends towards union with God *(credere in Deum)*" (*The Assurance of Things Hoped For: A Theology of Christian Faith* [Oxford: Oxford University Press, 1994], p. 5).

12

exists, and the reason one has faith to do what God has commanded is because one believes that one ought to do what the God who is loved commands — because it is God.[17] In Locke, on the other hand, one believes because one can demonstrate that God exists and because there is evidence for what is believed *outside* the personal relation that tends toward union.[18]

What this difference amounts to can be fleshed out by highlighting some crucial features that attend Locke's picture. These are features that tend to be even more important than the particulars of the picture itself and that have survived criticism of those particulars. They are features that give the picture its very shape.

Locke in discussing the rationality of faith is not trying to make reason the *source* of all our beliefs, but he is trying to make reason our guide, indeed, our sole guide.[19] In order to do this, he insists on a certain indiffer-

---

17. Cf., e.g., Augustine: "The devil believes, but does not love: no one loveth who doth not believe. . . . Therefore where there is love, there of necessity will there be faith and hope . . ." (Tr. in Io. 83.3).

18. To be sure, Locke does not overlook the problem, and argues that repentance and good works are necessary for faith; one can't *just* believe the same things that demons do and be counted a person of faith. (Cf. *The Reasonableness of Christianity*, secs. 164-67.) But that is *the* issue, not an inconvenient corollary. However, some gesture of complete fairness should be made to Locke himself. As is apparent in *Reasonableness,* Locke does, although somewhat grudgingly, hold together the three essential aspects of faith: intellectual appropriation, repentance — i.e., the act of turning to God to hold onto God as the source of salvation — and the living out of the Christian life. For that reason, his own faith, even if of doubtful doctrinal orthodoxy, probably should not be put into question. However, there really is something unstable about the way he holds them together, or at least the way he writes about them. Rather than taking the act of turning to God and holding onto God as the fulcrum that balances the practical Christian life and the intellectual appropriation of what is to be believed, he seems to have shifted the fulcrum to the intellectual appropriation; everything else now hinges on it. Thus upon being criticized that he is only proposing a mere historical faith, he is rather insistent that believing, that saving faith, is believing these historical propositions. That is why they were proposed in the first place, he claims. So one of the reasons that the issue of what the demons do or don't believe is irrelevant is that these propositions were never meant to be proposed to them for belief unto salvation. It is only when he senses that such a response may not be fully satisfactory to the critic who claims that this is only a historical faith, that he turns to consider repentance. This shift of weight to the intellectual destabilizes the integrity of faith as it had traditionally been understood.

19. Wolterstorff, *John Locke and the Ethics of Belief,* pp. 86-87.

ence to any matter under the consideration of the understanding. We are to be neutral as to the outcome, and should not assent to any conclusion that the understanding does not approve, no matter how much we would like to see it as true. This, of course, is what is at the heart of the matter of the "ethics of belief." We should not give any higher degree of assent to a proposition than the evidence for that proposition warrants. This would seem to be sound epistemological advice. Closer consideration, however, shows us that by insisting on this indifference a whole range of ways of forming beliefs is excluded. Locke understands this perfectly well since there are ways of forming beliefs that he really *does* want to exclude. One way is spiritual enthusiasm;[20] another is authority.[21] Within his own historical context, this is understandable. Writing in a world, as Descartes had before him, that was rent and fragmented by competing doctrinal authorities and spiritual prophets, Locke was particularly concerned to avoid what he called "the wounds of reason," which he considered both spiritual enthusiasm and reliance on authority to be. His insistence on reason thus needs to be seen as more than just a respect for reason. There are also cultural and political overtones, as indifferent reason becomes the polestar for a deep reorienting of the sorts of beliefs that had previously shaped and determined human life. To the extent that human life was coming apart in his age, the effort deserves respect. However, his emphasis on reason also comes to exclude certain vital aspects of human life together. "Authority," for example, can be understood as the root of an irrational "authoritarianism." It can also be, as the people who saw a difference between Jesus' teaching and that of the Pharisees understood, an indispensable interhuman mark for guiding human life.

To speak of "authority" as an interhuman mark for guiding human life lets us understand what is excluded by Locke's insistence on "indifference." It also lets us see somewhat more clearly how Locke's understanding of faith differs from Augustine and Aquinas. Whereas for those two faith conceptually involves an essential interpersonal element, e.g., the love of God, in Locke it is precisely the interpersonal that is excluded, or at least somewhat extraneous. Even if we grant Locke the legitimacy of his concerns about "the wounds of reason," by insisting on indifference, a whole range of reasons for approaching life in the way we do, reasons based on our per-

---

20. Essay IV.19.
21. Essay IV.20.17, p. 364.

sonal and interpersonal interests and concerns, is excluded. This just does not make sense. "Is it reasonable to expect a person to defend his or her religious convictions without making any reference to the kinds of religious questions and interests that inform and shape these beliefs?"[22]

Locke's approach has far-reaching consequences. It certainly involves a way in which we approach God different than that of Augustine or Pascal; whether, for example, we approach God with cognitive "indifference" or with a certain passionate interest, as Kierkegaard was later to insist. It also involves very different ways in what we take God's words to reveal. As Jean-Luc Marion states, "Christ calls himself the Word. He does not speak words inspired by God concerning God, but he abolishes in himself the gap between the speaker who states . . . and the sign. . . . In short, Christ does not say the word, he says *himself* the Word."[23] In Locke, Christ says words, he imparts information to be judged impartially. Similarly, miracles in Locke are evidence; they are not the "turn of the Spirit" to speak.[24]

2.3. Hume's Undoing of Locke's Optimism

It is certainly not the case that Locke's arguments have survived criticism intact. It is also not the case that the picture he paints is handed down to later philosophy whole cloth. His optimism certainly has not survived. But the shape of what is handed down is first given in Locke. As his way of shaping questions about faith was accepted and later enhanced, it further sharpened the differences between theologians such as Augustine, Aquinas, and Calvin and the modern view of faith, making those theologians difficult to understand sympathetically for many modern philosophers. Just how can be seen by returning briefly to Hume.

Hume, in the first place, undoes Locke's optimism chiefly by undermining Locke's arguments. Most importantly, as can be seen in the *Dialogues,* demonstrations of God's existence are excluded. At best, when Philo is finished, one is left with a weak analogical argument for a maker of the universe, and perhaps a vestigial sense of awe in the face of nature,

---

22. David Wisdo, *The Life of Irony,* p. 23.
23. Jean-Luc Marion, *God Without Being* (Chicago: University of Chicago Press, 1991), p. 140.
24. Marion, *God Without Being,* p. 142.

which for Hume is more powerful than any argument — and that is not very powerful. Furthermore, Hume is able to introduce a nearly unshakable doubt about the serviceability of miracles as evidence.[25] So at the end of the day we cannot demonstrate that God exists, and even if we could, we do not have sufficient evidence to say anything about God. The philosophical beauty of Hume's arguments is that they are based on an extension of Locke's own epistemological principles. If Locke's optimism and arguments are undone, however, his overall vision concerning the concept of faith itself, and its relation to reason, is not. Indeed, Hume has simply shown that Locke failed to play out the full implications of that picture. For that reason, the picture has actually remained remarkably intact along with some of its key elements. What is important is what Hume does not challenge.

What is it that Hume does not challenge? In short, the need for reason to approach questions of faith indifferently, and the casting out of certain ways of thinking about how religious faith operates. For example, in discussing the reports of miracles, Hume, too, is worried about the role of tradition and authority, seeing in them all sorts of possibilities for charlatanism, and thus he, too, excludes these interpersonal ways of knowing. But Hume goes far beyond Locke, exploiting inchoate possibilities of Locke's vision, especially his methodological indifference of reason. While a certain kind of indifference or neutrality is required for any genuine philosophical discussion, i.e., an ability to see one's conversational partner's point of view, with respect to discussions of religious faith Hume, in fact, turns that procedural indifference into a presumption of agnosticism, if not atheism. Here faith requires explanation and defense as something that goes beyond what intelligent human beings might normally engage in. He does this in part by taking away Locke's grounds for optimism. More important, though, is the way he transforms questions that are matters of the heart into questions of neutral intellectual explanation.

In a discussion of what he calls "Hume's Legacy,"[26] D. Z. Phillips describes just what Hume has done. At first the question of whether there is a God or not seems a straightforward one. But how can one decide whether there is a God or not? That, too, seems an obvious question. But, Phillips

---

25. In *An Enquiry concerning Human Understanding*, sec. X, "Miracles."
26. D. Z. Phillips, *Religion Without Explanation* (Oxford: Basil Blackwell, 1976), ch. 1.

notes, once one starts to answer this question, especially in reply to those who look at the world and say they do not see any reason to affirm that God made it, one "assumes that belief in God must be founded on evidence, on an inference in fact, an inference based on features of the world about us."[27] Here Hume's criticisms have their point: Hume does not simply provide evidence and counter-evidence to answer the question, but ultimately suggests that the whole project is misconceived.[28] The upshot is that "Hume's point is not a purely agnostic one. He is not simply saying that we can never know whether anyone made the universe. He is questioning the intelligibility of such talk."[29] And once Hume is able to do this, "intellectual integrity, then, does not lead us inevitably to look for an ex-

---

27. Phillips, *Religion Without Explanation*, p. 11.

28. Phillips argues that Hume does this in three stages. First, he simply points out the ambiguity of the evidence. It isn't immediately obvious that the world is like a machine, despite the success of Newtonian science. But he goes farther by suggesting that there is actually a *disanalogy* between the world and a machine. While it may show evidences of design, the world also appears to exhibit chaos and arbitrariness in its workings. Its workings in this case may simply be explained by physical laws which are sometimes beneficial, but which, as Darwin was later to exploit, are just as often "red in tooth and claw." The point was not wasted on later scientific naturalists who found scientific explanations to explain the world as fully as anything might be explained, and often with fewer annoying counter-instances. The third step, however, is the most damaging. It is at this level that Hume can call into question the very intelligibility of thinking that the world has an intelligent cause.

Hume's point is a subtle one. He suggests that in arguing from analogy we usually take similar effects to proceed from similar causes. Thus if we know something about the flow of blood in mammals and we encounter a fur-bearing viviparous creature, we have some reason to think that blood flows in it. But what is the relation between a human building a machine and a god designing a universe? What sort of causality could we even be talking about here? Humans have bodies and can effect changes in the material world. God does not have one. But what is even more damaging is a problem that comes in asking about the universe itself. The universe, Hume argues, is not an object like others, and it is misleading to talk about it as if it were, applying all the categories we normally apply to physical objects. Rather, the universe is just the collection of what is. Thus once you have given an explanation of the cause of every single thing in it, you have given all the explanation there is to give. So what sense does it make to ask about its cause, and what sort of causality could we even be talking about that would produce a universe? As Bertrand Russell was later to put it, just because everybody in the human race has a mother, it does not mean that it makes sense to ask who is the mother of the human race.

29. Phillips, *Religion Without Explanation*, p. 19.

THE ACT OF FAITH

planation of all things in God."[30] We can stand on the intellectually respectable ground of agnosticism, if not atheism itself.

Thus Hume extends and completes Locke's vision. Philosophically, of course, even Hume has not had the last word. Arguments can be launched to counter his arguments.[31] It is virtually an industry among some Christian philosophers to do so. The effort, though, does not move us out of how Hume and Locke have taught us to talk about faith, that is, by first deciding the question of God's existence with an epistemological indifference, and then looking for evidence, real evidence that is not simply a superimposed explanation of what is adequately explained otherwise. It does not move us out of the presupposition that talking about God cannot be conceptually or epistemologically on a par with any of our other talk; nor does it recognize that faith, even if it involves belief, might be conceptually different than belief in natural objects. So now belief that God exists, and much more so *faith* in God, becomes an "add-on" to what else we believe and needs to be explained in other more basic, more "natural" terms. We are not moved to ask the question of why there is something rather than nothing, nor do we know how to respond to the question. The psalmist asked, "When I look at Thy heavens, the work of Thy fingers, the moon and the stars which Thou hast established; what is man that Thou art mindful of him and the son of man that Thou dost care for him?" (Ps. 8:3). Locke's vision, especially as completed by Hume, simply does not let us see how the psalmist can answer this question, and claim without hesitation: "O Lord, our lord, how majestic is Thy name in all the earth!"[32]

The problem is that Hume, and any number of thinkers after him, take talk about God as if it were an explanation, an explanation that functions like explanations in physics. Hume was able to make belief and faith in God an add-on to more "natural" assumptions, and explanations of nature

---

30. Phillips, *Religion Without Explanation*, p. 21.

31. For example, his dismissal of the intelligibility of talk about the universe as a whole has been effectively challenged. Even if it does not make sense to ask about the cause of the universe as if it were an object like any other, it does, nevertheless, make sense to ask why there is anything at all, or why there are the things there are rather than others. This would at least get us back to agnosticism. Cf. William Rowe, "Two Criticisms of the Cosmological Argument," *The Monist* 54 (July 1970).

32. Diogenes Allen in *Christian Faith and the Postmodern World* (Louisville: Westminster/John Knox Press, 1988) develops at length how this question can be answered within the context of Christian faith.

came to dominate God talk. That has important consequences: to the degree that talk about God is assumed to be something like an explanation, faith inevitably comes to be seen as first and foremost a matter of belief that the proposition "God exists" is true because it explains something; it is only upon establishment of that belief that faith can reasonably be a matter of entrusting one's soul to God. And to the degree that "God" is no longer an obvious explanation, as it was for Locke, it is an extraordinary belief and stands in need of defense by ordinary modes of explanation. Why did this not particularly bother Hume[33] or many of his successors, including ones who did not share his skeptical conclusions? The question takes us into a larger intellectual cultural context.

2.4. The Conceptual Shift of the Modern World

Because very early on in the *Summa Theologiae* Aquinas provides five proofs for the existence of God and then proceeds for the next several questions to talk about what sort of qualities God as the first cause of the world might have, he has often been taken to be responding to the sort of questions Locke and Hume posed, making those questions appear perennial. He was not; those questions are not perennial. Attention to Aquinas shows that he set his proofs within an unabashedly theological context, one that assumed faith from the outset. This can quickly be seen by observing that when Aquinas poses the question of whether God's existence can be proved, the initial reason he gives for an affirmative answer is not the proofs themselves, but because St. Paul in Scripture says that it can; he then goes on to explain that there are some theological truths that can be known apart from faith proper.[34] What is clear is that Aquinas is hardly "indifferent"; his understanding of God as first cause of the world is construed within faith.

Reason and faith were not for Aquinas, as they were not for the an-

---

33. That it did not bother Hume is obvious in that throughout the *Dialogues* Demea insists that he has different reasons for believing in God than those of argument. Nowhere does Hume ever explore what these might be, and he seems to assume that they cannot be anything other than Philo's own sense of wonder at the universe, a wonder that appears to stem from its inexplicability. But there are very different sorts of wonder that usually motivate Christian belief. Cf. below, Chapter 7, 2.3.

34. S.T. I.Q2, art. 2.

cients or early medievals, neatly separated out to deal with distinct realms of nature and the supernatural, nor was theology an exercise of arguing oneself into faith from a consideration of a pure, separate nature that is the primary intellectual *donnée*.[35] Nature and supernature were not impermeably separated. Nature was itself a gift, and made for the supernatural; natural thought was made to receive ultimately the thought of the transcendent God. For that reason alone, human thought could never be distant and uninvolved in its thinking about God. Thus as Aquinas thinks about the relation of faith and reason, his solution is not to sharply distinguish them and separate them into discrete realms. It is to address himself to the issue of how to think about a single world in which grace permeates nature. To do so is the highest science and the "wisdom above all human wisdoms." So when Aquinas then "proves" God's existence he is not making a beginning on a *tabula rasa;* he is explicating what it means for God to exist, the God on whom all things depend in all ways. He is trying to lead the faithful mind to understanding; he is not trying to establish faith, and certainly is not doing so from a more secure foundation in nature.

If this was the case for Aquinas (even for Aquinas!) and for the Christian intellectual tradition up to the Renaissance and Enlightenment, then it is not at all obvious that God needs to be talked about as an explanation like others, or even should be. And God was *not* talked about as an explanation in theology much before the Enlightenment, or as a subject on which a thinker could be indifferent or subjectively distant. What then gave the Lockean-Humean picture its compelling force? It was not simply Hume's conclusions, since these are disputable, then and now. Rather, it was a vision of how things needed to be talked about that came to be shared even by many who vehemently disputed Hume's conclusions. It was a vision that, in fact, affected how theology in the past was read and how theology to come would be done.

A good part of the story is about the metaphysical assumptions inherent in modern science about an objective, independent nature. Galileo had distinguished between primary and secondary qualities, the latter of which depend on human perception's distinctively human qualities. Banishing

---

35. Cf. Henri de Lubac, *The Mystery of the Supernatural,* trans. R. Sheed (New York: Crossroad, 1998). De Lubac argued strenuously that the modern separation of nature and the supernatural was foreign to Aquinas, and needed to be seriously rethought in modern theology.

them from scientific calculation made the primary physical reality a mathematical abstraction that did not require human sensibility. Descartes in distinguishing mind and matter introduced a very strong notion of objectivity: a world without subjective colors, a world that goes on while we sleep. Nature is what-is apart from our interaction. The task of the mind then was not to learn to interact with nature, but to mirror it faithfully. Both Locke and Hume in their empiricism continue this tradition, and reflect it in their standards for knowledge.

With the exception of Hume, these were also religious men, however. How then did they come to subsume theological thinking under the model of mathematical physics? Why didn't they see the need for personal appropriation, or see that objective indifference was not the way to approach theological questions? In large part, it was the fault of theology itself, which[36] was as much the problem as the victim; the story of the shift begins not in philosophy but in theology. Faced with the overwhelming blood-soaked religious conflicts of the seventeenth century, theologians, in an effort to save religion but also to avoid the disputes of confessional theology, sought (not unlike Locke later in the century) to put theological questions in terms of natural philosophy — in terms of what was commonly accessible and less personal. But in doing so they lost the spiritual focus of questions of Christology, ecclesiology, and pneumatology that had really been the primary topics of Christian faith, and sought first to establish by universal reason the existence of God. They approached theology not as the historical *depositum fidei,* but as an argument. Earlier theologians, especially Aquinas because of his attempts to establish the existence of God so soon in the *Summa Theologiae,* now came to be viewed not as writing from within and for faith, but as philosophers who were trying to establish the *possibility* of faith.[37]

---

36. Cf. Michael Buckley, *At the Origins of Modern Atheism* (New Haven: Yale University Press, 1987). Hans Urs von Balthasar has made similar claims; e.g., regarding the naturalist, materialist ideal of Descartes he claims: "An ideal of this kind could never have arisen if the whole of reality had not already been stripped of its living depths and spontaneity, its own truth, goodness and beauty, and had thus been set in unmediated contradiction to the *res cogitans*. The foundations of our 'modern' materialism were laid long ago in the intellectual history of our Western, Christian tradition" (*The Glory of the Lord V: The Realm of Metaphysics in the Modern Age* [San Francisco: Ignatius Press, 1991], p. 29).

37. Cajetan's glosses on Thomas in the sixteenth century are usually regarded as the culprit for making Aquinas look like this to subsequent ages.

THE ACT OF FAITH

Once theology had established the question of God as a question to be addressed as a question of reason and not as the experience of grace, it was not difficult for the ensuing Enlightenment simply to pick up the question in that shape.[38] And pick it up as a question of natural philosophy is exactly what they did, moving from Descartes's arguments for the existence of God as the presupposition for physics, to Newton's establishment of God as the corollary of the great system of nature. In all cases, the tendency was to move questions of faith proper out of the range of what could be discussed rationally, and to move religion into the range of questions raised and dealt with in natural philosophy. Once theology became a set of arguments akin to those in natural philosophy, it is of course not hard for someone such as Hume to exploit the unfortunate equation. The sort of thinking it led to is illustrated by Newton and his protégé Samuel Clarke — and it is well to remember how impressed Locke was by Newton.

God was crucial from the very beginning of what Newton saw himself doing in the *Principia Mathematica*. For while Newton had uncovered the principles of physical nature, he did not see nature simply as the outworkings of those principles. He also saw it as a great system of balance and interworkings. It was quite clear that the mechanical force of gravity was not able to account for "the system which it continually affects and to which it gives unity and coherence."[39] It was God who alone could do that. In Clarke's explanation of what Newton was up to, the force that made the system cohere was dominion, and it was "dominion which makes god be god."[40] Absolute space and time, which were eternal, and which, Leibniz complained, had become co-eternal with God, were for Newton, according to Clarke's explanation, simply God's *sensorium* by which he impressed this dominion and was everywhere present to the system. God was here certainly an explanation for the universe. But far from seeing this as naturalizing God, Clarke saw it as establishing religion. Because the universe showed intelligence, God existed. But because God must also be free, and chose to establish a universe in which intelligence reigned, God must also be wise. Because wise, God must have supreme moral virtue. QED the first

---

38. Buckley is confirmed in this judgment of how Aquinas and the earlier theological tradition came to be read in a very different light by G. de Broglie, "La vraie notion thomiste des 'praeambula fidei,'" *Gregorianum* 34 (1953): 341-89.
39. Buckley, *At the Origins of Modern Atheism*, p. 128.
40. Buckley, *At the Origins of Modern Atheism*, p. 135.

basis of religion, Clarke thought. (Cleanthes' argument is clearly here already present in Clarke.) This system also has the wonderful virtue of uniting religion and natural philosophy.

The glories of the unification, however, mask important, subtle conceptual changes. First, there is a very different way of thinking about God. E. A. Burtt's comparison of Newton's teleology with that of scholasticism remains classic:

> For the scholastics, God was the final cause of all things just as truly and more significantly than their original former. Ends in nature did not head up in the astronomical harmony; that harmony was itself a means to further ends, such as knowledge, enjoyment, and use on the part of living beings of a higher order, who in turn were made for a still nobler end which completed the divine circuit, to know God and enjoy him forever. God had no purpose; he was the ultimate object of purpose. In the Newtonian world, following Galileo's earlier suggestion, all this further teleology is unceremoniously dropped. The cosmic order of masses in motion according to law, is itself the final good. Man exists to know and applaud it; God exists to tend and preserve it. All the manifold divergent zeals and hopes of men are implicitly denied scope and fulfillment; if they cannot be subjected to the aim of theoretical mechanics, their possessors are left no proper God, for them there is no entrance into the kingdom of heaven. . . . God, now the chief mechanic of the universe, has become the cosmic conservative. His aim is to maintain the *status quo*.[41]

What is now is what has always been meant, and is all that is meant; it is the standard and judge of thought.

Second, while this system has its virtues of intellectual coherence, they were not to last long anyhow. Once religion and natural philosophy were united and discussed under the same sort of rubrics, it was not at all difficult for later philosophers and physicists who worked out the unfinished details of Newton's physics to argue quite the contrary, to show that God was *not* needed to make the system work. As the French physicist Laplace was later to remark to Napoleon when asked where God was in his book: "Sire, I have no need of that hypothesis." But not only is God no longer

41. E. A. Burtt, *The Metaphysical Foundations of Modern Science* (Atlantic Highlands: Humanities Press, 1952), p. 297.

THE ACT OF FAITH

needed to make the system work, in the hands of those who actively disbelieved, natural philosophy now was in a position to explain religion itself as a strictly natural phenomenon. For example, religion according to these thinkers is the result of uninformed human minds seeking an explanation for the beginning of the universe, which they superstitiously called "God." So began an intellectual history, continued in Nietzsche and Freud, in which religion was simply part of the natural history of the universe.

Thus we find in the history of natural philosophy itself a parallel to Hume's arguments. What has at least happened in this story is what has been called "the domestication of transcendence."[42] God has been reduced to something like a natural explanation, the "top story of the universe" but part of it nevertheless. The nature of God has become commensurate with the sort of evidence used to establish God's existence. Furthermore, whether "God" is even intelligible now becomes a central topic of discussion. Of course one can subjectively maintain a methodological indifference to such a god. By aligning its project with natural philosophy, theology made itself into something it was not and thereby sowed, out of that internal contradiction, the seeds for its own intellectual discreditation.[43]

3. THE SPECTATOR'S VIEW

3.1. The Exclusion of the Personal and Historical

What this history suggests is that the Lockean-Humean vision is not just the result of an argument, but the articulation of an age's approach to Christian faith, and even the formulation of a theology that is no longer Christian except in name, for it no longer thinks as Christianity thought. It is important to recognize the full depth of the consequences of that approach for thinking about faith. The life of faith — its full range of commitments and activities — was sectioned off from having any real place in public intellectual discussion. A process begun early in small sophisticated

---

42. William Placher, *The Domestication of Transcendence* (Louisville: Westminster/John Knox Press, 1996).

43. This is a story that has repeated itself more than once. Cf., e.g., John Milbank, *Theology and Social Theory: Beyond Secular Explanation* (Oxford: Basil Blackwell, 1990), who suggests that certain theological moves created the domain of the secular, which has now come to be the normative intellectual ground for the modern world.

intellectual circles, it has now become far more extensive: faith is now relegated to "spirituality," to the realm of the private, to "mere" personal commitment. Such sectioning off at least restricts the logical space in which faith can operate. Its public appearances then become determined by a much different sort of logical space, often quite foreign to it, and one in which faith may have very little to say. But let us be more precise about what was sectioned off and what triumphed. It was not simply the "doctrines" *per se* in which faith found its orientation. To see it that way is already to be subject to the vision. Rather, it is the triumph of the spectator over the participant and the triumph of third person language over first person language.[44]

What does the triumph of spectator language mean for the act of faith or for the person who is faithful? Surely it means at least having to take an artificial, although, by now, a seemingly natural, distanced stance to the one to whom she is committed. But this also means that the act of faith itself becomes ahistorical, at least in the sense that history as the novel, agonized, and joyful life of human beings is largely irrelevant to coming to faith or to holding on to it.

Christian faith is personal. But it is not personal in the sense of having a "cosmic friend." It is a relation with God, but God known and relating to us in the Incarnate Word, Jesus Christ. The faith of a Christian makes one an heir to a promise, and to the history of that promise. It unites one to a historical community, the *communio sanctorum*. Augustine once called faith "a partnership with the past" (Tr. in Io. 45.9). Not simply a theory held in common, this partnership is revealed in the very way that theology itself was taught. For the ancients and medievals that partnership was reflected in theology's use first of the Bible and then of a collection of theological texts gleaned from the church fathers. Doing theology, thinking faithfully, was therefore an activity within a continuing

---

44. "One *neither* experienced anything of god nor discerned within oneself a pervasive orientation that could tell as theological evidence. One was informed about god from the outside — as one might be informed about the existence of the New World or deduce the corpuscular theory of matter. . . . In one way or another, religion involves god as a living presence; philosophic inference demonstrates that there is a god as 'a friend behind the phenomena.' . . . There was an unrecognized progressive movement in this ongoing dialectic of content. In their search for proof of the divine existence, the theologians had shifted from the god defined by and disclosed in Christ and religious experience to the god disclosed in impersonal nature" (Buckley, *At the Origins,* pp. 348, 350).

THE ACT OF FAITH

and somewhat open-ended conversation with the members of that community. Even the Reformers, although they arrived on the scene in the midst of change and show signs of having feet in both worlds, carried on their project by a continual stream of quotations of past thinkers. They, too, consciously participated within that history. But all that changes as theology begins to unite itself to natural philosophy.[45] Authorities now are still cited, but are cited for their arguments, not their personal authority and exemplification of the life of faith. Their presence — and the very idea of thinking within a relation of personal presence that history can provide — no longer forms the matrix, the mothering context, of lived faith. This has serious consequences for how past authors are read. For one who no longer lives and breathes in that historical matrix, it is difficult to understand how earlier writers did assume it, no matter how logical, systematic, or innovative within the tradition they might have individually been. One tends then to read such authors from a strictly modern vantage point and to assume that they are *just* formulating arguments.[46] How one thinks about partnerships in the present affects what we assume the past must have taken partnerships to be. (For Dilthey this was, in fact, an explicit hermeneutical rule.)

What deserves underlining here is the personal and self-referential quality of faith and theological interpretation. Faith is an actual dealing with persons, including God, and it is a personal dealing, not an argument about a neutral self-standing nature. But if faith is a personal commitment, involving self-knowledge, it cannot be divorced from the situations in which we gain self-knowledge, especially the history of the community of faith in which one participates and in which one exercises faith. It has no prior and overarching law inexorably guiding its direction. For that reason, one cannot understand it as a spectator sport.

The failure to recognize this essential personal quality of faith and the-

---

45. On these points cf. Buckley, *At the Origins*, p. 43. Buckley does note that Aquinas's much more systematic presentation, though, makes it easy for a later generation to replace presentations such as Lombard's.

46. Susan Bordo in *The Flight to Objectivity: Essays on Cartesianism and Culture* (Albany: State University of New York Press, 1987) argues that Descartes and his contemporaries were threatened by a "loss of home" as the medieval world collapsed. Their emphasis on "individuation" constituted a separation from "mother." In their quest for certainty they compensated for the loss of this mother, this matrix. The self could now generate its own certitude.

ology has resulted in a "dissociation of sensibility" for Christian thought.[47] The dominance of the Lockean-Humean vision in things religious, and the triumph of an impersonal method in things scientific, has forced Christian thought, as well as the humanities, to see itself in the light of that vision. Neither can, however, see its own activity very clearly in that light or understand its own history very well. Within the vision it cannot understand its history and future as "the response of the will or the heart to the One in whom we believe."[48] It cannot even understand its own most basic activity, prayer. For prayer is not just a feeling, pure subjectivity, but also a coming to know, and a genuine thinking of the object of faith. When knowing is thought to be gotten only by other means, by distanced and indifferent means, claims to *knowing* God in prayer are not very intelligible. Within the vision, Christian faith and thought then have to justify their relevance in terms that are not relevant to their own activity; either that or face their own irrelevance.

3.2. First and Third Person Views

It would be, of course, historically inaccurate to suggest that nobody recognized that there was a problem, that deep things of very different orders were being forced together. Obviously Pascal did, and so did Leibniz, who was gravely concerned over the theological implications of Newton's metaphysics, and who worked tirelessly to think out a metaphysical system that had the virtue of integrating without reductionism the principles of nature *and* grace. But there were also those who, like Paley,[49] tried to advance arguments designed to beat Hume at his own game without ever realizing that what was at stake was the deep issue of how Christian faith is actually

---

47. As coined by Andrew Louth (from T. S. Eliot) in *Discerning the Mystery* (Oxford: Oxford University Press, 1983), ch. 1.

48. Louth, *Discerning the Mystery*, p. 3.

49. Paley's *Evidences of Christianity* and his *Natural Religion, or Evidences of the Existence and Attributes of the Deity Collected from the Appearances of Nature* were immensely popular in the nineteenth-century English-speaking theological world. The former, published in 1794, went through fifteen editions by 1811; the latter, published in 1802, went through twenty editions by 1820. These were standard theological textbooks throughout much of the century.

THE ACT OF FAITH

thought, or who, on the other side, thought to dismiss Christianity as intellectually irresponsible.

But even when a problem was recognized, it was not always clear that it was the right problem that was coming to light. It is one thing to recognize the shortcomings of rationalism and the distinctive origin and concerns of religious thought and quite another to understand what it means to think faithfully. The problem and solution for many of the greatest thinkers who put themselves to it concerned only the former. It was a matter of solving the relations of science and religion, and philosophy and theology, by paying due service to religious thinking but then looking for a larger intellectual system in which to subsume it, a system already determined by "scientific" rational demands. Hegel is a prime example, but there are others. Kant, for example, sought to shift the locus of talk about God from nature, where Newton had put it, to the moral. For Kant, God was an inescapable postulate of the moral life, without which moral rationality would forever be undone. In moving talk about God outside the realm of natural philosophy, he explicitly sought to make room for faith. But this is not thinking God, it is finding room for God in a way of thinking already set. Schleiermacher, on the other hand, found the religious in the inner life, in a universal consciousness and "feeling of absolute dependence."[50] From there he sought to deduce the content of what is believed. Within the context of a vision that so thoroughly misunderstood the act of faith, both efforts were admirable. Unfortunately, they actually underline the problem rather than ameliorating it. In both cases, faith became a universal question, like a philosophical one, subject to a third person method. In both cases, while large and extensive claims for faith were made about its importance in human life, the space in which faith was to operate was not generated in the matrix of faithful activity; it was space defined and

---

50. As Hans-Georg Gadamer remarks, though, it was typical of Schleiermacher "to see this everywhere" (*Truth and Method* [New York: Crossroad, 1986], p. 165). It is significant to note Schleiermacher's own religious beginnings in Pietism, which had reacted sharply to sterile, rationalistic versions of Christianity. But Pietism does not recover historical Christian faith; by trying to cut to the basics, it frequently rides roughshod over historical differences. Ironically, it thus comes to a position not unlike that of the Enlightenment Deists where religion is not just moral, but chiefly moral. (Cf. Claude Welch, *Protestant Thought in the Nineteenth Century* [New Haven: Yale University Press, 1972], vol. 1, p. 29.) It is a matter of being a good person. The hangover in American popular religion remains.

left over by the more rationalistic worldview. While they talked about personal categories, and often very well, those categories ultimately were understood in the context of a third person worldview, or generated one themselves.

There were, however, genuine alternatives throughout the nineteenth century: Søren Kierkegaard,[51] Samuel Coleridge,[52] John Henry Newman,

---

51. Kierkegaard is often taken to be an irrationalist in matters of faith, denying that reason could get us to faith, insisting that a "leap of faith" is required. Like Pascal, he is taken to make faith a matter of willing despite, or even deliberately against, the evidence. His point is far more subtle, for his argument is with a view of reason that has consistently misrepresented faith by making discussion of it conform to ways of talking that are alien to it. He does so on the behalf of a better understanding of what exactly faith is. So in works such as *Philosophical Fragments* and *Concluding Unscientific Postscript* he is *not* offering an apologetic of any kind for the Christian faith. He is simply trying to say where faith has been misunderstood, and he does so on the basis of its own claims.

So where has it been misunderstood? Chiefly in that the world has failed to recognize that there is a wide conceptual gulf between the sort of knowing given in objective demonstrations and evidences (even when they are possible, which they rarely are for unique occurrences) and the personal appropriation of God that faith is. Faith occurs when we are confronted by the "paradox" of God having become man, a paradox that confronts us as proclamation. What is proclaimed can only be given by God, and thus the very possibility of faith remains with God and not humans. When so confronted, we have to respond personally — "subjectively" or "inwardly" or "passionately" — if we respond at all. But the response cannot be from a distance or to what is at a distance. Rather, the response consists in the transformation of ourselves, of how we understand ourselves and of what is possible for us. In accepting and holding dearly to the proclamation, we possess what we did not possess before. We learn to rely on God, and in doing so, the very passion of holding onto God is God's own passion. It is God's action in us. And *thus* is the will and person engaged. Faith is "Christ in me" (St. Paul), a relation with God in which God and the human are engaged.

Kierkegaard is therefore not a "subjectivist" in the sense that faith is a subjective feeling that operates parallel to the objective, rational world. God is objective and stands *extra nos*. But one does not know God except as one concomitantly knows oneself and the world in God's light. To have that light is to have faith.

52. Coleridge, too, was deeply concerned to deal with the demands of genuine religious knowing — and those were not the demands of a theory but of a way of life. Thus he sought to explicate Reason as being a knowledge of the self in relation to the whole, a knowledge that was imaginative and intrinsically moral. But most important was the level at which Reason becomes personal fidelity. The knowledge of God particularly was a form of personal knowing, requiring personal fidelity, for religion is finally "the relation of a Will to a Will, the Will in each instance being *deeper* than Reason, of a Person to a Person." (Quoted in Welch, *Protestant Thought in the Nineteenth Century*, p. 121.)

THE ACT OF FAITH

William James,[53] and Maurice Blondel,[54] to name the most striking. For each, the problem was not so much a problem of how to think *about* Christian faith, but one of a *way* of thinking, of what it meant to think as a Christian in the first person. Newman's account, which we shall develop here briefly and then again in the final chapter, is in its outlines perhaps the clearest account of the problem and alternative. Consciously indebted to Aristotle's concept of *phronesis,* Newman argues for a view of religious understanding and judgment that is a matter of personal capacity that cannot be given by "logical science" as he calls it.

Newman is clearly conscious of the Lockean-Humean vision, and explicitly argues that Locke was wrong in asserting that our degree of assent ought not to go beyond the certitude of the evidence. Newman is at pains to argue that we do find certitude beyond that given by bare evidence. The reason? Certitude is not a quality of the evidence, but a result of the thinking mind. It is not a title attached to and inherent in the evidence, but what *we* come to by engaging the evidence, often by long experience of dealing with it. For example, detectives, even if they must prove a case by other means to a less experienced jury, know from their experience just who committed a crime. As Aristotle suggested when describing *phronesis* — the human capacity of moral judgment — knowing what good is to be done in a particular situation depends upon a developed capacity of the

---

53. William James, in his reply to Clifford, "The Will to Believe" (in *The Will to Believe and Other Essays in Popular Philosophy* [New York: Longmans, Green, 1898]), hardly develops the issue to the depth to which Kierkegaard, Coleridge, and Newman go. Yet this essay in battling against the grain is deservedly celebrated for its observation that in important matters of life our live options are forced upon us. To have a life that means anything at all we must choose. Clifford's cool survey of the possibilities and suspension of judgment simply runs against life as we know it. It should be noted, though, that James's title is misleading insofar as the problem is not the will to believe (which reflects modern distance) but the believing will.

54. Blondel, especially in his *L'Action* of 1894 sought to show that reason is by itself incomplete, and stretches out toward an end it can never fully conceive. It demanded faith as its completion. But this, of course, meant that the problem of faith in its modern, "extrinsicist" formulation of distanced rationality was desperately inadequate: "it does not suffice to establish separately the *possibility* and the *reality* . . . of the supernatural. . . . It is still necessary to show the *necessity for us* to adhere to this reality of the supernatural." Faith depends on a personal act that extrinsic reasons cannot make for us, but in their inadequacy only point us to. (Cf. Roger Aubert, *Le probleme de l'acte de foi* 3ième ed. [Louvain: E. Warny, 1958].)

virtuous, a capacity born of long experience with particular cases as well as general rules. Thus Newman claims:

> Instead of trusting logical science, we must trust persons, namely, those who by long acquaintance with their subject have a right to judge. And if we wish ourselves to share in their convictions and the grounds of them, we must follow their history, and learn as they have learned. We must take up their particular subject as they took it up, beginning at the beginning, give ourselves to it, depend on practice and experience more than on reasoning, and thus gain that mental insight into truth, whatever its subject matter may be, which our masters have gained before us. By following this course, we may make ourselves of their number, and then we rightly lean upon ourselves, directing ourselves by our own moral or intellectual judgement, not our skill in argumentation. (GA, 342)

Judgment in concrete situations is a personal capacity. It is not innate, but developed by experience, and on the basis of the convictions and principles that we might hold. Such a capacity is what Newman called the "illative sense." The illative sense is being able to draw together ambiguous concrete facts into a coherent whole, and is gained by practice. Newman saw the illative sense as holding for human reasoning generally, and thus saw Locke as generally wrong. But he was particularly concerned to show that it was the proper way to think of reasoning within faith. Faith is not a choice to believe certain things, with or without evidence, but a capacity of the thinker to understand the form of communal and personal histories, especially in light of the moral demands of conscience. It is the ability to *discern* God's grace either in the Christian story as a whole or in how that history comes to bear in particular circumstances. It is not, however, something that can be had apart from its own exercise; it is inaccessible to distanced reason. Distanced reason even tends to undermine it. Arguing against Paley's attempts to demonstrate the existence and providence of God from the design of the world to the disinterested reason, Newman voiced his doubts about the project:

> Men are too well inclined to sit at home, instead of stirring themselves to inquire whether a revelation has been given; they expect its evidence to come to them without their trouble; they act, not as suppliants, but as judges. Modes of argument such as Paley's encourage this state of mind;

they allow men to forget that revelation is a boon, not a debt on the part of the Giver; they treat it as a mere historical phenomenon. (GA, 425)

It is in this vein that Newman can claim, as he tries to show the divine sense of a particular example in Christian history, "this phenomenon again carries on its face, *to those who believe in a God,* the probability that it has that divine origin which it professes to have" (GA, 439). Certitude produced by illation is gained by living out and thinking out in life and history the beliefs that make up our lives and history. The point of the illative sense, in any field of inquiry, is therefore not to produce arguments to defeat the one who disagrees; it is to bring one's own mind to judgment, to complete one's own desires to know and to act.

We do not need to deal with all the questions that Newman's "illative sense" raises, other than to note that he certainly did not have in mind any thought of isolated minds pursuing their own individual truths, even though truth is always held individually. When there is disagreement, "logical reason" needs to be brought in as a sort of umpire. But there is a difference between umpires and players, and players do manage to play with each other, often without recourse to umpires. Newman at every turn is struck by the very apparent phenomenon that human minds do agree in the conclusions they reach from living out their principles, and that they can be helpful in instructing and correcting each other as they pursue the conclusions of their moral and intellectual commitments. Illation is not an isolated process, but one that involves dealing with other people, and committing oneself to living within a tradition and to learning the "grammar of faith" from those who already know it.

Thus we get some initial sense of what is missing in the modern vision of distanced reason, in the triumph of the spectator over the participant. Faith is essentially personal both in the sense that it involves by God's proclamation the transformation of a person's moral and intellectual capacities, and in the sense that its exercise, its activity, is in the world of personal engagement and cannot be understood apart from that world.

Yet those who voiced this were often voices crying in the wilderness. Since Hume, most theology in the western world, although it always felt a great deal of dis-ease with the intellectual climate in which it found itself, actually found itself trying to defend itself in the terms of what made it uneasy, and it continued to misrepresent a great deal of what it was about, whether by trying to find rational foundations for Christianity or by finding ways around them. If, however, thinkers like Kierkegaard, Coleridge, Newman, and Blondel were isolated figures in an earlier age, at the beginning of the twenty-first century there is good reason to take what they were saying far more seriously. The Lockean-Humean vision has been recognized and has been questioned, although hardly by everyone. But it is not enough simply to doubt it. It is also crucial to have some sense of where it goes wrong. For this reason we need to look briefly at its own intellectual limits, what it failed to say and what it did not comprehend. That should, in turn, give some sense of how we might be better able to discuss what faith encompasses and in what terms it needs to be thought.

4. SHATTERING THE MIRROR OF NATURE

4.1. The Mirror of Nature

At the heart of the intellectual enterprise of the modern world that we have been describing has been a quest for certainty, and a horror of undisciplined speculation and subjectivism. Key to that quest has been an attempt to *ground* knowledge on unassailable foundations. That was Descartes's self-confessed project in the *Meditations,* and in one way or another the heritage he bequeathed to the modern world. After Hume it was largely assumed that it is empirical matters of fact that provide that foundation. But also key to the quest has been the attempt to articulate a rational method that would serve as a guide to reason, determining what is reasonable to say about matters of fact and what is not. Most radically, this latter element involved an attempt to spell out a canon of criteria, a canon of rational form, of what counts as rational. Such a canon by its very nature is a matter of a distanced, third person perspective since it spells out what counts as rational everywhere and every time. It most decidedly does not depend on personal capacities. Knowledge gained from observation of what is and put in universal rational form is a "God's-eye view of the universe," for it depends on no perspective. This was a far cry from the ancient task of refusing to let one's mind be overcome by the distortion of the passions.

The high-water mark of this quest came in Logical Positivism, which reigned throughout much of the first half of the twentieth century, and which in its assumptions and its downfall shows the problems of the mod-

THE ACT OF FAITH

ern view. For the logical positivists, philosophy was *not* a quest for wisdom or even knowledge *per se* — the latter was given by science, which dealt with matters of fact — but an enterprise that was to ground the sense and logic of what we said about empirical reality. It was dedicated to explicating as thoroughly and completely as possible the logical form that meaningful propositions take. In Wittgenstein's early work, for example, which attempts to show what it is logically possible to say and not say, the logical form of the world as it were, they saw (somewhat mistakenly) a complete formal representation, a mirror image, of the world. This is the formal world in which experience takes place, and which alone can meaningfully articulate knowledge. To see their admiration of this project helps us understand what the point of the "verification principle" at the heart of their project really was. The verification principle — "all meaningful statements are logical constructions out of sense data" — is relatively easy to understand in these terms. By observation we see what is; that by itself does not give scientific knowledge. However, we can build complex theoretical statements when those statements translate observations by a set of logical equivalences, thus never adding to or subtracting from the content of the observation. This can be done because logical form is universal and formal. With this understood, it will be helpful to look briefly at what the verification principle tried to do and at its failure, as it illustrates very well the problem of distanced knowledge.

A simple example shows how the principle works. Scientific theory often contains terms that are not the result of direct observation. We, for example, do not see atoms or quarks. What we do is see disturbances in cloud chambers and read measurements from instruments such as galvanometers. Does this mean that atoms and quarks are empirical fictions? Not if what we mean by atoms and quarks in scientific statements can be seen as a direct, although complex, literal translation of the observations we have made of cloud chambers and galvanometers. This much makes perfect sense and helps us understand even something of scientific work.

The verification principle, however, as a principle for *all* meaningful statements is not anything so innocent as a mere helpful guide to understanding the nature of theories. It also excludes any statement from meaningfulness that cannot meet its criteria. For example, as A. J. Ayer asserted,[55] ethical and religious statements are meaningless, perhaps simply

---

55. A. J. Ayer, *Language, Truth, and Logic* (New York: Dover, 1946).

statements of emotion, because they cannot show themselves as such translations. Recalling Hume's principle that one cannot derive "ought" from "is" (the so-called "fact/value" distinction), the problem is that any number of mutually incompatible religious or ethical statements are supposedly based on the way the world is. Or, whatever they are claiming — e.g., "You shall love the Lord your God with all your soul," etc. — makes no empirical difference to the observations of what is. They are thus contentless. To put religious belief in these terms and to have to defend it in them — it is after all meant as a criterion for all rational statements — is a daunting task, and efforts to defend religious belief in these terms have been notoriously unsuccessful.

4.2. The Destruction of Positivism

There is a problem with the verification principle, however, that is devastating to the entire project of empiricism as well as to the project of setting out a criterial understanding of distanced reason. The problem is that the principle itself cannot be shown to be a statement that is the logical equivalent of sense experience. It is neither analytic — i.e., a matter of pure logical form, a matter of formal translation — nor is it empirically testable. But here rather than jump to the conclusion that religious belief can no longer be excluded as meaningful, it will be helpful to see precisely why the principle and the entire project of giving a criterial canon for understanding is misdirected. This, in turn, will give some further direction to just how faith does need to be discussed.

The literature engaged in marking the downfall of positivism's project and its alternatives is sophisticated and enormous.[56] The problem involved

---

56. To cite simply some important classic texts: Wittgenstein's own reconsideration of his earlier project in *Philosophical Investigations* (New York: Macmillan, 1958); W. V. O. Quine, "Two Dogmas of Empiricism," in *From a Logical Point of View* (New York: Harper & Row, 1963); W. Sellars, *Science, Perception, and Reality* (London: Routledge & Kegan Paul, 1963); T. Kuhn, *The Nature of Scientific Revolutions* (Chicago: University of Chicago Press, 1962); H. Putnam, *Reason, Truth, and History* (Cambridge: Cambridge University Press, 1981); R. Rorty, *Philosophy and the Mirror of Nature* (Princeton: Princeton University Press, 1979). Helpful for sorting out the issues that arise from the reconsideration of the project is R. Bernstein, *Beyond Objectivism and Relativism: Science, Hermeneutics, and Praxis* (Philadelphia: University of Pennsylvania Press, 1983).

can be put relatively simply, though, by looking at the example of scientific practice given above where the verification principle was seen to have its best application. At first blush, building theories out of empirical observations would seem to be exactly what scientists are doing. Closer examination, however, shows that the situation is far more complicated than that, for the process cannot be neatly sectioned out of a larger world. For example, what does it mean to observe a cloud chamber or a galvanometer? One would not only need to have the concept of a cloud chamber *per se*, but in having that concept would also need to have some sense of how to read it, just as doctors need to know how to read x-rays, and can see in them things that escape the untutored eye. But to have such a concept, and to be able to describe it meaningfully, depends on an entire set of practices that at least require being trained in science, as well as in the practices and the language used by the culture in which one is working. The problem is that in making observations the reports we could carry away are virtually infinite; we have learned, then, to exclude certain ones and to value others. But the principle of choice we use is not possible outside those practices. Indeed, having the concept of a cloud chamber means being able to use it and to give theoretical discussions. But doing those things in turn depends on a whole set of concepts and practices that are themselves interlinked in a way distinctive to a culture in which science is practiced. In this way, as Thomas Kuhn observed, all observations are already theory laden, and make sense within that theory and the larger intellectual milieu of the theory. This applies not only to observations, but to the logical form in which we describe our observations. So *if* the verification principle makes any sense at all it makes sense *only* within a set of practices that assume it. That is why it is self-refuting. Whatever else it is, it is *not* a God's-eye view of rationality.

Wittgenstein put the problem this way. Soon after he had developed his "picture theory" of logical form in the *Tractatus Logico-Philosophicus*, that is, that there was a single logical language in which to describe all events, he realized that there was a singular problem with it. Even if such a language were possible, even if one could give a glassy mirror reflecting the logical form of how things are, one has to know how to apply it. Even if there are rules for such application, one still has to know how to apply the rules. And so on, *ad infinitum*. The application is not in the rules themselves. The *connection* between the proposition and reality is therefore not in the picture itself. It is in our doing and in our use of the picture. Thus he came to argue that to have a concept was also to know how to apply it — not as something separate from the concept, but as something within it. But if this is so, concepts are not glassy essences; they are embedded within practices and make no sense apart from them. To know the grammar of a proposition was to know how to use it. "How strange," he says, "if logic were concerned with an 'ideal' language and not with *ours*. . . . Logical analysis is the analysis of something we have, not of something we don't have. Therefore it is the analysis of propositions *as they stand*."[57]

Now the point to be taken away from this is not that there is no truth — there may be and we may even have found it; rather, it is that there is no external prior guarantee nor any set of rational criteria that stand outside our actual historical practices that allow us to say that "the concepts themselves determine what philosophical arguments are right. . . ."[58] Nor can there be, since criterial principles do not *determine* truth and rationality; they articulate our understanding of the propositions we actually have. They are not prior to the exercise of reason; whatever rational principles there might be are embedded in our reasoning, and our reasoning is not comprehensive.[59]

If there is no prior criterial canon of rationality, no God's-eye view, at least for us, then so must the distanced spectator's view of knowledge be questioned as the final court of thought. In fact, the very attempt to gain such a view needs to be seen as desperately confused. But if this is so, then several of the assumed "dualisms" of modern philosophy that depend on

---

57. Ludwig Wittgenstein, *Philosophical Remarks*, ed. Rush Rhees (Chicago: University of Chicago Press, 1975), p. 52.

58. Putnam, *Reason, Truth and History*, p. 111.

59. Putnam argues: "The gambit . . . that refutes the logical positivists' verification principle, is *deep* precisely because it refutes every attempt to argue for a criterial conception of rationality, that is because it refutes the thesis that nothing is rationally verifiable unless it is criterially verifiable. The point is that . . . [the positivists] often spoke as if their arguments had the same kind of *finality* as a mathematical proof or a demonstration experiment in physics. . . . In short, if it is true that only statements that can be criterially verified can be rationally acceptable, that statement itself cannot be criterially verified, and hence cannot be rationally acceptable. If there is such a thing as rationality at all — and we commit ourselves to believing in *some* notion of rationality by engaging in the activities of *speaking* and *arguing* — then it is self-refuting to *argue* for the position that it is identical with or properly contained in what the institutionalized norms of culture determine to be instances of it. For no such argument can be certified to be correct, or even probably correct, by those norms alone" (*Reason, Truth, and History*, p. 111).

the picture also need to be rethought. One is the distinction between mind and body as distinct substances, for if mind is distinct from body, it is assumed to be distinct because the mind can take this view from nowhere, because it can mirror nature and the logical form of nature perfectly. Another is the distinction between "facts" and "values." It is in challenging this latter distinction that we come closer to our point.

4.3. Fact and Value: The Inevitable Question of the Person

Hilary Putnam's strategy in attempting to dissolve the distinction between facts and values is particularly helpful. Although we tend to lump facts and objectivity together on one side and values and subjectivity on another, things do not split so easily. Even science, which admittedly is much more "fact-heavy," cannot as a practice be understood without some reference to values. For example, not only do scientists quite apparently make judgments on aesthetic grounds as well as on empirical ones — between two competing theories of equal explanatory power, we always choose the simpler — science's own commitment to truth is not wholly a matter of empirical truth as the bottom line, but something much larger. Why, for example, do we construct representations of the world? "I would answer that the reason we want this sort of representation . . . is that having this sort of representation system is *part of our idea of human cognitive flourishing*, and hence part of our idea of total human flourishing, of Eudaemonia."[60] Not only does science embody certain internal values in its practice, those values are inescapably intertwined with our larger sense of the value and goals of life. And, it is often because we have the ideas of human flourishing that we do, that we have the facts that we do. That is not to say that we make them up, but simply that without certain values that constrain and direct our practices we simply would not have the representations of the world we do. Without them we would not have the same conceptions of the facts that we, in fact, do have.[61] Similarly, it is because of what we take to be the facts that we have the values we do.

60. Putnam, *Reason, Truth, and History,* p. 134.
61. In US 4, Newman, without attempting to make this an apology for Christianity, suggests that the sort of cooperation needed for scientific work depends upon a set of interpersonal virtues such as Christianity lays out as human duties.

Putnam's argument raises significant questions for discussion, ranging from how facts and values interact (if one can even put the question that way) to the ideology of science and its role in determining social power. Our interest here is in using such an argument to effect a shift in how we might talk about faith. The shift is *not*, however, to talk about faith as chiefly a matter of values now that values can no longer be regarded as merely subjective, although the language of faith will inevitably involve value talk more than physics will. It is not a matter of finding intellectual space for faith. The problem is not that easy. Rather, the problem of distance, the spectator's view, in talking about faith *is not and never was simply a problem of rationality*. If science, or any other cognitive enterprise for that matter, has *always* involved a set of historical human practices that have been intertwined with value commitments, then it is not simply a view of rationality *per se* that makes it difficult to think through the life of faith. It is also those value commitments and the vision of human flourishing that encouraged an age to dream of a pure, distanced rationality. If the commitment to the spectator's view *is* intertwined with a deep-seated value of the modern world, it is not enough to lift the harsh intellectual strictures that positivism claimed to lay on the language of faith. Simply lifting them, but valuing everything else the same way, will change little. Indeed, if the short history of post-positivism and postmodernism in intellectual culture shows anything, it is *not* a new and apologetic welcoming of traditional understandings of faith, even if there is more intellectual openness to diverse forms of reasoning than before. The problem now does not seem to be intellectual at all. But it may well be personal. The problem then is not an intellectual one, of faith versus distanced reason; it may well be a problem of values all the way down. Thus the dissociation of sensibility that theology suffers may not simply be one of having to discuss concepts that belong in personal categories in terms of impersonal ones; it is also the dissociation of having to discuss religious concepts in the wrong personal categories. For as it turns out, reason always has been personal, whether it recognized itself that way or not.

We can be somewhat more precise in defining the problem. In his penetrating *Sources of the Self*, Charles Taylor argues at length a point about the inescapable relation of facts and values. Taylor suggests that we live our lives within inescapable moral frameworks, moral because they involve a constitutive sense of a good for human life. These frameworks, however, are not metaphysical constructs, placed "out there" somewhere, to which

THE ACT OF FAITH

we consciously subscribe, nor are they things we choose to believe or not. Where they bear on human life is that they shape our identity, our moral self as it were, giving us a sort of "moral space" in which we operate, a space that gives us our bearings *vis-à-vis* each other and the larger natural world. We understand ourselves through our relations with others and those relations are constituted by a shared sense of the goals and directions of human life. We do not invent these, because we are never outside such frameworks. We come to be personal agents precisely as we come to share them, as we are inducted into the life and language of a culture. Despite the efforts of the modern age to find a "view from nowhere," to argue that we can do without such frameworks, it is because they give us an identity that they are inescapable. "[T]he claim is that living within such strongly qualified horizons is constitutive of human agency, that stepping outside these limits would be tantamount to stepping outside what we would recognize as integral, that is, undamaged human personhood" (Sources, 27). Intellectually, arguing for dispensing with these frameworks makes no more consistent sense than arguing for the verification principle does; it assumes a framework and moral space that we have failed to recognize. To do without such spaces actually would mean destruction of the human agent who does the arguing, as there would be no goals or values in common with those whom one engages in conversation. We would have no standing as persons with them, or they with us.[62]

The bearing that the "moral self" brings to understanding the act of faith is this: Christian faith is an act of the moral self, and involves living within a certain kind of moral space. But, so too is distanced, third person rationality. The problem of faith in the modern world is then not strictly intellectual, as Pascal saw early on. It is one of competing moral selves and moral spaces.

Understanding the plight of faith then means that we need to have some sense of the moral space of distanced rationality. What ends of the

---

62. "In the light of our understanding of identity, the portrait of an agent free from all frameworks rather spells for us a person in the grip of an appalling identity crisis. Such a person wouldn't know where he stood on issues of fundamental importance, would have no orientation in these issues whatever, wouldn't be able to answer for himself on them. . . . [A] person without a framework altogether would be outside our space of interlocution; he wouldn't have a stand in the space where the rest of us are. We would see this as pathological" (Sources, 51).

self did and does it serve? While it is the job of the next chapter to develop an answer, a sketch of where the problem lies can be given here.

4.4. The Ends of the Self

What ends of the moral self does distanced rationality serve? Why was the Lockean-Humean vision morally satisfying or demanding? Locke in the first part of his opening sentence of *An Essay Concerning Human Understanding* gives the clue: "Since it is the understanding that sets man above the rest of sensible beings, and gives him all the advantage and dominion which he has over them . . ." (Essay, I.1.I). Rationality and understanding are what give us power over things, for it is by being able to survey possibilities and to understand them that we have control over our destinies. By disengaging ourselves from the world and treating it mechanistically, we can, as Descartes and Hobbes had already aspired to do, reassemble it. But it is not only the natural world from which we disengage ourselves; what this disengagement also "calls for is the ability to take an instrumental stance to one's given properties, desires, inclinations, tendencies, habits of thought and feeling so that they can be *worked on,* doing away with some and strengthening others, until one meets the desired specifications" (Sources, 160). Even the idea of having a "self," a set of memories, properties, etc., is new here, and the result of being able to take a third person point of view to one's own person. This results in what Taylor calls the "punctual self," an agential self that is no longer constituted by natural and social relations and that shrinks to a willing agent choosing from distantly surveyed alternatives.

Within the world of the seventeenth century such distancing made some sense. The social world of religion and culture was fragmenting, presenting what appeared to be intractable problems *within* the religious and cultural world. Stepping outside must have seemed a necessity. But it is clear that stepping outside was no mere political expedient. It was a thoroughgoing project that in time came to define the modern world and its moral space. With it came a radically different sense of the self that affected any number of endeavors. Locke's political philosophy, which begins with the (nearly) isolated individual choosing and arranging the polity he will join, is parallel to, and culturally and religiously just as important, if not more so, as all of his work on the nature of the understanding. There we find a self that is free, autonomous, and self-creating,

THE ACT OF FAITH

and it is those qualities, Locke thinks, that make man in God's image, not his communion with God.

Similarly with Kant. When answering the question "What is Enlightenment?" he answered with the bold motto: *"Sapere aude!"* "Dare to understand!" Understanding is what frees us from dependence on another for guidance, from our self-imposed(!) immaturity. "All that is required for this enlightenment is *freedom:* and particularly the least harmful of all that may be called freedom, namely, the freedom for man to make public use of his reason in all matters."[63] *This* is the sort of moral space that makes distance desirable, and that creates the modern moral self. The oft-quoted Iris Murdoch poignantly summarizes that self:

> How recognizable, how familiar to us is the man so beautifully portrayed in the *Grundlegung,* who confronted even with Christ turns away to consider the judgement of his own conscience and to hear the voice of his own reason. Stripped of the exiguous metaphysical background that Kant was prepared to allow him, this man is with us still, free, independent, lonely, powerful, rational, responsible, brave, the hero of so many novels and books of moral philosophy.[64]

The faithful self looks much different. The traditional language of faith includes individual personal capacities such as *thinking with assent,* prayer as supplication, humility, obedience, and faithfulness, and communal ones of intimacy and interdependence such as St. Paul's organic image of Christ's body suggests, with all members inescapably bound up with each other. The traditional language of faith does not jibe well with a sense that we are isolated, free choosers. Thus the modern disjunction of faith with contemporary intellectual life is not just a problem of reason, but a problem at its root of how we see ourselves as moral selves. It is a problem that does not simply divide believer and unbeliever, but affects even believers. Even church people often see their religious associations in the terms of the Lockean self: as instrumental, voluntary associations in service of developing one's own empirical self.[65]

---

63. Kant, "What Is Enlightenment?" in Karl J. Friedrich, *The Philosophy of Kant: Immanuel Kant's Moral and Political Writings* (New York: Random House, 1949), p. 134.

64. Iris Murdoch, *The Sovereignty of Good* (New York: Schocken Books, 1971), p. 80.

65. Cf. Robert Bellah et al., *The Habits of the Heart: Individualism and Commitment in American Life* (New York: Harper & Row, 1986).

Reason and the Reasons of the Heart

* * *

As we now turn from the intellectual questions presented by the modern world about the act of faith to the deeper questions of the self who asks those questions, a degree of nuance needs to be added. Contrasting the apparent virtues of the self after the Enlightenment — freedom, power, rationality, autonomy — with those of Christian faith as it was understood before the Enlightenment — humility, obedience, intimacy, letting oneself be shaped by a unique history — puts in high relief the differences between the two understandings of the self and the moral spaces in which they dwell. High relief, however, should not be mistaken for the depth of the problem, nor should it obscure or dismiss genuine overlap. Christianity, for example, has always understood that pride is an obstacle to faith. But the modern virtues are not pride *simpliciter,* nor is there no overlap between them and the virtues and questions of faith. There are intellectual questions to which faith addresses itself and which need to be addressed to faith. Many of the personal and social values of the modern world are the direct development of Christian concerns for the dignity of the individual human being. The deep issue is the way that they are held, for moral frameworks are totalizing. Consider an example. At the end of Book I of the *Confessions,* Augustine describes himself, his talents, and his concerns:

> For at that time I existed, I lived and thought and took care for my self-preservation. . . . An inward instinct told me to take care of the integrity of my senses, and even in my little thoughts about little matters I took delight in the truth. I hated to be deceived, I developed a good memory, I acquired the armory of being skilled with words, friendship softened me, I avoided pain, despondency, ignorance. In such a person what was not worthy of admiration and praise?

Indeed. Everything Augustine mentions (well, most everything) could be cited by a twenty-first-century American as qualities of the self that are worthy of admiration. But Augustine goes on to invoke an important moral framework to his description that leads him to conclude something very different about who he is and what he ought to do than we might:

> But every one of these qualities are gifts of my God: I did not give them to myself. They are good qualities, and their totality is my self. Therefore

THE ACT OF FAITH

> he who made me is good, and *he is my good,* and I exult to him. . . . (Conf. I.xx [31])

Or, as he puts it at the beginning of the *Confessions:* ". . . you have made us for yourself, and our heart is restless until it rests in you" (Conf. I.i [1]).

For Augustine, nature, even his own nature, is not something neutral waiting to be disposed of by his choice. It does not at any time stand outside God's grace, even though he may have tried for several years to see it that way. From the very inside of his being he is a creature of God; his nature is the one God gives. To be a self, to think, to act, is therefore to do so within that framework of God's goodness. It is, as Pascal saw, a question of the heart. Similarly with Aquinas when he works out his proofs for the existence of God. He is not trying to retrace the steps of the act of faith nor trying to determine his future path. His is a mind that is reaching out to grasp as clearly as it might the path of his life, its source, and its goal that makes his mind what it is.[66] The modern sense of the self is different. The self, and the nature in which it acts, stands independently; it then moves to the question of whether to give itself to God and to the problem of how to bring God into relation with it. On the two sides of these two ways of understanding the self lay very different ways of understanding the nature and use of our talents, and very different ways of imagining what the ends and duties of the self are.

We therefore now turn to look at the modern self to understand those duties and the limits of its imagination.

---

66. On understanding Thomas's proofs this way, cf. Henri de Lubac, *The Discovery of God,* trans. A. Dru (Grand Rapids: Eerdmans, 1996), esp. ch. 3, "The Proof of God."

CHAPTER II

Moral Space

1. THE NOTION OF MORAL SPACE

The moral space in which we dwell, public or private, is not simply there, not simply something we move around in and then decorate according to whim and will. Nor is it conceptually accessible from all vantage points. It is something that is constituted by having certain concepts that are not so much descriptions of a reality that is just "there" as they open that space and are the vehicles used to move within it. To have certain concepts is to find certain kinds of space and to be able to move within them. Not to have them is to live in a different life world. To use them is not just to describe something out there; it is also to say something about ourselves. Faith is just such a concept, for it opens a life world; to have faith is to live and move and have one's being within that world.

There are at least two important implications to talking about the space of our lives in this way. The first has to do with what is involved in talking about "moral space." Moral space is not simply a space found within a neutral, Newtonian grid, an area reserved for moral action in an otherwise larger, non-moral sphere. It is the space of life itself; it constitutes the possibilities that we have for understanding ourselves as persons. Our identity as persons is formed within such space. But not only is our identity dependent on the moral space in which we dwell, so is our action. Or, perhaps, because our actions are the practices in which our concepts are rooted and played out, and we are constituted by our actions and their shape, it is better to say that moral space is the space that is the playing out of ourselves as living human agents. What we can imagine that we can and should do and what we should be in life is our moral space. Moral space is also a realm of moral imagination. Imagination need not be fantasy and projection, for we do not make up moral space; we live it. Moral imagination is the ability to play out the possibilities of a moral space. Moral concepts and identity-constituting concepts are not chosen from a neutral vantage point and simply "applied," for to do that would be to choose without a sense of self or value, but are something more like defining capacities exercised within a life world. For example, Aristotelian *phronesis* is a matter of seeing and doing just actions; it is an act of moral imagination that exploits the possibilities of justice within that life world. Similarly, "faith" can be a form of moral imagination, the ability to live out a world in which Christ is Lord.[1]

The second consequence of talking about moral space is that it is important to recognize that over the course of Western history the defining assumptions of our moral space have shifted. Spaces have been created and lost as a result. One that has been created is the very idea of the secular as we presently understand it. The public space we now assume — the secular, which used to be the *interregnum* prior to the kingdom of God — was created in the modern period by staking out the realm of "*factum* as an area of human autonomy . . . and *dominium* as a matter of absolute sovereignty and absolute ownership" according to John Milbank.[2] Its present existence had to be created, and that was done, Milbank notes, ironically, by bringing certain parts of the theological vocabulary into prominence. Now, that history is important to recognize because it forces us to see that the "secular" and "natural," which we assume as normative, depend upon us and our history. They say something about us when we use them. Neither is at the outset any more the *index et judex sui et falsi* than anything else. Thus a "Newtonian" picture of an absolute, universal, neutral space is

---

1. There have been a number of recent works on moral imagination, including its relation to faith. Cf., for example, Garrett Green, *Imagining God: Theology and the Religious Imagination* (San Francisco: Harper & Row, 1989); Mary Warnock, *Imagination* (Berkeley: University of California Press, 1976); David Bryant, *Faith and the Play of Imagination* (Macon, Ga.: Mercer University Press, 1989); Walter Brueggemann, *Texts under Negotiation: The Bible and Postmodern Imagination* (Minneapolis: Fortress Press, 1993).

2. John Milbank, *Theology and Social Theory: Beyond Secular Reason* (Oxford: Basil Blackwell, 1990), p. 15.

not itself actually neutral but bespeaks a certain sort of self-constituting moral world, with its own form of moral imagination, one shaped by a spectator's view of how to approach moral, scientific, and political questions.

This provides an important vantage point for understanding some deeper points about what is involved in the Lockean-Humean vision discussed in the previous chapter. Although it involved a crucial intellectual shift in the understanding of faith and how to discuss it, it was not *just* an intellectual shift or intellectual misunderstanding. The shift to a spectator's view from a participant's view is also a shift in the moral space of the Western world and in our understanding of what it means to be a self. Understanding this provides an important perspective on how one can even discuss the act of faith as a present possibility. It is not enough to point out the intellectual shortcomings and misrepresentations inherent in the spectator's view. For if faith is the key to one sort of moral space, and the spectator's view the key to another, then it is extremely problematic to try to imagine the world of faith — at least in any continuity with thinkers such as Augustine, Aquinas, or Calvin — without first coming to grips with the very different sense of what it means to be a self for anyone living in the modern world. What is at stake is *not* two theories or explanations of the world as the Lockean-Humean picture would try to have it, but two very different sorts of moral space with differing acts of imagination.

To put matters that way is to put them so sharply that it would appear to be impossible for one person, living in a specific moral space, to understand life in another. It suggests that we cannot talk with any coherence about other moral spaces. Other spaces would simply seem inconceivable ways of living to us. While that does happen, to lay much emphasis on the fact is also surely overstating the case, especially with respect to our own history. Historical shifts are never fully revolutionary; if what comes later undoes in important ways what preceded it, it also brings something of the past into the present, although it inevitably reshapes the defining assumptions of the past. There is never absolute discontinuity between two periods of history. And that means that there are almost always some sorts of conceptual bridges. Not only can we see the faces of our ancestors in ourselves, but we may even in so seeing find solutions to our problems in the modern world. And to the degree that we can, we can reconstitute and find present room in moral spaces first lived in during the past. But to do this it is necessary to come to some understanding of the moral space in which we live: of how we came to have the commitments we have, of just what they are and what their forms are, and by that to uncover not only their promises but their falsities as well. From that we can understand what choices we have made, and which ones we can make.

2. THE CENTER OF VALUE

2.1. From a Human World to an Anthropocentric World

There is an oft-told story that Copernicus's heliocentric hypothesis marked the end of the ancient and medieval world by displacing humans from the center of the universe. The story goes that medieval man did not go quietly, and fought by entrenched opinion and base authority Galileo's further working out of Copernicus's earlier suggestion. Not only, though, is that story terribly simplistic, it is not true. Just the opposite occurred. To be sure, the human was displaced by the new science, but not as the center of *value* in the universe, which nobody thought anyhow; rather the human model for explaining action and causality was undone. What was destroyed was the Aristotelian system of causality, a system that had taken human intention and action in a world of human interaction as its basis. The Aristotelian four causes — material, efficient, formal, and final — were largely causes in the sense that they answered the question "On what account, for what reason did x occur?" Within human action, formal causes and final causes — the reasons for which something is done — make perfect sense. Applied to the larger world, they gave a world that was at root spiritual and moral, a world in which purposeful human action and interaction fit harmoniously with the rest of nature. This world was undone, first by Galileo, and then by Descartes and Newton, making the physical world a world of matter, all of a piece, without purpose, blindly obeying physical laws of nature.[3] Yet it was also at this point, when the world was disenchanted and became less person-like, that humanity itself

---

3. Cf. Pietro Redondi, *Galileo Heretic* (Princeton: Princeton University Press, 1987). It seems that the church's reaction to Galileo had less to do with the heliocentric hypothesis *per se*, than it did with Galileo's reducing the heavenly bodies to mere flying rocks, and proposing a system of causality that made hash of theological explanations such as the transubstantiation of the Eucharist.

came more and more to be the spiritual center of the world, with less and less reason to look outward for direction and purpose, finding it safely ensconced within itself. Indeed, where else could it be found?

The shift to an anthropocentric understanding of the world was gradual, of course, like most historical shifts, with new insights embedded within the older worldview. But shifts there were. Although he had him still within the older celestial hierarchy and could discourse on what was not dignified in him, Pico della Mirandola in 1488 could nevertheless talk about man as being the center of the world, containing within himself the seeds of all things. In Pico's *Oration on the Dignity of Man,* when God creates he puts man "at the midpoint of the world." He then speaks to his creation thus:

> We have given to thee, Adam, no fixed seat, no form of thy very own, no gift peculiarly thine, that thou mayest feel as thine own, have as thine own, possess as thine own the seat, the form, the gifts which thyself shalt desire. A limited nature in other creatures is confined within the laws written down by Us. In conformity with thy free judgement, in whose hands I have placed thee, thou art confined by no bounds; and thou wilt fix the limits of nature for thyself. I have placed thee at the center of the world, that from there thou mayest more conveniently look around and see whatsoever is in the world.[4]

Thus to man is given the charge to be "the molder and maker of thyself; thou mayest sculpt thyself into what shape thou dost prefer." To be sure, man does not automatically pattern himself on the model of the angels; he must still look to higher natures. But it is his choice and he has within himself all things. We can see a similar shift to anthropocentrism in changes from the medieval period to the Renaissance in art. The nearly two-dimensional icons produced by the ancients and medievals whose only background is light itself gave way first to paintings with three-dimensional backgrounds of secular life outlining the holy figures in the foreground. In time those secular background figures, great and small, came to be the central focus and subject matter.

This, of course, is still a long way from Percy Bysshe Shelley's rantings against the divine as tyrannical, and his praise of Prometheus's revolution-

---

4. Pico della Mirandola, *Oration on the Dignity of Man,* trans. C. G. Wallis (Indianapolis: Bobbs-Merrill, 1965), pp. 4-5.

THE ACT OF FAITH

ary gift of reason and self-determining freedom that gave man his natural birthright.[5] Yet at the same time that Copernicus makes his discovery, a more comprehensive shift bringing humans to the center of value is also going on. It is a shift that, in time, will amount to much more than the "seeds of all" that Pico found planted in the human breast. When Descartes, for example, writes his *Meditations,* in form he closely follows a meditation undertaken by Augustine. But rather than finding a place for himself in the universe in the idea of perfection on which he depends,[6] he finds a standard for reason that will allow *him* to construct a world and to liberate himself from matter and the passions. Descartes's dualism shows "the way to an 'innerwordly liberation' of the soul" (Sources, 146). Unlike Plato and Augustine, who looked outwardly with love and attention to the world order ordained by God in order to find sense and value, for Descartes this order is nowhere to be found. But the discovery of inner rationality does give him a power to construct order, and to find self-mastery.[7]

Here is a decisive shift that brings an increasing sense of humans directing their own destiny. To be sure, Machiavelli had already heralded something of the sort in political theory, but his innovations are tinged with a strong pragmatic need simply to stabilize human life in a time of turmoil. What now comes into sight is something more than establishing a peaceful order; by an act of radical reflexivity, humans now can establish their own inner order and own selves. This is not simply a matter of taking responsibility for one's own life; it is creating one's self on the lines of a political order as if the individual were his or her own state. Nowhere is this so clear as in Kant, who takes the term "autonomy" to describe his moral ideal. Before Kant, "autonomy" had been strictly a political term applied to the self-rule of states; now it describes the individual's moral life. The moral life of dealing with others no longer depends on friendship but on

---

5. In his *Prometheus Unbound.*
6. On Augustine's meditation in *On Freedom of the Will,* cf. ch. 3, sec. 1.3.
7. For Descartes, "there is no such order. Being rational has now to mean something other than being attuned to this order. The Cartesian option is to see rationality, or the power of thought, as a capacity we have to *construct* orders which meet the standards demanded by knowledge, or understanding, or certainty. . . . If we follow this line, then the self-mastery of reason now must consist in this capacity being the controlling element in our lives, and not the sense; self-mastery consists in our lives being shaped by the order that our reasoning capacity constructs according to the appropriate standards" (Sources, 146-47).

reason and diplomacy, just as it does in negotiations between sovereign states.

At least two important beliefs emerge here that shape the modern sense of moral space and identity. First, is the belief that we *have* a self as well as the freedom to determine our selves. Just what is at stake here can be seen by considering an alternative view. Aquinas defined the soul as *forma unica corporis* — the unifying shape or form of bodily life. The human soul or subject on this view is the unifying activity of one's relations, not something separate from them. In the modern world, however, by an act of radical reflexivity we have learned to take a distanced stance to our own activities, which we can then go to work on. We become our own construction projects as it were (hence the obvious point and popularity of self-help books). We can survey our qualities and expand and improve them. To the degree that we can, we can add a certain sort of richness to the empirical self, which is largely contingent.

The second consequence of this ability to order life, and concern for doing so, is both a greatly enlarged and vital concern for ordinary life, and an assumption that it is what is really important. In part, this concern comes about negatively through the historical destruction of the hierarchies of the older world order. More positively, it is because "the full human life is now defined in terms of labor and production, on the one hand, and marriage and family life, on the other" (Sources, 213). Human life can and ought to be fulfilled within this world; it can also be fulfilled by diligent human effort. The fact that human life was materially improved by increasing commerce and technology underlined and contributed to the assumption.

Concern for ordinary life is a crucial and far-ranging aspect of moral thinking in the modern world. It encompasses not only a concern for the success of life — a concern for prosperity in broad and narrow senses, but also a concern over suffering that undoes a successful life. The ancients and medievals, who were not without compassion, could order suffering to *amor fati*, and use it for higher callings. For the modern self suffering is an evil precisely because it frustrates self-realization. Moreover, as ordinary callings come to be seen as valuable in themselves, a certain respect for equality also comes to the fore. Hierarchies differentiated as they oppressed. Their loss could only mean a newfound respect for all of humanity. This concern for ordinary life and equality has theological import as well. If ordinary life is important, it is important in good part because it is important to God. Therefore God does not call us out of the world, but within it. When Athanasius said "God became man so that man might become God," he meant that humans would be deified and transformed; the modern world took the Incarnation as deifying and hallowing human life in this world. So even God's chief concern is with life in this world, with the fulfillment of human life, with relieving suffering and oppression, and with establishing equality.

The indisputable moral importance of this affirmation of ordinary life cannot be overstated for the modern world. Extended into the areas of individual rights, our distaste for elitism, and concern for equality and problems of human suffering, it is bedrock moral ground for us. But it has another side as well, for it is not by itself necessarily a *concern* for another, nor does it necessarily entail our dealing with our neighbor or looking at her except through the lenses of our own experience. The modern sense of justice extends to others by canons of reasonable fairness the concern we have for ourselves. For example, it is sympathy that is the root of moral action for Hume, with sympathy largely a matter of not wanting to happen to others what we dislike happening to us. In Locke, as well as later liberalism, the social contract is made out by the demands of reason for individuals seeking to protect their own lives and property; law keeps us from running into each other. For Kant, that we are to treat no person as a means, but only as an end, is because others, like us, possess reason. In these ways, the concern for ordinary life has a tendency to be not only anthropocentric but also individualistic, and even egoistic.

There are significant tensions within the moral space of the modern world and its sense of the self, tensions that show the imprint of the differing sources from which it draws. On the one hand, the affirmation of the ordinary comes from the Jewish and Christian traditions of love of neighbor, and especially the Protestant emphasis on the priesthood of all believers, as well as its refusal to make faith and its vocations hierarchical. Neither can the moral impulse behind the Enlightenment be forgotten. The seventeenth century had genuine reason to doubt the efficacy of traditional moral authorities, authorities that had clearly contributed to the bloodshed of the Wars of Religion and the Civil War in England, wars that showed no hope of reconciliation. Some other way clearly had to be found to keep human life intact; that humans should construct a world for humans was an imperative. On the other hand, the Enlightenment began to mark the loss of a spiritually charged world that we did not create and that we had to go outside of ourselves to love. The loss was not just the result of finding within human strength and ingenuity the ability to construct its own world. This was also an anxious world, and its own uncertainty became its chief problem. Not only does anxiety keep us self-involved and at a distance from others, from extending ourselves and welcoming another, it also produces demands for hyper-certainty, control, and prediction. And thus is born an emphasis on distanced reason, an instrument for constructing a world, and in that also comes a loss of moral space configured by direct human interaction.[8]

2.2. Human Space as a Construction Site

So was born a new sort of moral space and a new moral and political philosophy. Moral interactions between humans are now to be managed by reason. It is reason, neutral and universal, that constructs the protecting state and manages the social contract; it is to guide our moral action in a human world. Now to put it that way would not at first blush have appeared so very strange to the preceding world. Platonists, Aristotelians, and Stoics as well as Augustine and Aquinas would have said nearly the same thing. But there is certainly a very different emphasis being placed on reason and its use now. For the Stoics, reason let us see the order of the world in order to consent to it and love it. For Aquinas and the natural law tradition, the natural law was not a general law of nature, but the reason inherent in our nature and in things. To live according to it was to live according to an *ordo amoris,* and to be reasonable was not to look to a standard and apply it; it was to become the standard. It was to interact in a truly human way. But now reason is distanced reason, something more like an instrument to achieve fulfillment, an application by the neutral self of a universal law. It is less a way of being in the world and something more like a way of brokering the world. This is the reason of the manager so effective at producing, extending, and serving the construction projects.

Why that is a troublesome moral project can be seen by looking at

---

8. On the seventeenth century's quest for certainty and shift to demands for certainty in reason, cf. Stephen Toulmin, *Cosmopolis: The Hidden Agenda of Modernity* (Chicago: University of Chicago Press, 1992).

what is involved in a well-known claim of Hobbes concerning the nature of political philosophy:

> The skill of making and maintaining commonwealths consists in certain rules, as do arithmetic and geometry, not, as tennis-play, on practice only; which rules neither poor men have the leisure, nor men that have had the leisure have hitherto had the curiosity or the method to find out.[9]

What Hobbes means here is rather straightforward, and is particularly helpful in coming to grips with the modern view of moral reasoning. For Hobbes the task of making commonwealths is that of discovering certain rules, especially rules and principles for understanding human nature, and then constructing commonwealths according to them so that the ends proper to human nature may be fostered. Those ends are also a matter of rules. Hobbes does not doubt that such rules and principles actually exist and can be spelled out. Under the early spell of Descartes's project and full of enthusiasm for being able to explain material existence mechanically, he explicates at length in Part I of *Leviathan* the causal chains of human behavior so that he can construct a state suitable to such a being. That human practice has constructed different sorts of commonwealths on the basis of experience and practice Hobbes does not doubt. What he does doubt is that those commonwealths are very good, for, he reasons, they *cannot* be well founded. Even commonwealths that have been long lived he regards as no valid counterexample. He argues:

> But, howsoever, an argument from the practice of men that have not sifted to the bottom, and with exact reason weighed the causes and nature of commonwealths, and suffer daily those miseries that proceed from the ignorance thereof, is invalid. For though in all places of the world men should lay the foundation of their houses on sand, it could not thence be inferred that so it ought to be.[10]

It is for this reason that philosophy cannot be like tennis. Practice and experience may, indeed, hit upon a happy solution in areas such as politics. Practice and experience, however, Hobbes thinks, can never serve as a sure

9. Thomas Hobbes, *Leviathan*, Part II, ch. 20.
10. Hobbes, *Leviathan*, Part II, ch. 20.

foundation on which to build our associations, for they involve no real knowledge of what holds those associations together. Their success is a bit of an accident; even when successful, there is nothing in them that can guarantee their permanence or success. Only a foundation of deductive reason, he thinks, can do that.

Hobbes's theory serves as a particularly transparent example both of how we think about constructing selves and their environments as well as the importance of distanced reason. It also serves as an example of modern moral reasoning, positive and negative. Positively, for instance, Hobbes would have us look at ourselves and others with a certain sort of moral objectivity. In historical context his theory is actually a sincere and imaginative attempt to deal with a situation that was devastating to human souls. There is a negative side to this theory, however, for if this ability to distance ourselves from ourselves has some positive value, it also hides the fact that it is dealing with any sort of context at all. It hides the fact that our social relations *are* like tennis, and that in light of a particular experience — the English Civil War — Hobbes is trying desperately to make a winning shot. Rather than claiming neutrality and distance to be a *wise* solution, at least in this situation, he is claiming to give a *necessary* solution for all times and all places. Not only does he call for a distance to ourselves; his solution forgets the people he is talking about and thus he eliminates vital resources, historical and habitual, needed to deal with particular situations.

This is dangerous for several reasons: by forgetting that thinking about our social relations is an activity of historical human knowing, we easily fall into the error of believing that there simply is an answer "out there" and that all we have to do is describe it, and that any fool with the right method can describe it. So we forget that we, the describers, are active beings in search of knowledge for some valuable reason, that we do live within moral frameworks. We forget that what we do and can know depends upon how we approach what we want to know. In such forgetting, it becomes all too easy to believe that what we have discovered by our objectivity is, in fact, purely, simply, and totally what is the case. When we do forget in this way, if there is anything else to know, we do not have left any habitual practice of knowing it. We also by practice habituate ourselves to think that persons are just the way we have described them, and that we can know all about them by analysis. We develop a habit of radical reflexivity that keeps us continually at a distance from ourselves. In the end,

THE ACT OF FAITH

then, if we keep telling ourselves that we are that way, we soon lose the ability to see ourselves any other way.

2.3. Moral Distance

2.3.1. The Utilitarian Version

There is a paradoxical nature to modern moral reasoning. On the one hand, there is a genuine concern for human life. The moral insights that we and other humans are not means, that there is a fundamental moral distinctness to humans, that there is a vital separateness to each human that we cannot presume to violate, are important and deep reaching. On the other hand, this radical reflexivity, this ability to distance ourselves also keeps us locked in on ourselves. The life world, the rough and tumble of human give and take and human contact and the matrix of human development, is set at a remove. History, our history, becomes not simply accidental, but radically contingent, and changeable at will. It is a burden to us. Our life's goods are seen as exchangeable and willed and no longer constitutive of and rooted in our historical communities. Our actual engagement with others is also always undertaken at a remove. Distanced reason and the spectator's viewpoint is therefore not simply a matter of reason, but an integral element of a new moral space, and a highly frustrating one at that. Paradoxically, at the very moment we come to appreciate the distinctness of each human life, we lose contact with it.

The problem is one that has dogged liberal modern moral and political philosophy, especially in the forms that try hardest to be rational, such as utilitarianism and social contract theory. In part, this is surely due to a reductionism that seeks general, publicly accessible features of human life upon which to reflect. This reductionism is perhaps inevitable simply because universal, objective, and distanced reasoning depends on general notions and not concrete particulars. It has to appeal generally, and not simply to those who have highly developed sensibilities. Bentham's highly rationalistic utilitarianism, a form of later Hobbesianism, is a prime example. Bentham sought to reduce human behavior, happiness, and motivation to the twin principles of pleasure and pain, and then sought to calculate how best to achieve the greatest happiness of all. He thought he could perform this calculation by the principle of utility, which calculated the specific amount of pain and pleasure to come out of any given act, and which then told the specific amount of happiness that would result from any given act.[11] The problem with such systems, however, is that they inevitably run roughshod over our "thick" moral concepts, the morality we have achieved, like tennis-play, by history and practice. Bentham's version of utilitarianism more than sufficiently has this quality, and is utterly without nuance; for him "pushpin is as good as poetry." Later utilitarians have tried to add that nuance. But it is not possible to fully encompass the moral concepts of the lived life world within this approach.

Consider the far more finely tuned version of Richard Brandt's "conscience utilitarianism," a recent attempt to make a utilitarian approach congruent with our thick moral concepts. Much more bending than Bentham's "act utilitarianism" (the calculation of utility for every moral act), it involves attempting to determine what optimal social moralities there might be by figuring out what states of affairs fully informed people in general want and then linking that outcome with the actions necessary to achieve it, as well as with the "motivations and aversions" (Brandt's definition of "conscience") that bring about such actions. By such linkage he thinks we can determine rationally what sorts of aversions and motivations ought to be instilled in members of society in order to achieve maximum utility, and which ones, personally and socially, ought to be and can be rejected by rational reflection. Brandt tries hard to avoid the old hardline reductionism of utilitarianism, and to propose the more modest task of analyzing (but still read "transforming") moral questions in terms of states of mind such as "motivations" and "aversions." Although he is trying to retain the sense of thick moral concepts, this analysis, he thinks, is rationally necessary, for traditional terms such as "good," "better," "right," and "wrong" are "far from satisfyingly clear."[12] The analysis is simply to give us clarity. Once we go through it "the answers to our normative questions can

---

11. In a Hobbesian-like move, Bentham claims of the principle of utility that is alone rational: "The *principle of utility* recognizes this subjection [to the governance of pleasure and pain], and assumes it for the foundation of the system, the object of which is to rear the fabric of felicity by the hands of reason and law. Systems which attempt to question it, deal in sounds instead of sense, in caprice instead of reason, in darkness instead of light" (*An Introduction to the Principles of Morals and Legislation* [Oxford: Clarendon Press, 1876], ch. I.I).

12. Richard Brandt, *Facts, Values, and Morality* (Cambridge: Cambridge University Press, 1997), p. 8.

THE ACT OF FAITH

then be derived from learning exactly which of these states of mind would exist in a person who was fully factually informed — roughly about everything knowledge of which would tend to change that state of mind."[13] This analysis then allows us both to take seriously thick moral concepts and empirical psychological facts and to link them. Thus we can understand which ones are important and which ones rational reflection can dissolve when they are irrational. The point is to see that "the acquisition of desires/aversions and values is a lawful process and some of the causal links — conditioning and stimulus generalization — are very important for living. But it also seems as if many effects of this process are also subject in a lawful way to being undermined by vivid reflection on facts."[14] Brandt's discussion of motivational theory, and how information can and ought to change our view of things, does come as close as any utilitarianism has to fitting itself to the moral world in which most of us live.

Yet, even so, he ends up in much the same place as his predecessors, namely with a theoretical approach that is unself-reflective and unself-conscious, and that misses the personal context that the older sense of "conscience" bears. There is a sense in which he simply fakes the morality of conscience. Just how can be seen by considering a brief passage from the Czech writer Ivan Klíma's novel *Judge on Trial*. It is the accusation of a wife to her husband, a judge in the highly rational system of Eastern European socialism during the Cold War:

> "Adam, I've been pondering on you for all of the past ten years. Sometimes when I felt I couldn't stand it any longer — your remoteness from me and from us — I've told myself that you probably can't help it. That they changed you during the war and stole something from you that you can never get back."
>
> "What do you think they stole from me?"
>
> "Everything, apart from your reason. You're sometimes tender — because you know you ought to be — but not because there is any tenderness in you."

This conversation, which, in fact, any number of wives have had with "rational" husbands, is the flavor of Brandt's "conscience utilitarianism." It begins to dawn on the reader that nowhere and never in his explication of

---

13. Brandt, *Facts, Values and Morality*, p. 9.
14. Brandt, *Facts, Values and Morality*, p. 59.

the idea in *Facts, Values, and Morality* is it ever suggested that somebody who is thinking about the right thing to do might actually ask another person what he or she thinks, even if it happens to involve them. After all, if you're fully informed, you're fully informed. Nowhere in plotting the optimal social morality is it ever considered that you might ask somebody's permission as to whether or not he wants to join in such an enterprise (unless this is part of the standing "social constraints"). In that sort of context "sympathy" and "empathy" are discussed, but again as qualities of the calculator. The person one might actually sympathize with is eerily absent from the discussion. That sort of moral reflection has nothing to do with the thick concept of conscience. For conscience is not simply a matter of "motivations" and "aversions" as Brandt would have it; it is actually taking a good, close look at the people you happen to bump into, and taking them seriously.

It is clear that there is a moral allegiance that operates in *Facts, Values, and Morality*. But it is not conscience. It is an allegiance to a system of quasi-scientific, objective, ahistorical, and distanced third person rationality. Now, Brandt has gone some considerable distance to link that commitment to our moral commitments to people. But the problem is not distance; it is one of commensuration.

2.3.2. The Social Contract Version

The problem of moral distance also appears in the Lockean tradition of the social contract. This tradition, to be sure, avoids the blatant reductionism of utilitarianism. Because it also seeks to put human moral interaction under the rubric of a contract, it would appear to depend upon and encourage human engagement. But on what grounds and to what degree? Ultimately it is still distanced and consciously avoids precisely the moral commitments that lie closest to our moral identity. Or, perhaps better put, by avoiding them, it transforms the nature and space of those commitments to the degree that it excludes them from discussion.

The problem is that it tries to put humans *behind,* and not within, their moral frameworks. By sharply redefining what constitutes the public and the private, by engaging a Newtonian picture of moral space, it excludes from discussion the very commitments that earlier ages thought most important for moral discussion. The tendency is illustrated most succinctly in Locke's justly celebrated *Letter Concerning Toleration.* The

THE ACT OF FAITH

circumstances of the letter are well known. Locke, himself an exile in Holland at the time, argues for toleration of dissenters from official English religion. But he does not argue like Gamaliel in the *Book of Acts,* who argued for toleration of the Christian sect within Judaism by suggesting that intolerance might be a matter of opposing God, who would overcome anyhow if these people were right. Locke does not seek common religious ground. Rather, he first defines the commonwealth as a "Society of Men constituted only for the procuring, preserving, and advancing of their own *civil Interests,*" with civil interests being "Life, Liberty, Health, and Indolency of Body; and the Possession of outward things such as Money, Lands, Houses, Furniture and the like."[15] Then, because a church is, according to Locke, "a voluntary Society of men, joining themselves together of their own accord,"[16] it is clear that religious commitments lie outside the purview of the State, except insofar as those commitments might impinge on civil interests. Although Locke himself would have been willing to admit a far greater degree of impingement than his successors might, a decisive move has been made. We choose our ultimate moral frameworks, and they are not a matter of public discussion.

The "social contract" is not, despite outward appearances, a moral negotiation at all; it is a negotiation meant to protect our prior, individual choices about the good. Locke describes the social contract using the fiction of a state of nature, which already avoids the biblical picture, and ultimately assumes his own theory. In the state of nature he describes man in two contrary ways. He is both content and self-sufficient by the use of his reason, but also anxious for his person and possessions because of the arbitrary execution of the law of nature and the unreasonableness of men in the state of nature. Thus he negotiates a contract with others, demanded and formed by reason, to preserve his life, liberty, and possessions. He does so with people of similar intent. This demand for a contract, and its form, he presents as a law of nature.

There is, however, an ambiguity in exactly what a "law of nature" means. To the ancients and medievals, to fulfill the *natural law* meant to fulfill human nature; natural law was morally normative. It was not like the law of gravity, a law of nature, which simply describes natural pro-

---

15. John Locke, *A Letter Concerning Toleration,* ed. James Tully (Indianapolis: Hackett Publishing, 1983), p. 27.
16. Locke, *A Letter Concerning Toleration,* p. 28.

cesses. Perhaps in a time of terminological change, the difference was not apparent to Locke. But one soon sees that Locke's "law of nature" is not morally normative, for what stands prior to the invoking of the law of nature is ultimately the right of self-preservation that is Locke's moral bedrock. That is what is morally normative, and it cannot be negotiated. The "law of nature" that leads us to negotiate the social contract is simply the rational requirement of finding the procedural means for defending this right. It has no particular moral content itself.[17] Morality is not in the negotiation at all; one steps outside one's sense of the good in order to negotiate its protection. Nor is the negotiation for this reason really social, a matter of persons negotiating with each other and shaping their sense of the good by the push and pull of human contact. Neither do they realize their moral nature in that push and pull, nor are they expected to do so.

Thus the social contract is not actually social, but a form, even a defining form, of individualism. What we are negotiating in the public realm is not the moral at all, which is universally given as self-preservation; all else is choice, albeit, by the ethics of belief, it should be reasonable choice. This is not necessarily selfish, although it has aptly been styled "possessive individualism." But it is important to recognize that what is negotiated is the procedural guarantees of liberty, and defenses of our right to be self-contained and to be left alone, to choose what goods we will pursue. There is nothing normatively moral in the negotiation itself, no discussion of who we ought to be. Human nature is not fulfilled or bettered in the interaction, and reason used to negotiate the contract is not moral reason, but as in Locke's philosophy of religion, a neutral, distanced guide. This tendency is not only Locke's, but haunts contemporary versions of contract theory, such as Rawls's, as well.[18]

---

17. In this argument I am loosely following Leo Strauss's *Natural Right and History* (Chicago: University of Chicago Press, 1953), esp. pp. 215-33. Strauss notes also an important contradiction in Locke's story. On Locke's own principles for reason, the natural law cannot be innate. It can therefore only be discovered within civil society where there is sufficient discourse and time to discern it. But, of course, for Locke civil society is the *result* of the negotiation.

18. The upshot of Locke's approach, particularly when it is combined with a Kantian view of reason and the person, is seen in John Rawls's influential *Theory of Justice* (Cambridge, Mass.: Harvard University Press, 1971). Seen as an alternative to the utilitarianism that dominated moral theory and liberal political policy of the previous hundred years, Rawls's attempt was to reinterpret the Kantian transcendental ego and establish a rational system of pure procedural justice. Like Locke, he did so by constructing a hypothetical situa-

This raises three sorts of problems. First, it is highly questionable that we can or ought to see ourselves this way. To see ourselves as distanced from our concrete commitments this way is actually *damaging* to them; it is *not* neutral,[19] for distance is not neutral itself, but constitutes a substitute moral framework. Second, even the various social goods that we are negotiating are themselves not "neutral" but gain much of their desirability from the historical communities in which they exist and are bound up with concrete, historical, moral communities.[20] Third, there is no genuine negotiation between persons. Who we are is bound up with our commitment to the good; to leave it aside and to negotiate communal norms is tantamount to letting a computer run the figures.[21]

---

tion, the "veil of ignorance," where negotiators are to reason out the contract as if they were not aware of how exactly they themselves would be affected if it were enacted. This device, Rawls argued, would allow fairness to be the ultimate outcome, for reason would demand of each of us that we would never choose to make any position in the social world so disadvantaged that we would be unwilling to accept it for ourselves. Further, if there were to be inequalities we would only accept them if somebody's advantage would ultimately benefit all.

In Rawls's work reason is morally more normative than in Locke since it actually demands certain outcomes, although it remains procedural. But it also spells some far-reaching consequences for how the moral self is to be understood. One, it does not substantially change Locke's individualism one whit. Two, and connected to the issue of individualism, it requires that we be able to see ourselves as selves who can make moral decisions without "thick" moral commitments, that we can reason morally without calling into play any other sense of the good than self-preservation and the demands of universal reason. In short, while avoiding the reductionism of utilitarianism, it actually sketches a normative theory of the self as transcendentally reasonable. All other commitments are choices of the self, and not ultimately contributing to our moral identity and reasoning.

19. Cf. especially Michael Sandel, *Liberalism and the Limits of Justice* (Cambridge: Cambridge University Press, 1982): "But we cannot regard ourselves as independent in this way without great cost to those loyalties and convictions whose moral force consists partly in the fact that living by them is inseparable from understanding ourselves as the particular persons we are — as members of this family or community or nation or people.... Allegiances such as these are more than values I happen to have or aims I 'espouse at any given time.'... They allow that to some I owe more than justice requires or even permits, not by reason of agreements I have made but instead in virtue of those more or less enduring commitments which taken together partly define the person I am" (p. 179).

20. Cf. Michael Walzer, *The Spheres of Justice* (New York: Basic Books, 1983).

21. Peter Winch points out: "Rawls' contract is an entirely abstract construction, a theoretical device. Normally the point of saying that a common arrangement must be ar-

2.3.3. Reactions and Tensions

Of course, not all of the modern West's energies have gone into developing disengaged, instrumental reason for the use of the individualist self. There have been strong and vital reactions, beginning soon after the Enlightenment. Rousseau, for example, saw in a way that Locke did not that the human self *is* shaped by historical and social factors. The problem then was to choose the right ones, the ones that would promote real human freedom. Nietzsche argued that the rational morality of his age, especially its attempts to be benevolent, was simply a matter of *ressentiment,* born out of weakness, and a refusing to deal with nature itself. Such thinkers, by trying to force a return to nature and to ground humans in nature, provide an alternative to disengaged reason that has been vastly influential in shaping the modern self. They also signal a tension within the features of modern culture, or perhaps even a set of countervailing forces that, together with more rational approaches, help form the moral space of liberal democratic societies of late capitalism. Each gives distinctive flavor to the modern sense of self, even if they are often held in tension. The tension, however, is often regarded as creative, and not contradictory. This is right since both are indi-

---

rived at by 'negotiation' is that one must wait on the result of the negotiation in order to know what the arrangement is going to be. One may, of course, make more or less well-founded and shrewd predictions about the likely outcome, but such predictions must await verification or falsification by events. There is room for surprises. Rawls, however, does not say: put the interested parties together, set suitable limits to the kinds of consideration to be deemed relevant to the negotiation, and then retire to see what happens. He *calculates* the result. In other words the outcome is not a genuinely negotiated one at all: the idea of a 'negotiation' is nothing more than a logical device for presenting a certain form of argument, the conclusion of which can be appraised by anyone. This is of course connected with the fact that Rawls' contracting parties are not human beings at all, but rational constructions. And the notion of 'reason' or 'rationality' that is deployed is a purely *a priori* one: not derived from any serious examination of how such terms are actually used" (*Simone Weil: The Just Balance* [Cambridge: Cambridge University Press, 1989], pp. 184-85).

Rawls's most recent work, *Political Liberalism* (New York: Columbia University Press, 1993), has sought to avoid the first of these problems, and relatedly, the second as well, by limiting itself to a "more genuinely political solution." But it is not clear that it succeeds, as it depends on a presentation independent of "any wider comprehensive religious or philosophical doctrine." And to the degree that it does so depend, it does not avoid the criticism that it is not we who actually negotiate, but a pale, thin shadow of our concretely committed selves.

THE ACT OF FAITH

vidualist. The reaction to rationalism, in fact, both ensures the triumph of the individual and offers a sort of virtual theology to undergird it.

The reaction to rationalism is various and complex. By concentrating on one historical manifestation of it, namely romanticism, however, its most salient features can be highlighted. The romantic rejection of rationalism, even in Pietism, which contributes to it, was not a conservative rejection. The rejection of science as authority, and even the scientific image of the world and human beings proposed by thinkers such as Hobbes and Newton, was *not* an invitation to return to traditional authorities and texts. That was not what William Blake meant when he portrayed Newton at the bottom of the sea of materialism. Romanticism was not only an even stronger refusal of the authority of the past, it was also a rejection of present authority in favor of freedom that was quite willing to reject *what* scientific reason was proposing, namely a universe ordered by laws. Materialist physics did not give the deep truths, the existential truths that make one alive. The romantic reaction appears irrational, and even nihilistic. Although it was not without its destructive revolutionaries, early and late, like most important reactions its deep motivation really came from its own positive sense of the value of human life that it believed rationalism had betrayed. Life involved more of spirit than rationalism allowed. Humanity had been cut off from itself and its deepest sources of value by its rational constructions and attempts to mold life artificially.

There are two chief features to the romantic view of the self. First is its commitment to freedom, and its horror of heteronomy. A life that is truly free is one in which the principles of action are chosen, chosen from within, and committed to. Motivation and intention mean more than result. If Kant is a "restrained romantic," he is still a romantic in this sense. Second, romanticism believed that modern humanity was cut off from the spirit inherent in nature, which alone can give authentic life. In calling for a return to the sources of nature, however, romanticism was not looking for anything like an intellectual alternative to science; it was not interested in discovering the truth about nature. Indeed, the problem of rationalism was that it tried to objectify nature. The romantics were not going to make that mistake again; they were interested in living from nature. Isaiah Berlin notes of Schiller, who signals this attitude well:

> [Schiller] introduces for the first time what seems to me to be a crucial note in the history of human thought, namely that ideals, ends, objec-

tives are not to be discovered by intuition, by scientific means, by reading sacred texts, by listening to experts or to authoritative persons; that ideals are not to be discovered at all, they are to be invented; not to be found but to be generated as art is generated.[22]

Nature, on this view, is not outside us. It is a force at the root of humanity itself that gives it dignity and to which we have access through our impulses and their articulation. We have access to nature through our own nature, and we have a deep, even moral need to express that inner nature, for our power for life is in our doing, our expression. Now, because it does pay attention to our nature as the voice of nature, the source of value, romanticism is far more sympathetic to our inner life than disengaged reason. It is even more sympathetic to theology, at least for those thinkers who have been able to interpret God "in terms of what we see striving in nature and finding voice within ourselves" (Sources, 371), although it has no sympathy with any form of heteronomous authority.

Expression of this inner nature is crucial for one to be a self, for nature itself is infinitely striving forward, and to partake of it is to give it voice and move ahead oneself. The romantics were consistent here. Speaking is not speaking *of* nature; it is a symbol of nature, not so much as signaling nature through a verbal signifier, but as giving life to nature in a way that will not betray its infinity and creativity. Symbols have to be created, and life has to be symbolic. If symbolism is often vague, and deliberately so — Baudelaire said that it was no virtue to be understood — it is somehow truer, and surely more interesting than any objective truths we utter. Symbolism connects us to nature, and if it contributes more to evoking feeling than rational thought, for the romantics that is the way it should be. Creative art rather than contemplative science is life. But moreover, it is necessary that one express nature. So the freely creating human will is one of the paramount synthetic features of romanticism.[23]

---

22. Isaiah Berlin, *The Roots of Romanticism* (Princeton: Princeton University Press, 1999), p. 87.
23. Cf. Berlin, *The Roots of Romanticism*: "Th[e]se are the fundamental bases of romanticism: will, the fact that there is no structure to things, that you can mould things as you will — they come into being only as a result of your moulding activity — and therefore opposition to any view which tried to represent reality as having some kind of form which could be studied, written down, learnt, communicated to others, and in other respects treated in a scientific manner" (p. 127).

THE ACT OF FAITH

Charles Taylor's description of the broad rebellion against rationalism as "expressive individualism" insofar as it partakes of romantic ideals is therefore apt and lets us see how both disengaged reason *and* the reaction to it stand on a continuum. *Both* are radically anthropocentric and even egocentric, for the individual remains the center of action. This works out in at least two ways with respect to the individual's relation to others. For expressivism, communities are often obstacles to nature, as Rousseau suggested. Or, if they are valuable they are valuable because they are vehicles for self-expression. When they don't work that way there is a moral imperative to change them, for they have become obstacles. On both counts, however, modern communities and relations, and thinking about communities and relations, are often less genuinely communal and interactive than poly-individualistic. Feeling the aridity of isolated, possessive individualism, the subject finds itself needing relations; it is even now defined as "being essentially relational," as it is in much contemporary theology and certain forms of communitarianism. It is the individual self that is being related, and it is truncated when unable to put itself in enriching relations. So there may even be a *right* to relations, which is a really odd way of seeing things. Here, especially when any sort of appeal to an external order is missing, an appeal one could make in both Platonism and Christianity, moral depths become located *within* the soul, not actually in interactive relations. The richness of relations does not really come from the relations themselves, or from the letting another into one's life; it comes from the nature within. Thus there is a decided tendency in expressivism to subjectivism as well as a deep moral commitment to anthropocentrism, since moral sources are found fully within.[24] Expressivism adds relations to the soul; it is not genuinely relational.

---

24. Cf. Sources, 389-90: "That examining the soul should involve the exploration of a vast domain is not, of course, a new idea. The Platonic tradition would concur. But this domain is not an 'inner' one. To understand the soul, we are led to contemplate the order in which it is set, the public order of things. What is new in the post-expressivist era is that the domain is within, that is, it is only open to a method of exploration which involves the first-person stance. That is what it means to define the voice or impulse as 'inner.'

"Of course, Augustine had a notion of something 'inner' which similarly stretched beyond our powers of vision: our 'memory.' But at the base of this is God; to penetrate to the depths of our memory would be to be taken outside ourselves. And this is where we achieve our ultimate integrity as persons, in the eye of God, from the outside. In the philosophy of nature as source, the inexhaustible domain is properly within. To the extent

To criticize the different sources of the modern sense of the self and the moral space in which it dwells, however, is not the same thing as to criticize the shape that results from their interpenetration, for each can bring a remedy for the insufficiencies and excesses of the other. The picture here seems much brighter, and even comfortably familiar. Romanticism and its heirs certainly give to liberalism in both its contract theory and utilitarian versions a broader sense of human imperfection, a deeper sense of what constitutes human flourishing, as well as a need for self-understanding and toleration. For example, within the framework of Lockean contract theory where the pursuit of the good is an inescapably individual choice, it can give a deeper sense of what those choices can and ought to be. (Locke talks about little more than the pursuit of property and self-dominion.) It also — and this is appealing to theology — gives a sense of a mysterious something larger than ourselves in which we participate, which we cannot control and which we can never describe accurately, but must talk about with passion, concern, and commitment, and which can break in upon us. Disengaged reason, on the other hand, tempers the nihilistic fire of romanticism and its reliance on sheer will and feeling. We do often need to get distance, rational distance, on our needs and desires and personal projects. It thus offers a sense of order and fairness that romantic rebellions are prone to override to the great destruction of human flourishing.[25] One gives heart, the other order.

It still, of course, remains to be asked whether this is the moral space in which Christian faith moves, or in which it could move. Perhaps it is, if the problem is simply a degree of distance to the other, neighbor or God, and how to ameliorate it. But if the problem is modernity's unflinching

---

that digging to the roots of our being takes us beyond ourselves, it is to the larger nature from which we emerge. But this we only gain access to through its voice in us. This nature, unlike Augustine's God, cannot offer us a higher view on ourselves from beyond our own self-exploration. The modern, post-expressivist subject really has, unlike the denizens of any earlier culture, 'inner depths.'"

25. Cf. Berlin, *The Roots of Romanticism*: "The result of romanticism, then, is liberalism, toleration, decency and the appreciation of the imperfections of life, some degree of rational self-understanding. This was very far from the intentions of the romantics. But at the same time — and to this extent the romantic doctrine is true — they are the persons who most strongly emphasised the unpredictability of all human activities. They were hoist with their own petard. Aiming at one thing, they produced, fortuitously for us all, almost the exact opposite" (p. 147).

sense of self-possession and willed self-determination, and its sense of the normal, then we may have simply described the triumphant failure to find any truly deep, abiding consent to a Good that calls and indwells us, and the openness necessary to be taught by it. Giving any sort of full picture of how modern liberal sensibilities work with respect to these questions, and any answer to them, remains for a later portion of this work. Before we can say much about these questions, what the moral space of premodern Christian faith has been — and the sense of the self with which it operates — itself needs to be told.

CHAPTER III

The Concept of Faith in the New Testament

Wittgenstein put the problem we face about belief this way. We tend to assume that belief — and by that he meant "belief" generally, not just religious belief — is a matter of bringing the thinking subject into a relation with an external object, a fact.[1] What does he mean? Consider the biblical material: There it is, somewhere outside us, containing numerous accounts of facts. To believe it on the assumption that Wittgenstein worries about is to bring our minds into a relation with those facts. We picture that relation like this: the Bible tells a story, it presents the facts; to believe it is to believe the facts in a way that is similar to believing what *The New York Times* might say about recent election results. Of course, to look at it this way is to raise all sorts of "scientific" and historical questions. Are the facts that the Bible relates themselves the real facts? It then takes critical examination of this question, a matter of plotting the biblical telling of the facts onto a time line of "real" facts to ascertain whether we are justified in believing what the Bible says or not. This is the Lockean view of things.

This is a highly misleading way of looking at the Bible. In fact, it misses the whole point. The Bible was not written as a factual account, at least not as *The New York Times* is written; it wasn't written as fiction, ei-

---

1. "Here it appears superficially as if the proposition *p* stood to the object *A* in a kind of relation" (*Tractatus Logico-Philosophicus* 5.541). Wittgenstein goes on to attack in *Philosophical Investigations* x, xi, the picture that this engenders, namely that belief is a state of the soul, as if we could look into someone's head to see what he believes.

THE ACT OF FAITH

ther. More important, it wasn't written to outsiders. It was written by people of faith to people of faith, an act of personal communication. It has the authority of personal communication in which the tellers of the stories are moral witnesses writing to other witnesses. The way they tell the story and their own stories are intricately bound up with the facts they tell; what the relevant facts are cannot be separated from that. From beginning to end they are telling what they see; they don't see facts and *then* put an interpretation on it: "So we interpret it, and *see* it as we *interpret* it."[2]

This observation applies not only to how we should understand the biblical writings, but also to the sort of faith they call for and address. The Bible talks about having faith in God and having faith in Jesus Christ. In doing so it is not trying to bring people to believe it, as if the nature of belief were already understood and common, as if one simply had to believe the facts. What is talked about *and* the way it is talked about *and* the way it is received is distinctive to what it means to have faith. St. John in a frequently cited and frequently abused passage claims at the end of his gospel: "Now Jesus did many other things in the presence of his disciples, which are not written in this book. But these are written so that you might believe that Jesus is the Messiah, the Son of God, and that through believing you may have life in his name" (John 20:30-31). Since he writes to believers and not the Roman authorities, he is not trying to get his readers to start believing as a result of his prose, but is telling them the things essential to living in faith. We may give bread to somebody who is hungry so that they might live, but we are not bringing them to life in doing so, for they already are living. There would be little point in giving them bread otherwise. But we give them bread so that they might live in the sense that being alive, they need nourishment. So too the biblical material. It is the address of the Word through words that those who read them may have the life of faith. That, of course, is why the story is told each Sunday; it is not to convert those in the pews. The story is the daily bread of the community that brings it to live with each other and in God. It opens up a certain space,

---

2. L. Wittgenstein, *Philosophical Investigations,* xi, p. 193e. For a discussion of this in Wittgenstein and its particular relation to religious belief, cf. Peter Winch, "The Expression of Belief," in *Proceedings and Addresses of the American Philosophical Association* 70, no. 2; "Lessing and the Resurrection" (unpublished ms.); and my "Faith, Belief, and Perspective" in *The Philosophy of Peter Winch* (forthcoming).

and faith is the way we move within that space. Thus Wittgenstein's observation:

> Christianity is not based on a historical truth; rather, it offers us a (historical) narrative and says: now believe! But not, believe this narrative with the belief appropriate to a historical narrative, rather, believe, through thick and thin, which you can only do as the result of a life. *Here you have a narrative, don't take the same attitude to it as you take to other historical narratives!* Make a *quite different* place in your life for it — there is nothing *paradoxical* about that![3]

So the conceptual problem of faith is both to show that faith *is* personal and a matter of participation for the biblical writers and the theological tradition, and to describe the life-world of faith — its sensibilities and virtues, its dispositions, both communal and individual. The task of conceptual uncovering is also a task in the service of recovering that life-world now in a world in which we stand so other to ourselves, to others, and to a God who is, while transcendent, ever Subject in all that we do in faith.

1. FAITH AND FAITH IN CHRIST

Faith is not, of course, an invention of Christianity, but something it shares with Judaism through the Scriptures it calls the Old Testament. The Old Testament provides the linguistic background to New Testament calls for faith and prepares the ground for Christianity's historical self-understanding of its religious and narrative coherence. St. Paul, for example, roots his understanding of Christianity in his reading of the promises of God and Israel's history as stories that are centrally concerned with faith from beginning to end. So while Christianity makes the importance of faith to be faith in Christ, and emphasizes a certain way of understanding that faith, particularly derived from Paul and John, the Old Testament highlighting of faith as central to religion gives an important sense to what *faith in Christ* might mean.

---

3. Ludwig Wittgenstein, *Culture and Value,* trans. Peter Winch, ed. G. H. von Wright (Chicago: University of Chicago Press, 1980), p. 45e.

THE ACT OF FAITH

1.1. The Old Testament Background

With one possible exception (Isa. 26:2), the Old Testament does not have a noun for what we would call "faith." Rather, it is forms of the verb '*mn* (from which derives "amen") that most often designate "faith" and its various meanings. It is an activity or disposition to activity. The range of meaning of '*mn* and its forms is similar to that of the English word "believe." It can designate simple belief, say, in a report, as well as deeper moral responses such as "trust," "commitment," "obedience," and "faithfulness." It often does designate or assume, even in a religious context, simple belief, such as believing that God exists or that God is present in Israel's history, that God has historically done certain things. This meaning of faith, however, as in the New Testament, is not full religious faith, which is something much deeper. If the fool says in his heart that there is no God (Ps. 14), he is not denying that God exists, or even that God has led his people out of Egypt into Canaan; he is failing to live out the life of obedience and gratitude that such a personal and communal history would demand. He acts as if God does not see what he does. So he is a fool not because he is ignorant, but, as with all fools, because he ought to know better. The fool can be said to believe in some sense. That sense, however, by itself is not religion. But, if simple belief is not by itself true religion, true religion is still not separable from believing certain things about the God of Israel. In the case of the all-important Exodus tradition, for example, full religious faith does involve memory of what God has done.

Yet within that tradition faith always involves the deeper responses of confidence in God's ability to preserve his elect nation, and obedience to his commandments, especially the avoidance of idolatry. And it issues in praise. It is at the deeper level of "trust" and "obedience" that one begins to see the religious importance of faith in the Old Testament and the commitment it entails. Most religious uses of the verb carry these meanings. The Exodus tradition makes clear that the faithfulness of obedience, rooted in the memory of what God has done for Israel, is the lifeblood of the nation's existence. Keeping the covenant leads to keeping the gift of the land; to fail in faithfulness, and ultimately in memory in any real sense, is to lose that gift.[4] But as is also clear, because faithfulness is rooted in a his-

---

4. Cf. for example, the promises and warnings in Deuteronomy.

tory with God and in a covenant it also touches on the deepest parts of Israel's identity, which makes it deeply personal and intersubjective. To have this history as one's own is to find oneself being led to a life of holiness. In Deuteronomy, for example, when a son asks his father what the meaning of the statutes and ordinances of the Lord is, the father is to reply with the history of the Exodus (Deut. 6:20-25).

Faith, then, although it includes belief, in its most important religious sense is never mere belief. What is believed *about* what God has done for Israel has deeper connections to God's purposes and Israel's very identity. As soon as Israel has been delivered from Egypt and brought to Sinai, God declares the purpose of the Exodus: "You have seen what I did to the Egyptians, and how I bore you on eagles' wings and brought you to myself. Now, therefore, if you obey my voice and keep my covenant, you shall be my treasured possession of all the peoples. Indeed, the whole earth is mine, but you shall be for me a kingdom of priests and a holy nation" (Exod. 19:4-6). To be holy, which is to keep God's covenant, is Israel's defining destiny and *raison d'être*. It is not an external command, but one that is ultimately internalized and that fulfills the one who is faithful: "Blessed is the one who walks not in the counsel of the wicked, nor stands in the way of sinners . . . but his delight is in the law of the Lord, and on his law he meditates day and night. He is like a tree planted by streams of water, who bears its fruit in its season and whose leaf does not wither" (Ps. 1). To hear God's word is to be claimed by it; to live according to it demonstrates the power of the word, and reflects God's glory by the very indwelling of the word that God directs to his people.[5]

What, then, is the specific shape of faith in the Old Testament? There are two standard and paradigm examples of faith in the Old Testament that exemplify the moral shape and quality of faith. The first shows the nature of faith as *trust;* the second shows the nature of faith as *discernment and waiting.* Individually and together they also show how just how faith in God is personal. These two examples are the stories of Abraham

---

5. Cf. Hans Urs von Balthasar, *The Glory of the Lord: VI; Theology: The Old Covenant* (San Francisco: Ignatius Press, 1991). E.g., quoting Deut. 30:11-14 — "The word is very near you; it is in your mouth and in your heart, so that you can do it" — von Balthasar comments: "It is precisely this immediacy, which penetrates mouth and heart, that demonstrates the power of the word. It does not, however, intend to be a power that does violence but rather one which summons insistently: in the word, the infinite 'I' summons the finite 'I' to be fully itself" (p. 57).

THE ACT OF FAITH

in Genesis, and certain pronouncements Isaiah makes to King Ahaz. The stories of Abraham are particularly important insofar as Abraham is a prime exemplar of faith in Judaism, and through Paul, in Christianity as well.

In the stories of Abraham that stretch from Genesis 12 to Genesis 25, there are several episodes that specifically deal with Abraham's faith; all are bound up directly or indirectly with God's promise to Abraham that he will make of him a great nation. All when treating of Abraham's faith, do so as a matter of his trust in God and God's promises. In Genesis 12, Abram, who prior to this is given only a genealogy, is told at the age of seventy-five to leave his father's house and God will make of him a great nation. Wordlessly, Abram leaves his home and begins a series of lengthy wanderings. In Genesis 15, he is told again that he will be the father of a great nation; when he complains that this is not likely since he is childless (complaining is apparently not incompatible with trust), God calls him out of his tent to stand under the stars of heaven and declares that his descendants will be as numerous as those stars. It is written then that "he believed the Lord; and the Lord reckoned it to him as righteousness" (Gen. 15:6). Lacking descendants, and with Sarai his wife far beyond childbearing years, Abram begets a son, Ishmael, of Sarai's slave, Hagar. In Genesis 17, God reiterates his promise and, signaling Abram's new stature because of the promise, renames him Abraham and his wife Sarah. The covenant is sealed by the rite of circumcision. In Genesis 18, upon the appearance of three mysterious visitors, he is told that the covenant will be fulfilled by a son, born of Sarah, not Hagar, an event that comes to pass three chapters later with the birth of Isaac.

We are not given any account of Abraham's inner reflections through *any* of this, and it would be unwise to attribute any in particular to him or to rest a case on these reflections. But we are, nonetheless, given certain striking actions by him that do define what it means to say that he is an exemplar of faith. One central characteristic of Abraham that perdures throughout these narratives is that Abraham trusts God, and trusts God unconditionally. His trust *is* the point of the stories individually and as a whole; it consists in shifting himself and his interests from the center of moral gravity. All of these stories involve a certain testing of Abraham, but "testing" is not tempting him to do otherwise than he should, but getting him to do what he should, namely to exhibit an unreserved ability to act in response to God's behest. His faith is his willingness to leave all personal

The Concept of Faith in the New Testament

security and specific hopes behind when he leaves his home to risk all for this promise.[6]

But then comes one of the most troubling passages in the Bible: Abraham is told he must take Isaac and offer him as a sacrifice. Again wordlessly, Abraham carries out his awful task all the way to the point that with his knife raised, he is stopped in mid-thrust, and a ram is given to him as a substitute for Isaac. The story disturbs us in its implications: faith appears to be a blind, unreasoning, and heartless obedience. Within the context of God's promise within which Abraham is acting, however, it still has disturbing aspects but somewhat different ones. For Isaac is not just Abraham's son; he is the promised child, the one on whom all of Abraham's hopes, and all of his history for the last thirty years or more, rested. To sacrifice Isaac was not only to sacrifice a beloved son, but also to let go of every concrete expectation Abraham might have had for the future. *That* surely is the point of the story as a story of faith. By not trying to possess and hold the promise, by not trying to determine where it should go, Abraham had put all his hope in the promise, as well as his concern for Isaac and everything he meant to Abraham, in his trust of God. That was the way to hold the promise most surely. Kierkegaard observed, ". . . you had to draw the knife before you kept Isaac."[7] Abraham's faith was not his willing-

---

6. It is also arguably involved even in his acceptance of Ishmael, Hagar's son, as the son of promise. While some exegetes have seen in the begetting of Ishmael a certain wish to force the issue by taking an overly natural way out of the problem of Sarai's age, a failure to understand the promise in the right terms, there is good reason to read the story otherwise. Abram is *not* personally delighted by the son of a slave being the heir of the promise (Gen. 15:2), and to the degree that he *is* later delighted by the announcement that Sarah will bear a child, he seems to have acceded to a situation that was not *his* first choice in the case of Hagar and Ishmael. Here, as with the Isaac story, Abraham seems to be willing to accept the promise on terms not of his own making, and that is important to understanding his faith, the nature of his trust.

7. Søren Kierkegaard, *Fear and Trembling,* ed. and trans. Howard V. and Edna Hong (Princeton: Princeton University Press, 1983), p. 23. Edward Mooney in commenting on Kierkegaard's exegesis of the Isaac story notes: "Abraham must relinquish (or show that he has already relinquished) Isaac as the unique center of his world. Worldly attachment, on this view, cannot serve as the unique center of aspiration and devotion. Resigning Isaac is resigning such worldly attachment. . . . Relinquishing Isaac as absolute center of value means that Abraham must relinquish any claim to possess, master, or control the meaning Isaac will have as the aged patriarch advances toward his death. Isaac was to be the promise of his immortality, the consolation of his mortality, the continuance of his

THE ACT OF FAITH

ness to sacrifice Isaac, it was his willingness to sacrifice his own expectations. The moral center of his life was no longer himself; that is how the promise is held most securely. Such faith is intimately connected to the very content of the promise.

The Abraham stories illustrate the first of the deeper senses of religious faith in the Old Testament. Faith is trust in God, a trust that receives the promise of God, the life of God, especially by renouncing control of the outcome. But it is also a trust that is rooted in the dealings one has already had with God. Excepting his initial encounter with God in Genesis 12, Abraham's willingness to go along with God always has a history of God's faithfulness behind it.

The second aspect of faith, waiting and discernment, is illustrated in a narrative that comes from the early years of the prophet Isaiah. It is a time when Judah has been forced into a cruel dilemma. Israel and her ally, Syria, have concocted a plan to rebel against their fearsome suzerain, Assyria. Believing that numbers would make the difference, they ask Judah to join the alliance. If it does not join, they themselves will attack Judah. The dilemma then is either to join the alliance and face likely destruction by Assyria, or not to join and face destruction by the allies. King Ahaz believes himself forced to choose. Meeting him at the upper pool, Isaiah firmly declares that the plot of the allies will not last, that Yahweh is in charge of the outcome. He then declares, playing on two forms of the verb *'mn*, which is brought out helpfully by the New Revised Standard Version: "If you do not stand firm in faith, you shall not stand at all" (Isa. 7:9). Isaiah's point is this: That God has already set in motion his purposes to do something about Israel and Syria. That is not to be doubted. Ahaz's response therefore ought to be to trust that; Isaiah tells him to "take heed, be quiet, do not fear, and do not let your heart be faint . . ." (Isa. 7:4). Should he fear, and take matters into his own hands, it would be faithlessness, not simply as a matter of disbelieving God, but primarily as a matter of opposing him. Thus Ahaz will not stand at all. The point is underlined when Ahaz refuses the advice and calls in Assyria to protect Judah from the alliance. Isaiah promptly denounces him and declares that like the

---

seed. Abraham must be weaned from any presumption that in this way his future can be foreclosed. He cannot presume to master history through selfless care of Isaac" (*Selves in Discord and Resolve: Kierkegaard's Moral-Religious Psychology from "Either/Or" to "Sickness Unto Death"* [New York: Routledge, 1996], pp. 50-51).

flood waters of an otherwise gently flowing river, Assyria will overwhelm Judah.

What Isaiah recommends in requiring faith is therefore a certain kind of fearlessness that comes from trusting that God will do what he says he will do. That trust involves, as in the case of Abraham, a willingness not to control the situation or to let the horizons of one's own limited imagination determine what can be done. (Ahaz's imagination, if it is anything, is clearly limited.) The advice is not quietism, to do nothing at all; it is to wait and to act as directed. It is a call to discern God's hand, to be instructed by the prophetic word. When Judah is then subsequently overwhelmed because of Ahaz's apostasy, Isaiah deepens this message. Although there is no clear word about what the future will bring, no specific direction that is spoken of, and although Judah is now living in the midst of catastrophe, faithfulness and trust in God will now amount to this: "I will wait for the Lord, who is hiding his face from the house of Jacob, and I will hope in him" (Isa. 8:17). This message of waiting is further replayed in Isaiah's successor, "deutero-Isaiah," in his great message of hope at the time of Judah's return from the Babylonian exile. It is also important to New Testament understandings of faith, and to the theological tradition that treats faith as an active willingness to be instructed.

There is a certain difference in emphasis concerning faith in these two examples. Abraham's faith is largely a matter of *faithfulness*, a quality that he has; what Isaiah calls for is an active recognition and grasping of God's declaration, which he makes key to Israel's life. Nevertheless, the two emphases are not exclusive and, indeed, later Judaism tended to talk about them as implying each other.

1.2. Christ and Faith

Christianity inherited these understandings of faith. Jesus clearly recommends faithfulness to his hearers throughout the Gospels. This is faith as trust, of course, but it is particularly the sort of faith that reaches out and grasps the message that he is proclaiming. His hearers are called upon to wait upon and discern what God is doing; faith is seeing. This sort of faith is especially evident in the Synoptic Gospels.[8] Even though the message is

---

8. For a discussion of faith in the Synoptics, cf. Edward D. O'Connor, CSC, *Faith in the Synoptic Gospels* (Notre Dame: University of Notre Dame Press, 1961).

new — but new messages are not unheard of in Israel anyhow — the sort of response demanded shows clear overlap with the point of the Abraham stories and the sort of faith for which Isaiah is calling.

What new thing the New Testament writers clearly do add to faith, however, even in the Synoptics, is that faith is faith in Jesus. Early Christian belief embraced the resurrection of Jesus; indeed, the resurrection of Jesus was the chief element of early Christian preaching, the kerygma.[9] Believing and trusting this message need not stretch the Old Testament concept of faith very much beyond involving it in a new aspect of what its object, God, was doing. But the New Testament takes faith to be belief and trust in Jesus as the Christ, the Son of God. Less pronounced in the Synoptics, in Paul and John and the Letter to the Hebrews it becomes especially important. But therein lies a problem. What is faith in this sort of instance? Martin Buber, for one, saw in Christianity, especially Pauline Christianity, an utterly different kind of faith and pattern of religion than in Judaism.[10] Jewish faith he found rooted in the history of a community; Christian faith was the belief of individuals outside history.[11] This is disputable. To talk about Christian faith as faith in Jesus can involve two crucial questions: (1) Who is Jesus that we should have faith in him? and (2) What is faith in Jesus? These are not the same. In the first question we are asking for what he is, perhaps in order that we might decide to believe in him, whatever that might mean. If so, that is to look for a reason to move from unbelief to belief. This is by and large the Lockean position. It is individualistic, and it has dominated much biblical scholarship, including the various quests for the "historical Jesus." The second question, however, asks what life in Jesus, which is had by faith, is like. While it might appear that there is a natural progression from the first to the second question, from ground to application, contemporary approaches that assume this naturalness have effectively obscured the all-important perspective of the second, something the investigation into who or what Jesus is usually misses. In the New Testament, faith did of course begin in believing something about Jesus, namely, the resurrection. But faith and the resurrection were inseparable

---

9. Cf. Ian Walker, *Faith and Belief: A Philosophical Approach* (Atlanta: Scholars Press, 1994). Walker argues that faith is that which interprets events, and that the chief event central to faith in the New Testament is the resurrection.

10. Martin Buber, *Two Types of Faith* (London: Routledge & Kegan Paul, 1951).

11. Buber, *Two Types of Faith*, ch. 17.

for New Testament writers such as John and Paul, who think that faith is the way of life and experience. They make it clear that this faith is inseparable from the one resurrected; life in God is faith in Christ. Faith is trust in God; but in Christ it is a distinctive discerning and being instructed of God. Faith is shaped by the message and by the community that comes into existence and lives and participates in the Resurrection. It is part of the new creation in Christ.

2. PAUL

2.1. The Context of Paul's Writings

While faith in its various meanings, including faith in Jesus as the Son of God, is demanded throughout the New Testament as the relationship one ought to have with God, nowhere is the concept so fully developed as in Paul, excepting perhaps John. Paul's use of the concept of faith has set the all-important role that faith has played within the history and practice of Christianity as a whole. It was Paul's understanding of faith that inspired Augustine, especially in the Pelagian controversy, and Luther and Calvin in the Reformation. Luther, for example, took Paul's understanding of justification by faith to be the key to understanding the gospel itself, a hermeneutical key for reading all of Scripture. Luther's emphasis on faith, however, spawned the view that when Paul talked about faith, he was putting forth a doctrine of faith; that is to say, faith was not only what the gospel demanded as an adequate response on the part of the believer, but what the gospel was all about. Not only that, but in taking Paul's writings on faith as a doctrine, Luther and subsequent generations saw in the doctrine the deliberate working out of the heart of Christianity.

Luther recognized the importance of faith within Paul's thinking. It is doubtful, however, that Paul was actually putting forth a *doctrine* of faith, that is, a comprehensive theological framework covering all aspects of Christian life under the rubric of faith. Instead, Paul's concept of faith itself is encompassed within a much larger framework constituted by God's new action in Christ's death and resurrection, which is what Paul is primarily proclaiming. Paul's letters do not begin with a call to faith in Jesus from unfaith, nor does he have a well-worked-out view on why unfaith ought to become faith. Rather, Paul assumes a belief in the resurrection that is shared by the communities of the early church to which he writes. Thus Paul's understanding of "faith" needs to be seen within the configuration of what the early church, including Paul, actually believed and saw in their religious world, instead of being seen as a matter of Paul arguing his congregations into certain beliefs, including beliefs they ought to have about the nature of faith in order to have faith. More directly, in Paul the concept of faith operates and has its meaning within a certain life-world, a certain logical and moral space, shaped by the death and resurrection of Jesus. What "faith" means in its most important religious sense for Paul lies within this configuration of beliefs about the resurrection and early Christian practices that memorialize Jesus' death and resurrection.

Paul's religious world is unabashedly an apocalyptic one.[12] Paul sees the world in apocalyptic terms, and the resurrection, therefore, *is* for Paul the breaking in of a new reality in human life, an event that, after the defeat of the controlling powers over human life by the cross, initiates the beginning of a new life that will be completed in the future. Paul's various judgments, and the views that he holds about the law, about faith, about the Christian life, flow from that conviction. If Jesus is the Messiah, then the law has been invalidated by his death and resurrection. Sins are forgiven because the law is no longer left to condemn. Gentiles who were excluded by the law can now be heirs to the promises of God. Faith is indeed the basis by which they and the Jews are heirs to that promise (Rom. 1:16–5:21) and by which righteousness comes about. But faith, saving faith, is not an *a priori* category, it is the result of Christ's resurrection. Humans are made righteous by Christ's faithfulness and their faith is dependent on his. "[W]e know that a person is justified not by the works of the Law but through the faith of Christ *(dia pisteōs Iesou Christou)*. And we have come to believe in Christ Jesus, so that we might be justified by the faith of Christ *(ek pisteōs Christou)* . . ." (Gal. 2:16).[13] Faith is trust and discernment; it is also life in Christ. So faith is not a specific doctrine in Paul, nor is Paul advising his hearers to have faith, that is, to adopt a set of beliefs

12. Cf. J. Christiaan's Beker *Paul the Apostle: The Triumph of God in Life and Thought* (Philadelphia: Fortress Press, 1980). I follow Beker at a number of points in this section.

13. A long controversy has gone on concerning whether *dia pisteōs Christou* should be translated as "faith in Christ" or as "faith of Christ." Recent work has come down in favor of the latter. Cf. J. Louis Martyn, *Theological Issues in the Letters of Paul* (Nashville: Abingdon Press, 1997), ch. 9, for a discussion of the issue and review of the literature, esp. pp. 149-51.

that ensure right standing before God. Faith is a concept that he uses to say what God is doing in the world in Christ's death and resurrection and that describes how men and women move within that world.

What then is God doing in Christ? What does this life-world look like? For Paul, Christ's death is the end of the older powers of sin and death that dominated human life (Col. 2:15), and his resurrection is the beginning of new life, a new creation (2 Cor. 5:17), which will be consummated in the eschaton. The features of that new life include, by virtue of the cancellation of the Law, forgiveness of guilt and condemnation, bringing freedom instead of bondage (Gal. 4:1–5:1). But they also include the formation of a new community, and a new way of being with each other. No longer do the old antagonisms rule, for "there is neither Jew nor Greek, there is neither slave nor free, there is neither male nor female, for you are one in Christ Jesus" (Gal. 3:28). This is a community of love and patience and other virtues (1 Cor. 13; Gal. 5:22-23). It is also a waiting community (1 Thess.). But this is also a community that is organically knit together as one body with Christ as its head (1 Cor. 12; Rom. 12:12). Christ's body is not a mere metaphor, for these people are gathered together and live by the animation of the Spirit that is poured out in the resurrection. The new life is literally life in God through the Spirit that animates the community. Believers then are not individually justified by their beliefs; their faith is formed and lived out in the community's life together, a life of righteousness.

What then does this say about faith? In the writing of Paul, faith is both trust and waiting discernment, but it also moves toward a conception of organic life in Christ. This conception is of particular concern to us here, for it is crucial in setting the grammar of faith for the next millennium and a half. What it means within the context of Paul's thought is most clearly discerned in his letter to the church at Rome.

2.2. Faith in Romans

Paul wrote the letter to the Romans shortly after his reconciliation with the Corinthian congregation and before he journeyed to Jerusalem with the offerings of the Greek churches for the support of the Jerusalem church. The reconciling power of the gospel was at the front of his mind, not only because of the newly regained unity in Corinth, but also because the support of the largely Gentile churches for the Jewish church symbolized an

THE ACT OF FAITH

overcoming of the greatest division of his religious world, the one between Jew and Gentile. It was an hour fraught with significance. Romans may well have been a rehearsal of the speech that he would give when he got to Jerusalem, one that he might well make to the Romans since he wanted to use Rome as a base for future missions to the western Mediterranean. He needs to present his credentials to them. Since there are also apparent problems in the Roman church, a split between Jewish and Gentile believers, this speech is appropriate. It is also appropriate theologically. By stressing the invalidity of the law, Paul has created a chancy reputation for himself, both in Jerusalem and Rome, and he needs to explain himself. If the law is no longer valid, what happens to Israel? How is Christian faith in continuity with what came before? Paul's discussion of faith lies within the context of a larger point about the reconciling and unifying power of the gospel, the life of the Christian community, and within the context of a certain problem about the place of the law.

After a pleasant introduction to the church at Rome, Paul boldly gets straight to his point and the basis of his position on the law by quoting the prophet Habakkuk: "For I am not ashamed of the gospel; it is the power of God for salvation to everyone who has faith, to the Jew first and also to the Greek. For in it the righteousness of God is revealed from faith to faith, just as it is written, 'The righteous shall live by faith'" (Rom. 1:16-17). Paul clearly means to stand firm on the tradition's insistence that righteousness is both right standing before God and what God has promised. But by claiming that righteousness is by faith, and by quoting Scripture to make that claim, he is making two additional points: (1) that righteousness is by faith and, by implication, it is not by the law; and (2) that Scripture itself says so. It has always said so; faith always has been the key to righteousness. So what Christ reveals, and what Paul says that Christ reveals, and that faith receives, is not new or revolutionary; it fulfills God's original intent. Paul is instructing them on how to read the Scriptures. Paul gives what appears at first to be a very peculiar argument to support this contention. Initially (1:18-32) he unloads an indictment of the pagan world and its immorality, highlighting what to Jewish eyes are its most disgusting features. He continues (2:1-16) by arguing for the deserving punishment of this wickedness, pagans' or anybody else's — including the Jews', for that matter. To condemn another is to condemn oneself when one is guilty of the same thing (2:2-3). For those who do good on the other hand, there is glory (2:10). Jewish readers would heartily agree with all this. But then

Paul turns the condemnation around and lays it on the Jews. "If you call yourself a Jew and rely on the Law and boast of your relation to God . . . you, then, that teach others, will you not teach yourself? While you preach against stealing, do you steal?" etc. (Rom. 2:17-24). On the basis of this universal condemnation, Paul, again by quoting Scripture, can say that "none is righteous, no, not one" (Rom. 3:10-18). As a result, if one cannot fulfill the law, and no one appears to be able to do so, then the only way to righteousness is "the righteousness of God through faith in Jesus Christ for all who believe" (Rom. 3:21). The argument puts the Jews in a dilemma: not being able to fulfill the law, the only way to righteousness is by faith in Christ.

What is peculiar about this argument is the way that Paul appears to paint Jewish righteousness. On the one hand, it is rhetorically excessive. It is hardly likely that the Jewish readers of the letter are thieves, adulterers, temple robbers, and the like. One wonders why they would feel the effect of the condemnation at all, or feel anything other than irritation. On the other hand, the perfection that Paul seems to be demanding out of followers of the law is also excessive. Practicing Jews did try to uphold the law, but clearly recognized that nobody kept it perfectly; one needed to trust in God's mercy for forgiveness and atonement. God had even given in the law various rituals of atonement to help this happen.[14]

This, however, may be precisely Paul's point. Even the Jews did not expect perfection in matters of the law, but relied on the grace of God's mercy. If this is so, then Paul is not trying to force his Jewish-Christian hearers onto the horns of the dilemma — hypocritically standing on the impossible demands of the law or faith that admits Gentiles, which is an odd way to recommend yourself to an audience you hope will support you in future endeavors. He is appealing to Jewish-Christian experience of forgiveness by grace.[15] He is not proposing that faith is the alternative to hypocrisy, but suggesting that as believers they need to recognize what they have been relying on all along is God's grace. They have been relying on faith for righteousness, just as Scripture said they should. They need to

---

14. Cf. E. P. Sanders, *Paul and Palestinian Judaism* (Minneapolis: Fortress Press, 1977).

15. In support of this contention, cf. Rom. 4:7 where he quotes Ps. 32:1-2, "Blessed are those whose iniquities are forgiven and whose sins are covered; blessed is the one against whom the Lord will not reckon sin." Paul takes this as an example of the "blessedness of those to whom God reckons righteousness apart from works."

recognize this. And this means surely, don't be so hard on the Gentiles, the non-observers of the law. Recognize what you have in common with them: God's grace, which all believe has been revealed in Jesus Christ, and the reception of that faithfulness of God that saves you. Recognize your common faith and trust in him. It is that faithful response, and not doing the works of the law, that receives that faithfulness of God and lives it out.

The obvious but often ignored fact here is that Paul's audience, whether Jew or Gentile, is already Christian. He is not trying to argue them into a position, but is appealing to what they all accept; he is trying to get them to recognize just what that is. The problem with the works of the law, then, is not so much that it is an alternative choice confronting them, but that to assert the works of the law as the basis of the religious life, the new life brought in by Christ's death and resurrection, is in fact a kind of backsliding. For these people are not choosing at all; they have already made their choice. The question is how they will live that out, and Paul's point is that faith is the way to describe the question of their life in common. Faith is at the basis of their fellowship. People, Gentiles and Jews, may actually do what the law commands, and Paul does seem to think that what the law says about the elements of the righteous life is right; but it is not the law, but God's grace, that creates the community and fellowship. The problem then of relying on works of the law is particularly the boasting it creates, for that destroys fellowship and is faith's real contrary. Unfaith is then less a matter of disbelief, especially within the community, than it is matter of blindness to one's own situation and its parallel in the lives of one's compatriots.

But why not then simply uphold the law and recognize more clearly that God's grace and forgiveness are what is important? What is the point of Christ? What does *he* add to the forgiveness on which faithful adherents of the law had always relied? One response, of course, is the implicit one: Paul is arguing *within* the context of the revelation of Christ having taken place; he is not arguing *for* it. He has already accepted it and believed it and so has his audience. He is just working out what that means for their lives together. The second is that the law excludes the Gentiles, and in Paul's eyes the breaking in of the kingdom overcomes these sorts of divisions, as he had already pointed out to the Galatians and worked out with the Corinthians. This response he takes up explicitly.

In chapter 4 he takes up the case of Abraham to clinch his argument; if he were simply prooftexting his earlier quotation from Habakkuk, this chapter could follow directly upon that quotation. "Abraham," Paul argues, quoting Genesis 15:6, "believed God and it was reckoned to him as righteousness." Thus the promise of God was from the beginning (and Abraham was the beginning of the covenant) and has *always* been received by faith. The law only came later, and since God is always faithful to his promises, even the law could not change that original relation — nor, obviously, was it meant to, if God stuck by his original promise. Moreover, again citing the promise to Abraham, since the promise was that Abraham would be the father of many nations, not just one, clearly the Gentiles were included in the promise (Rom. 4:16-18). Thus reception of the promise, and creation of the community, "depends on faith in order that the promise may rest on grace and be guaranteed to all his descendants, not only to the adherents of the Law but also to those who share the faith of Abraham . . ." (Rom. 4:16).[16] Thus, he concludes in chapter 5, that we are all justified by faith through Christ's blood and will be saved by him.

This makes faith the adequate response to God's action and the basis of the Christian community and its unity. It receives grace; faith is a matter of living within the space created by the death and resurrection of Christ. Its sense lies within that space. Faith is not a way of entering that space; it is the way of living within it. Important as it is to understand Paul's notion of faith in this context, this much, however, actually says relatively little about its form or content. It is faith, not works, that defines the community, but even where that is not simply a negative point but a crucial and defining one for the basis of the community, there is still not much yet said about the actual ongoings of the community. Nor is it well spelled out what faith is other than the reception of God's faithfulness and trust, although it now starts to come clear that for Paul, belief in the resurrection merges into the much richer and more complex concept of faith proper.

For content one has to bear with Paul as he ceases talking about faith directly and begins to talk about life in Christ in chapters 6 through 8. The

---

16. It should be pointed out that when the promise to Abraham is appealed to in Galatians 3, Christ is taken to be what is promised. The contingent context of the letter clearly determines this different reading. It is not, however, incompatible with Romans insofar, as shall become clear below, that Christ actually incorporates within himself the community of believers.

discussion is occasioned by the unguarded comment that the law actually increased the trespass (Rom. 5:20), made just at the point that Paul seemed to be off the hook for disparaging the law. Paul's apocalyptic mindset is at the fore here. The problem is not with the law as such; it is with the fact that the Law, which never had the power to make one righteous — a power that belongs to God's faithfulness alone and is received by faith — is taken captive, as it were, by the powers of sin and death, the Patty Hearst of the spiritual world. "Did what is good, then, bring death to me? By no means! It was sin, working death in me through what is good. . . . For we know that the Law is spiritual; but I am of the flesh, sold into slavery under sin. . . . But in fact it is no longer I that do it, but sin that dwells within me" (Rom. 7:13-17). The law had pointed out what was good, but was without power in itself to effect that good. It consequently condemned deficiencies, holding one responsible for one's action, or at least holding the power of sin responsible, showing sin for what it is. But the law could not create human righteousness. With the coming of Christ's righteousness and forgiveness, however, not only is sin overcome, the law is no longer needed to condemn or even point the way, since in Christ one is made righteous (Rom. 8:1-4). Thus, of course, reverting to the law is reverting to an earlier and unhappier mode of existence.

One is made righteous "in Christ." This intrigues. Just as believers were once *in* sin, overcome by its power, and were instruments of it, despite deeply wishing that it were not so, so too, Paul sees righteousness as the converse, as being in Christ and in God's Spirit. His use of "incorporation" and "participation" language runs throughout these chapters, as it does throughout all his letters.[17] The believer is no longer in sin, because he or she has been baptized into Christ's death (6:3) and is united to him in his resurrection (6:4-5). Christ's death and resurrection are not external to believers, but internal. Chapter eight is particularly instructive. Walking in the Spirit (8:4) is being in the Spirit (8:9). Christ is in you (8:10) and being led by the Spirit is to be an adopted child and heir with Christ of God's promise (8:17), conformed to the image of the Christ (8:29). Thus nothing, including any cosmic power, can separate us from the love of Christ (8:35-39).

These sorts of statements run throughout Paul's letters, including

---

17. On this language and for a full presentation and discussion of the relevant texts, cf. E. P. Sanders, *Paul and Palestinian Judaism,* ch. 5.

phrases such as "Christ being in me," or "I in Christ." They are closely linked to the Pauline image of the church as Christ's body (Rom. 12.12; 1 Cor. 12). The Christian community is not simply a fellowship of like-minded believers, but people linked as brothers and sisters in the new creation that Christ brings. Because of their participation in Christ they have his Father as their common Father (not because God is father-like.) Or, as the body image indicates, they are organically linked as members of a living body, whose head, whose mind, and whose animating source is Christ himself. Christ is the soul of their souls.

Here is the content and shape of the faith that is the basis of the Christian community. If it is faith that links Jews and Gentiles, slave and free, male and female, it is because faith is participation in Christ. This is the new element in the biblical understanding of faith. Having faith is a matter of being a new self, one replete with certain moral and spiritual intertwinings with others in the community. Talents that are given to individuals only make sense and have a use within the community. Faith is played out therefore as mutual self-sacrificing love and help to others (1 Cor. 2). If justification by faith can sometimes make it difficult to assess just what works faith might do, by putting faith within this imagery, one can see how Pauline ethics can be done. In Romans 12, for example, it is the image of the body that initiates Paul's ethical recommendations in that letter; in 1 Corinthians 12, it concludes them. Faith therefore is not simply belief in Jesus; for Paul it is a concept linked to one's moral and spiritual identity.

Faith then comes through the hearing of the good news, the preaching of the resurrection (Rom. 10:14-15). Believing the gospel is a personal response of obedience (Rom. 10:16). The form of that faith is love (Gal. 5:6), which is exercised within a community formed by that preaching and animated and unified by Christ himself. Indeed, faith which is exercised within this community and makes sense within it can thus be said to be created by the preaching itself.[18]

But also, "faith is what it is because Christ exists."[19] Thus faith as tak-

18. "The preaching of the gospel is interwoven with the Spirit (I Th. 1:5) and thus faith is the result of this power of the word (Rom. 1:16; I Cor. 2:5). The message is called the preaching of faith because it creates faith (Rom. 10:8, 14-15, 17). Faith is the fruit of the Spirit (Gal. 5:22)" (Jürgen Becker, *Paul: Apostle to the Gentiles,* trans. O. C. Dean, Jr. [Louisville: Westminster/John Knox Press, 1993], p. 143).

19. Jürgen Becker, *Paul: Apostle to the Gentiles,* p. 143.

ing the word of Christ to heart is being in Christ, or having Christ in oneself, of being in the image of Christ and hence the Father, and walking in the Spirit. It is a transformation from selfishness to self-sacrifice, and also a consequent transformation from anxiety about one's status to confidence and hope. But Paul also understands, particularly after his unpleasant experiences with the fractured Corinthian congregation, that this participation is still treasure in earthen vessels (2 Cor. 4:7). Although one is in Christ, and has full confidence of Christ's faithfulness, one still has it as a matter of a sure hope, not as present fullness.

2.3. "Participation" Language

Albert Schweitzer early in the twentieth century initiated a new approach to Pauline studies by shifting the discussion of Paul's thought from doctrinal categories to ones that took seriously its apocalyptic context and Paul's "mystical" language of participation in the body of Christ.[20] Schweitzer's approach had little effect on expositions of Paul in subsequent years since it presented grave difficulties for making contemporary sense of Paul and his understanding of faith. "Participation" language seems desperately archaic and conceptually beyond anything we can presently make sense of, and any number of New Testament scholars have pointed that out. Yet that language is key to understanding faith in Paul and within the theological tradition through the Reformation, and to recovering a sense of faith that is not truncated by the modern sense of the self. The idea of "participation" signals the deep intersubjective nature of faith and a relation to what we are as selves, aspects that are missed if we do not take it seriously.

Rudolph Bultmann is a prime example of someone who presented Paul in quite a different sort of light than Schweitzer did. He remains one of the great twentieth-century interpreters of Paul, especially in his attempts to avoid Lockean versions of faith, and his drawing out aspects of Paul's thought important for understanding the relation of faith to the self. But there are within those contributions also severe exegetical and conceptual limitations.

20. Cf. Albert Schweitzer, *The Mysticism of Paul the Apostle* (New York: H. Holt & Co., 1931).

The Concept of Faith in the New Testament

From the very beginning Bultmann rejected the idea that the Reign of God was at all basic to Paul's thinking, even if it was central to Jesus' preaching. Instead, he put Paul squarely within Hellenistic Christianity; it was within that non-apocalyptic context that faith became for Paul a central concept. But it was not a matter of a concept that Paul would build a system out of, "a distantly perceived *kosmos* (system), as Greek science does. Rather, Paul's theological thinking only lifts the knowledge inherent in faith into the clarity of conscious knowing."[21] Paul saw faith as designating the relation between God and human beings, and saw what he was doing in talking about it as bringing that relation to consciousness. Thus Paul was particularly concerned with "anthropology," that is, the human's standing in front of and relation to God and how that affected human self-understanding.[22] Faith, then, and this is to Bultmann's great credit, is not believing something external to the believing self, such as a proposition; it is within the human experience of God, a response evoked by the kerygma.

By making Paul's work a matter of reflecting on faith, Bultmann saw Paul as making a case for faith wherein Paul first analyzes the position and predicament of the human being without faith and then shows faith as a response and solution to that predicament. Thus the person without faith is largely marked by self-striving and assertion. Using Romans 7 as a touchstone, Bultmann finds that for Paul the experience of the human being in this situation is desperately fragmented and unfulfilling. Attempting to find true life, one is divided as one's will struggles against itself. "Man, called to selfhood, tries to live out of his own strength and thus loses his self — his 'life' — and rushes into death. This is the domination of sin: All man's doing is directed against his true intention — viz. to achieve life."[23]

Faith is the solution to this self-fragmentation. It is the "radical renunciation of accomplishment, the obedient submission to the God-

---

21. R. Bultmann, *Theology of the New Testament*, trans. K. Grobel, 2 vols. (New York: Charles Scribner's Sons, 1951, 1955), 1:190.

22. "'Pauline theology' deals with God not as He is in Himself but only with God as He is significant for man, for man's responsibility and man's salvation. Correspondingly, it does not deal with the world and man as they are in themselves, but constantly sees the world and man in their relation to God. Every assertion about God is simultaneously an assertion about man and vice versa. For this reason and in this sense Paul's theology is, at the same time, anthropology." Bultmann, *Theology of the New Testament*, 1:190-91.

23. Bultmann, *Theology of the New Testament*, 1:246.

24. Bultmann, *Theology of the New Testament*, 1:316.

THE ACT OF FAITH

determined way of salvation, the taking over of the cross of Christ — is the free deed of obedience in which the new self constitutes itself in place of the old."[24] According to Bultmann, since faith comes from what is heard, the proclamation of Jesus Christ, it is ultimately a matter of knowing. But of what kind? "Ultimately 'faith' and 'knowledge' are identical as a new understanding of one's self. . . ."[25] That is to say, it sees the sinfulness of one's self-striving and sees oneself as now being in God's hand. But because it responds to the personal address of the kerygma, it is not simply knowing; it is also obedience, acknowledgment, and confession, all especially in the sense that these responses involve trusting and hoping in that message.

Faith as a new understanding of one's self is the hallmark of Bultmann's presentation of faith as found in Paul's writings — and in Bultmann's. The strength of his view lies in its stress on the personal transformation that really is at the heart of faith. "Faith" is not a simple recognition of an external — a being or statement or otherwise. It is a self-involving adherence that does not split thinking and assent. To have faith like this is to see things in a certain light, not the least of which is oneself. It is wisdom when combined with a certain ethical maturity.[26] Thus to be "in Christ" by faith for Bultmann is a distinctive way of doing and seeing things. Being "in Christ" is adverbial, for the phrase operates as a way of qualifying and distinguishing how something is done, although it is not a merely psychological qualification. Similarly, he goes on, "life in the Spirit" is a matter of giving over our old self-understanding to find the power to choose freely. The demand of the Spirit to act in a certain way creates the possibility of doing it and hence the freedom to do it. Thus "the bond with Christ which takes place in faith," which is often described in mythological terms, is "factually accomplished by the decision of faith."[27] At this point "participation" as any sort of union with Christ fades into existential self-knowledge that arises from self-reflection provoked by the *kerygma*.

How true is this to Paul? E. P. Sanders's 1977 work on participation language in Paul raises important questions about Bultmann's view as an exposition of Paul himself, especially about Bultmann's concern to

25. Bultmann, *Theology of the New Testament*, 1:318.
26. Bultmann, *Theology of the New Testament*, 1:327.
27. Bultmann, *Theology of the New Testament*, 1:351.
28. Bultmann, *Theology of the New Testament*, 1:454.

The Concept of Faith in the New Testament

deny that "Paul held a view which implies more than a change in self-understanding..."[28] and to deny the naturalness of Paul's use of participation language in his own context. According to Sanders, for Paul "the participatory union is not a figure of speech for something else; it is, as many scholars have insisted, real."[29]

Bultmann's presentation errs on at least two points, Sanders thinks. First, it is quite clear that Paul did not first analyze the existential plight of the human being before discussing faith as its solution. Rather, the solution, the experience of Christ's revelation and the possession of faith, preceded Paul's awareness of the existential problem. He did not reflect himself into faith. Second, Paul did take participation in Christ seriously, and it is precisely where he did begin. So the contrast is "not between self-reliance and reliance on God — two kinds of self-understanding — but between belonging to Christ and not belonging to Christ."[30] The problem of sin similarly is not a generalized existential failure but a problem of to whom you belonged, a problem that for Paul only begins to arise upon the experience of belonging to Christ, that is, within faith. This was an experience that to Paul's mind involved a real transfer into and participation in Christ's death and resurrection. Righteousness, the goal of religious life, really comes in a very direct way from Christ. Baptism then is not simply a rite, but a change in status and personhood. It, and the Eucharist, are literal means of participating in God's life that only come with Christ's death and resurrection. Early Christians understood this well and knew that entrance into the *ecclesia* by these rites signaled a change in how they would think and how they would live their lives.

Yet, Sanders goes on, while recognition of the importance of "participation" for Paul may have the effect of moving readers closer to the heart of Paul's thought, it also has the effect of making his thought less relevant.[31] We simply haven't any way to take this language, he thinks. Therefore, in the absence of having any category that would make such language more understandable, Sanders votes for Bultmann's existentialist understanding of faith in Paul as the best translation of Paul's meaning in the present circumstances.

Paul's language is foreign in a peculiar way to the modern mind, es-

---

29. Sanders, *Paul and Palestinian Judaism*, p. 455.
30. Sanders, *Paul and Palestinian Judaism*, p. 482.
31. Sanders, *Paul and Palestinian Judaism*, p. 520.

THE ACT OF FAITH

pecially the individualist mind; any attempt to make it less so needs to recognize at the end that there may still remain aspects to it that we will not easily and immediately grasp. But it is not impossible to give another way of approaching it that may be both more understandable and truer to Paul. The problem with "participation," of course, is its mystical qualities and overtones, perpetually embarrassing to modern scholars. Yet, grasping the designation rather than blushing over it may be useful. For example, mystical theology distinguishes between the interpersonal unity of mind and ontological or substantial unity.[32] Paul has been pressed into service for both, and it may well be impossible to say which best represents him. But the distinction is useful, since if the latter holds any water it is in the font of the former, insofar as any substantial unity of persons would be evidenced in their interpersonal unity of mind. That sort of unity, which ought not to be so very foreign to us, may then at least give us an approach to understanding "participation." Interpersonal unity of mind need not depend on a specific act of self-reflectiveness; it need only be a consciousness that one's self and identity are inseparable from a personal and communal space created by life with others through Christ. To have an identity is to live within a sense of good that lies at the heart of one's horizons and aspirations, a good that gives moral and narrative coherence to a person after all the postures and images have been stripped away. To have a Christian identity, to have faith, then, is not to speak *as* a Christian, the way a judge might say, "Speaking as an officer of the court. . . ." The judge personally may or may not personally agree with the judgment she renders. She may imagine herself as no longer being a judge without undergoing a crisis of identity. To speak of having faith in Christ, however, for Paul, is not to stand outside the sense of self that one has in relation to Christ, although one might reflect on it. To have a Christian identity, to participate in Christ, is certainly not less than to have a sense of self that begins and makes sense within the moral and personal space opened by the cross and resurrection of Christ, a space into which one feels called. "Participating in Christ," then, has meaning at least in the

32. Cf. Louis Dupré, "Mystical Union in Western Religion," in *Religious Mystery and Rational Reflection* (Grand Rapids: Eerdmans, 1998). Dupré notes that even mystics who stress substantial union "tend to use interpersonal language for expressing the state of union" and "even the most 'transcendental' mystic is constantly compelled to fall back on the language of love in the endeavor to express the content of the metaphysical raptures" (p. 127).

sense of living in the space opened up by his death and resurrection and sharing *(metechein)* in it.[33] Living in that space, having faith, means actively pursuing relations with God through Christ by participation in the sacraments of baptism and the Lord's Supper, as well as through prayer and interpersonal life in the Christian community and having one's identity formed through that kind of participation. Faith, then, for Paul is a habit constitutive of the self and its activity; it is one, however, that functions in the space of the covenant history, communal and personal. It is Christ's own action in the soul.[34]

To a certain undefinable extent these ways of putting things may not cover the full range and depth of participation language in Paul. One cannot forget Paul's emphasis on the newness, the inbreaking that changes so much and colors everything — although it is newness prepared from the foundation of the world. The deficiencies need not detain us; the Augustinian tradition in which we are interested is a conscious examination of

---

33. By not taking faith to arise directly from the reception of the news of the resurrection, but something dialectically linked to the experience of grace, Bultmann would, of course, find it difficult to talk about this space, especially as a logical matter, as being opened up.

34. In her own efforts to go beyond Sanders and Bultmann, Ellen Charry (*By the Renewing of Your Minds: The Pastoral Function of Christian Doctrine* [New York: Oxford University Press, 1997]) deals with Paul in a way that also underlines this question of identity. Charry argues that for Paul, to be Christian is to be taken up into the drama of God's plan for creation. For the pagans of Paul's time, this meant taking on a theological identity that differed sharply from their natural one (which, actually, in their own context was bound up with certain theological assumptions, political and social identity not being divorced from religion in the ancient world). For Jewish-Christians it meant sharing their history and hence identity. Both face a real change in their identity, in who they are. "For Paul and those who accept his gospel, one's theological identity becomes one's primary identity" (p. 42). But this is not simply something that occurs magically or *ex opere operato*. Although Paul does talk at times so that it appears that this change in self has fully occurred, given what else he says it is clear that it also depends on two further factors. First, after the recognition of the identity to which one is called, there is consecration, or "enchristing," a remodeling of the old person. "They are to become those whom they have been made" (p. 45). This is done by identifying with Christ and following his pattern. Second, there is the empowerment of believers by the Holy Spirit, a being overtaken by God. This is the participation and upbuilding of the community. But the community is one that is created by Christ's death and resurrection; life in it is participation then in Christ's life. In these ways, faith is more than a new way of understanding oneself. It is a new way of being a self. Reflective self-understanding follows from that.

THE ACT OF FAITH

faith as participation, and we shall have ample opportunity to revisit the question. However, it should be clear that "participation" ought to be linked to issues of identity, where identity is an issue of the good that shapes and forms the person. It also should be clear that if there is a problem here, the problem does not entirely lie in the conflict between mythological and scientific worldviews as Bultmann thought, but largely between ancient and modern views of the self. For faith, and the self, in Paul are ultimately concepts that make their sense within a personal world. It is a world where to have faith is to see questions of faith and thought and practice as questions touching not simply on self-understanding and choice of one's life's direction, but as questions ultimately about what it means to be a self. Christian faith is a question for Paul of how to be and to form that self in active relation to Christ. But it is not only Paul who thinks that way; the other two great theologians of the New Testament, John and the unknown author of the Letter to the Hebrews, think so too.

3. JOHN

It is the Gospel of John that is perhaps more responsible than any other New Testament writing for placing faith in Jesus at the heart of what Christian faith means. In John, the verb "to believe" *(pisteuein)* occurs ninety-eight times (although the noun only occurs once.)[35] Most often, especially when it is a case of "believing in," Jesus is the object of this belief; even "believing that" is usually directed to an explicitly Christological formula.[36] Moreover, it is quite clear in John that such faith is the condition of salvation. When people come to Jesus and ask him what they must do to perform the work of God, Jesus replies simply, "This is the work of God, that you believe in him whom he has sent" (6:29). Faith in Jesus, according to John, encompasses all of religious life.

For John, like Paul, faith is participation in Christ and is linked to who one is as a self. Or, more precisely, faith in Christ is faith in the Mediator who has his life in God and who gives the faithful a full share in that life. This is not an implication drawn from John's language and worldview.

---

35. A pattern of usage that parallels the Old Testament.
36. Cf. Rudolf Schnackenburg, *The Gospel According to John* (New York: Crossroad, 1982), vol. 1, pp. 559-63.

The Concept of Faith in the New Testament

John makes it an explicit and carefully worked out concern throughout his Gospel. But unlike Paul, for whom faith is in the apocalyptic risen Christ who brings the kingdom, faith for John is a matter of being confronted by Jesus and directly responding to him.

With the beauty of unified form, John writes his Gospel so as to make it clear that faith in Jesus Christ is the fulfillment of the human being's relation to God. The work of God is "to believe in him whom he sent" (6:30). What John writes, he knowingly writes in order to evoke and nourish faith (20:30-31). The key to how that is done is in the opening words of the Gospel:

> In the beginning was the Word, and the Word was with God, and the Word was God. He was in the beginning with God, and through him all things came to be, and without him nothing which is begotten came to be. In him was life, and the life was the light of human beings. And the light shone in the darkness, and the darkness has not overcome it. (1:1-5)

Believing God's revelation, what God says, his words, is believing in God's Word. What Jesus says to humans beings is God's direct address to them, and God is in that address. Thus Jesus teaches and talks at a length greater than in any other Gospel. Chapters 14–17, for example, are virtually unbroken discourse by Jesus. For this reason, then, believing his words is to believe the Word of God. To take them into one's life is to be taken into God's life. But the words that Jesus speaks are not divorceable from the person who speaks, and cannot be judged and understood apart from him and his actions. They make their sense only within him. To believe them, to have faith in him, is to know what sense they do make, and to believe them is to know how to see. It is especially to know how to see what God is doing. But that is not as a disengaged interpreter; one sees only in faith. Not to believe the words and the speaker is, for John, to think and know in an entirely unsatisfactory and unfulfilling way. It is to misunderstand.

This is illustrated in the way that John treats miracles. Miracles in the Gospel of John are signs *(semeia)*, and are, like words, signifiers of the one who stands behind them. They are intimately linked to Jesus' words and what God is doing in the world.[37] At one point Jesus can tell the disbeliev-

---

37. Cf. K. H. Rengstorf, *"Semeion . . . ,"* article in *Theological Dictionary of the New Testament*, ed. G. Kittel and G. Friedrich, trans. G. Bromiley (Grand Rapids: Eerdmans, 1968), vol. 6. Words and signs are directly related, for the word interprets the sign and the sign authenticates the word, "but both in such a way that they find their unity exclusively

THE ACT OF FAITH

ing crowd, "even though you do not believe me, believe the works..." (10:38). Yet it is clear that one does not know how to read those works apart from the one in whom all things were created. (John thus could not have made any sense of Locke's project of using miracles as neutral evidence to support the decision for faith.) Throughout the Gospel, Jesus regularly performs such signs, but when he does so, they are misunderstood by those who do not have faith rooted in his words,[38] particularly when Jesus interprets them by his words, as he does with most of his *semeia*. John 6 provides a helpful example.

In chapter 6, in one of the few stories that John shares with the Synoptic Gospels, Jesus performs the miracle of feeding a crowd of five thousand on a very few loaves and fish. The crowd, seeing what has just occurred, confesses that "this is indeed the prophet who is to come into the world." They are ready to make him their king, something Jesus wants to avoid, and so he withdraws to the other side of the lake. Encountering them again the next day, he points out that the reason they believe is that they ate their fill. But that is not the sort of bread he came to give them, nor the sort of faith he expects of them. They remain uncomprehending. After telling them that the work of God is to believe in the one whom he sent, they want a sign such as the bread given to their fathers in the wilderness. (But what has Jesus just done the day before but that?) Jesus now gives not another sign, but the words: "I am the bread of life" (6:35). This causes murmuring, which Jesus is able to rouse into a full-scale revolt by telling them that "unless you eat the flesh of the Son of Man and drink his blood, you have no life in you" (6:54). Now his words are the occasion for many of his followers to desert him. They do not know how to read the sign whose meaning he explains in his words; the words are offensive to them. But as his words make very clear indeed, the sign points to where life is to be found, and that is in him. By participating in him they have life. But they cannot do that without taking him at his word. Peter, on the other hand, when asked if he, too, wants to leave, shows some glimmering of how to read things when he declares: "Lord, to whom can we go? You have the words of

---

in the person of Him who has the right to use *egō eimi* of himself" (p. 252). "The *semeia* are the confession which God as Father makes of Jesus as his Son, while Jesus for his part reveals himself to be the Revealer of God by proclaiming his name" (p. 260).

38. On this point, cf. Craig Koester, "Hearing, Seeing, and Believing in the Gospel of John," *Biblica* 70, no. 3 (1989): 327-48.

The Concept of Faith in the New Testament

eternal life. We have come to believe and know that you are the Holy One of God" (6:68-69).

Peter's confession makes clear that faith is in Jesus' person, mediated by his words. Access to the Word is through his words and signs. But this isn't just taking him at his word; faith also clearly involves a sort of knowing, a sort of knowing how to read the signs, and to see what is going on. Miracles are not singing to the choir; rather, it is the choir that knows how to sing. Similarly, Jesus praises the man born blind in chapter 9 for being able to see when he says in front of Jesus, "Lord, I believe" (9:38), and criticizes the Pharisees who think they see, but do not, and who fail to get the sign at all.

The emphasis on faith as union with Christ or as participation in him also comes in John's sacramental imagery. Chapter 6 is again an obvious example. When Jesus tells the crowd that unless they eat his flesh and drink his blood, for John's readers who do participate in the sacraments, it is not only clear to what Jesus is referring, his words make clear exactly what the nature of the sacrament of the Eucharist is, namely, that "those who eat my flesh and drink my blood have eternal life," and that "those who eat my flesh and drink my blood abide *(menei)* in me, and I in them" (6:54, 56). Through the practice of participating in the Eucharist, they live in him. And that it is, indeed, he who is the Life in which the signs of the sacraments have their life-giving qualities is made pointedly evident in the crucifixion. There, when his side is pierced, the water of baptism and the blood of the Eucharist flow (19:35). The community of believers then not only participate in his life, they do so by participating in his death, and hence resurrection.

This well-constructed imagery, drawn from the church's own practice and experience, allows John to chart out a number of equivalences and analogies of union or series of mediations that he constantly interweaves throughout the Gospel. Most important is the union of Jesus with the Word, and the Word, and hence Jesus, with God (1:1-5; 10:30), as well as the unity of Father and Son with the Spirit of truth who speaks to the faithful what it hears from God (16:12-15). There is also the understood link between Jesus' words and his being the Word, and thus a link between believing those words and believing God. There is finally also the union of the believer and Christ, and hence of the believer with the Father through Christ's mediation. These analogies of union have their high point in chapter 17 where Jesus prays for the disciples, and for those who believe because of the words that they pass on:

THE ACT OF FAITH

> I ask not only on behalf of these but also on behalf of those who will believe through their word, that they may all be one. As you, Father, are in me and I am in you, may they also be in us, so that the world may believe that you sent me. The glory that you have given me I have given them, so that they may be one, as we are one, I in them and you in me, that they may become completely one, so that the world may know that you have sent me and have loved them even as you have loved me. Father, I desire that those also, whom you have given me, may be with me where I am, to see my glory, which you have given me because you loved me before the foundation of the world. (17:20-24)

This image of the unity of the believer with the community of believers, and its unity with Christ, and with God, is vital for John. On the basis of this unity, faith in Christ effects the life of God in believers and gives them eternal life, not as a reward for believing, but because faith shares in God's eternal life. *That* is the salvation that comes from believing. Faith, for example, brings peace, but not as the world gives peace (14:27). It also brings joy, a joy that is complete and that comes because of Christ's words (15:11). But the faith that shares in God's love also unites the community and gives to it social and ethical coherence as well. Those who love each other as Christ loved them, who are willing to lay down their lives for each other, are Christ's friends and each other's friends. Here is another equivalence, that between faith and love, one that underscores the importance of the concrete community of faith.

The community is formed and animated by the love of each for the others, a love John claims comes from God. It is also formed and animated by its hearing of Christ's words and participation in his death and life by the sacraments. Just as signs are interpreted by words and words confirmed by signs, the community's love is interpreted by Christ's words and sacraments, and confirms their efficacy in human life. In John, faith is a human act and experience that is shaped and lived out within a community. It is not an act or experience that is imported from elsewhere to initiate a community.

To have faith, then, for John is to have a certain, distinct kind of self and identity. He emphasizes this throughout the Gospel. Those who have faith are, like the Word, which is not born from blood or flesh, "born from above" and "born of the Spirit" (3:3, 6). While they are in the world, they are not of the world (17:16). These are the children of light, who

The Concept of Faith in the New Testament

flock to the light when it is shown (3:20-21). They are Christ's own and belong to his fold. Or they are, according to an image both organic and sacramental, branches to Christ's vine, cut off from which they can do nothing (15:1-11). While all this gives the Gospel of John a certain predestinarian flavor, some of that flavor seems to come largely from John's stressing the various analogies of union. It may also have something to do with John's purpose in writing the Gospel: to write so that in believing his readers might have life. He isn't dealing with outsiders. Nevertheless, there are instances in the Gospel where people do enter the light of this unity from darkness.[39]

It is frequently commented that in John, faith involves understanding or knowledge.[40] This is certainly the case insofar as it involves an ability to read the signs of God, and to recognize the light and those who belong to it. But insofar as it does involve knowing and understanding, it is not a substitute for either, a believing without knowledge or evidence. In John, unlike Paul, the need for faith will not pass away in the eschaton; it is the sort of personal knowledge that deepens. It is a knowledge that is embedded in the interpersonal practices of the faithful Christian community, understood as a community shaped by the living presence of the Word; and it grows into the full knowledge of God. It is helpful here to recognize this point in what John himself is doing in writing this Gospel.

John has without qualification been regarded as the least historically reliable of all the Gospels. Not only is he considered the latest, it is simply without question that he is not reporting Jesus' words verbatim, but is constructing a web of signs and words to make his point, namely that by wit-

---

39. For example, Nicodemus, who in his first interview with Jesus seems as thick and uncomprehending as anyone could be, nevertheless is described as coming to him as "out of the night," which may indicate not only benightedness, but also a desire for faith, a desire to get out of the night. When he then reappears at Jesus' death bringing the myrrh and aloes to anoint his body (19:39), it seems that he has succeeded. Similarly the Samaritan woman at the well, whose religious and moral life is a shambles when she encounters Jesus, comes to the understanding of faith, and the sort of spiritual worship that faith encompasses. She is able to pass these words on to others, who, upon meeting Jesus themselves, believe in him. (See Chapter 4.)

40. E.g., Bultmann, *Theology of the New Testament,* p. 73; Dulles, *The Assurance of Things Hoped For: A Theology of Christian Faith* (New York: Oxford University Press, 1994), p. 15; Schnackenburg, *The Gospel According to John,* p. 565.

THE ACT OF FAITH

nessing these things one may believe and have life. The imagery is not made up out of whole cloth. It is drawn from the church's actual life of practice: its ethical and social ideals for the community, the importance of the word, as well as prayer and sacraments. The knowledge of faith that John is talking about is a theological knowledge that is deeply rooted in a sense of the community's self-identity, and that has been practiced and found fulfilling. It may, in this way, contain more genuine knowledge of Jesus, of the Word behind the words, than critical history will ever provide. This is a knowledge of Jesus that comes from knowing Christ. This is how faith in the believing community has thought it knows Christ and what John thinks he is providing, that is, instruction for how faith might know Christ. And he does so by showing how the knower herself is constituted.

4. THE LETTER TO THE HEBREWS

The unknown author of the Letter to the Hebrews has a no less "high view" of Christ than John does. Christ in this letter is pre-existent, excelling all created realities, cosmic or human. He is "the character of the substance of God, sustaining all things by the word of his power" (1:3). Yet in this letter, faith is not quite participation in Christ the way it is in either Paul or John. Hebrews' conception of faith is deeply rooted in the Old Testament. In one definition, using a Jewish confessional formula, it is a matter of believing that God exists and that he rewards those who seek him (11:6). Faith here frequently means belief, and what makes one Christian is a matter of confession *(homologia)* (3:1). Specifically confessing Christ is the way one fully receives the promises of God. This is because Christ is the one who is faithful (2:17; 3:2, 6; 10:23), and is the pioneer and perfecter of faith (12:2). Faith in Hebrews particularly retains Old Testament qualities. It is the human side of the covenant, the "reception process, without which the gospel of reconciliation through the atoning sacrifice of Christ remains theoretical and unassimilated."[41] So faith in Hebrews is primarily directed to God; Christ is the one who gives the way of directing fully and accurately. He is the mediator between humans and God, not primarily because he is God present among us, although he is that, but because he fully

---

41. Barnabas Lindars, SSF, *The Theology of the Letter to the Hebrews* (Cambridge: Cambridge University Press, 1991), p. 108.

participates in human nature. He does not exactly bring faith; he perfects a faith that has been present in Judaism. In that he gives full access to God. He is faith's realization, immanent in his immediacy to the community.

To understand the full richness and complexity of an understanding of faith that appears on first sight to be less complex and rich than Paul's or John's, it is important to come to grips with the context of the letter. While it has proved virtually impossible to discover its exact historical context, this much is clear. The recipients are people who confess Christ, but who are on the verge of dropping this confession and returning to a Judaism that does not so confess him, replete with its full sacrificial system. They are probably Jewish Christians, and it is likely that the temptation to drop their confession has to do with some persecution they are facing, although the exact nature of that persecution remains a matter of speculation. Hebrews seeks to argue the community out of this backsliding by showing how Christ alone gives full access to God. Its argument is this: Jesus is the perfect mediator because he fully shares our nature and can sympathize with us and bear our sufferings to God without distortion and with sympathy. But he is also the perfect mediator because he is eternal and sinless and has no need in his sacrifice to make atonement for his own sins. So his sacrifice is full and complete, and there is no need to return to a sacrificial system where sacrifices are incomplete to the degree that they must be repeated. He alone gives full and perfect access to God, and is the pioneer and perfecter of faith.

Hebrews' chief exposition of faith *per se* comes at the end of this ten-chapter argument and is an exhortation about what to do, given what Christ has done and given the community's situation. Its advice is to hold fast to their confession and to have faith, which in this context means to persevere and hope, for this is Christ's way. It is also the way of the forerunners of Christ. At the beginning of chapter 11, Hebrews gives what has become an oft-repeated definition of faith: "faith is the substance of things hoped for, the conviction of things not seen." Hebrews has a certain Platonic flavor to it that is reflected in the use of the word "substance," although modern commentators try to avoid the suggestion, emphasizing a strictly Jewish usage and translating *hypostasis* as "assurance," as the Revised Standard Version does. Use of the term elsewhere, such as in 1:3 where Christ has the character of God's *hypostasis*, would seem to indicate that "substance" is the better, consistent translation. This Platonic influence is also needed to make sense of much of the argument of Hebrews, since it depends upon a distinction between the "really real" and what is a copy. For example, in 10:24 Christ did not enter a sanctuary that is a copy of the real one, but into the one where God really dwells. His sacrifice is complete *(teleios)* because perfect; others are copies. This does not mean, as it also would not in Platonism, that the copies are unreal. They simply are not full and complete; their reality depends upon participating in what is full and complete. Thus to call faith the "substance" of things hoped for is to talk about it as grasping and participating in the reality of those hoped-for things. In the numerous examples of Old Testament heroes that follow in chapter 11, it is clear that these are people who have grasped, who participated, in the reality of things hoped for, the really real, the perfect things, and the way they did so was by faith. Yet, strangely, while they did, it is also said that "they did not receive what was promised" (11:39).

Where Hebrews is un-Platonic is here, and not in the notion that faith participates in the reality of the perfect and unseen. Whereas philosophical Platonism saw participation as synchronic, Hebrews sees it as diachronic. For Plato, the perfect and copies of the perfect exist at the same time, as the idea of what a building ought to be and what it, in fact, turns out to be co-exist. But for Hebrews, the perfect is not co-existent in time with the copy, but is in the future; it is to be revealed. So the grasp of the unseen is hope, not insight; it is the grasp of a reality that is to come. It grasps the perfect fulfillment of a promise. This then actually gives the "copies," say, the sacrificial rites of Judaism, a certain *temporally* unsurpassable reality. They are not copies in the sense that nobody thought it out any better than Judaism did, but should have. Rather, in a much stronger and positive way, they are intimations of what was to come. But as intimations they are the demonstrating, the proving out or argument for that coming, but yet unseen, reality. That reality is real and is seen in the power that it had to affect the lives of those who lived by the promise. Faith is therefore not an intellectual grasp or glimmer of what God's promises bring; it is the reality of those promises in the situation of these heroes; it was what made their actions what they were. But this faith was also a matter of hope and perseverance because it was a witnessing to what God in his own time would fully reveal.

Faith in Hebrews not only carries the Old Testament sense of obedience and faithfulness, it also, and especially, carries senses such as patience, steadfastness, and perseverance.[42] It has a sense of "waiting for God," of waiting for God to reveal himself. Christ is the perfecter and pioneer of

---

42. Verbal and substantive forms of *hypomenein* are found at: 10:32, 36; 12:1-3, 7.

faith because he grasps and reveals fully that for which faith waits. But faith as waiting is clearly not passive. It has a certain power and a way of receiving the promise such that it embraces the power to make things, the things promised, happen. It particularly has the power to forge and maintain the identity of the community. It is helpful here to reconsider the context of the letter and the argument as a whole.

The community that received this letter was on the verge of forsaking its confession of Christ and returning to strictly Jewish practice, perhaps to avoid persecution. Here was a community that was about to lose its identity, for it was a community that was about to lose the faith that bound it together. It is in this light that we must understand the author's intent in writing the letter and the nature of faith he describes. Although he provides an account of why Christ is the fulfillment of all that these people had looked forward to, he is not trying so much, as many have thought he was trying, to prove that Christianity is superior to Judaism. At that time the distinction would not have made much sense, and the question could not have been asked in the way we ask it. Nor was he writing to the uncommitted; he was writing to people of faith, and he was trying to point out that they were about to lose their very identity. How? By losing their faith in the Christ, they would also lose their connection with their past, the history that gave them reason to make them look forward to the fulfillment of God's promise. Once they had lost that past, they would surely lose their future as well. In short, once they had lost their Christian confession, he hinted, they would lose their Jewish heritage as well. For, he argues, everything in that heritage had led up to this faith; to deny the faith now, once they had arrived at it, would be ultimately to deny the heritage too.

This can be put in yet another way, a way that the author of the letter himself tries. Much of the Letter to the Hebrews is a long and technical argument designed to convince these people who are about to give up their faith why they should not, namely because Christ does fulfill faith. In the eleventh chapter, however, that argument is dropped, and in his exhortation to the perseverance of faith, the author tries another tack. There he seeks to show, in concrete human and historical terms, precisely what that faith is that they are about to deny and what it means to persevere. He seeks to show how men and women who had faith had created that community and had looked forward to what these people were now thinking of forsaking. He thereby shows that real faith is something that creates community. Thus, the conclusion is that to break with the community is to

THE ACT OF FAITH

lose faith, and to lose faith is to lose one's community and identity. In short, he seeks to show the community that is united by faith, that is made by faith, and therefore the community that they are about to depart from; ironically, they think they are about to return to it. His way of showing that community comes in chapter 11, where he proceeds to list numerous characters from Abel to the prophets, lives that held together because of the faith they together held.[43] This cloud of witnesses, these lives of faith, is the substance of things unseen, the demonstration of things hoped for.

Faith in Hebrews, which is confession and hope and especially waiting and perseverance, is at its root being a certain sort of self that comes from identifying with a heritage and a people, and upon being able to identify with Christ as the one who leads that people to the fulfillment of the promise in a way that no one else could, for he is perfectly God and fully human.

---

43. One particular example from that list is especially striking, precisely because it illustrates better than most how communities are built by faith. It is the example of Moses, especially as he is described in a single phrase where it is said, "By faith Moses, when he was grown up, refused to be called a son of Pharaoh's daughter, choosing to share ill treatment with the people of God rather than to enjoy the fleeting pleasures of sin" (11:24-25).

One normally thinks of Moses as a great man of faith because of the extraordinary things he did. He is the one who faced down Pharaoh, who divided the Red Sea, who talked with God, and who delivered the Ten Commandments. All of these things were, of course, crucial to the community of the Hebrews; indeed, without them, that community never would have existed. But according to this phrase, it was none of these things that made Moses a real leader of the Hebrews. Rather it was the simple act of Moses' identifying with them, of seeing himself as one with them, even in their suffering.

The fact is that he didn't have to. Some scholars, citing the Egyptian root of his name, suggest that Moses actually was not born of a Hebrew slave, but was in reality an Egyptian through and through. Etymology aside, due to his upbringing, Moses could have considered himself to be one of Pharaoh's children, and could have enjoyed the life of a ruler, one of the power elite. But he did not. Indeed, it seems that when he looked at the Egyptians, the very people who had raised him, he did not see them as belonging to him at all. It was, rather, in looking at the Hebrews, insignificant and contemptible as they were to Egyptian eyes — and Moses' eyes were initially Egyptian — that he saw himself. He saw his life; he saw real life in them. He saw in these people the future of humankind, and he saw in them the fulfillment of God's promise. And, we might suggest, it was because he did that they came in time to be that.

Thus faith in Hebrews, even as a matter of waiting and perseverance, is at root a matter of being a certain sort of self and involves a certain kind of moral identity. It depends upon being able to identify with a heritage and people, and upon being able to identify with Christ as the one who leads that people to the fulfillment of the promise.

CHAPTER IV

Augustine

Augustine's *Confessions* is the story of a fragmented self that finds the way back to wholeness. But Augustine's life story does not begin with an awareness of that fragmentation; indeed, in its earliest tales, if one were to subtract Augustine's post-conversion commentary from the narrative, it reads quite differently. The *Confessions* as a factual *curriculum vitae* is the story of a gifted youth, raised by ambitious parents of modest means, who is no less ambitious than they but also with the intellectual and personal gifts needed to realize his worldly dreams. It is a story of a young upwardly mobile professional who has very reasonable dreams of reaching high levels of intellectual and political life. But along with this story is a second one that Augustine also tells. This is a story that begins when Augustine as a nineteen-year-old student first discovers philosophy in reading Cicero's *Hortensius.* This is where the fragmentation begins, or at least Augustine's recognition of it. In his philosophical life, Augustine hears the call of conscience, and sets his heart on truth, wanting to see things as they really are, and thereby to be wise. Being wise and knowing now makes a difference to who he is, for he cannot with any integrity see himself as striving for anything else. Yet he discovers he cannot bring his worldly ambitions into harmony with those of philosophy. He tells his reader that each time he tried to lift his mind's eye out of the abyss, it only sank back. In time he came to see himself as two wills divided: "I was in conflict with myself and was dissociated from myself" (Conf. VII.x.22).

This conflict of the self with the self is the all-important context of

Augustine's conversion and of his subsequent understanding of faith as a way back to wholeness. His conversion was no flash of light, no mystical ecstasy or great insight into the eternal verities. As he tells it, it came when he was naked to himself and utterly distraught with recognizing that he was unable to help himself, and that he did not know the way to truth. His conversion was a moral certainty about what that way is. Taking up Paul's letter to the Romans, he reads "Not in riots and drunken parties, not in eroticism and indecencies, not in strife and rivalry, but put on the Lord Jesus Christ and make no provision for the flesh in its lusts." It was then that the "light of relief from all anxiety flooded into my heart. All the shadows of doubt were dispelled" (Conf. VIII.xii.29). And as he simply states, "the effect of your converting me to yourself was that I did not now seek a wife and had no ambition for success in the world" (Conf. VIII.xii.30). Augustine's conversion is the fully accepted recognition of who he has been, and the consent to be what God will make him by God's help. His subsequent telling of his early life is then the telling of the painful growth of a self he had not earlier recognized and an acceding to another's authorship of his story, an authorship he had not recognized before. His subsequent search for truth and for the true author of that story is a search through the depths of the self, and through the motions of the will. Augustine seeks to bring his will, his identity, himself, into conformity with God.

Augustine's emphasis on the self has been charged with being the beginning of an unholy individualism in Western philosophy and theology. But if there is an explicit concern with the self that is not seen in Paul and John, Augustine's concern can hardly be called "individualism." That is what he is trying to escape. He needs to find himself *in* God, and within God to find how he is related to all else that God has made. His is a concern that the self be placed within a moral space that is defined and set out by God, entered into by personal and moral life in Christ. Augustine's repeated quotation of Isaiah 7:9, "if you do not believe you will not understand," involves for Augustine a program of bringing the self into line with what is to be understood and of identifying the self with that: the eternal God and his eternal order. Faith for Augustine, like Paul and John, is a matter of living life in God that the Word of God makes possible. Self-reflection is not an "objective" concern for the outer self, as it is in Locke, but a conforming to the image of God known in God's perfect image, Jesus Christ. For Augustine this is participation in God. It has its Platonic overtones, but its irreducible specificity is thoroughly biblical.

1. WILL AND ORDER: THE MORAL SELF IN AUGUSTINE'S *DE LIBERO ARBITRIO*

Because faith is life in God, what life in God means for Augustine is of first concern. It involves the relation of one's will to God's will, something that remains constant throughout Augustine's writings, even if the form of its articulation changes. In order, therefore, to uncover the nature of faith in Augustine, it is thus necessary to begin with Augustine's sense of self, particularly with his understanding of the will and the questions that it poses. This will be done by a close examination of Augustine's early *De Libero Arbitrio*. This book is not directly concerned with faith *per se*, although it is the first one where the Isaiah passage regularly appears. Rather, it is concerned with the problem of evil and the will. But as shall become clear, how Augustine treats that problem is very different than, say, how Hume treated it. And where it is different is highly revealing both of Augustine's moral context and of his understanding of the self, both of which are crucial determinants of his view of faith. While *De Libero Arbitrio* is, indeed, a philosophical defense of God's justice, it has another, equally important emphasis, a theological emphasis in which Augustine presents the Christian tradition's alternative to the modern sense of the self. In Augustine the self is not, and cannot be discussed as, a distant spectator to questions of God, or of good and evil; nor can it will itself on the basis of unengaged, unparticipated reason. For Augustine, questions of God and of good and evil are questions *to* the self, demanding its engagement.

1.1. What Is a Will For?

De Libero Arbitrio is a discussion of the problem of evil, and in it Augustine uses what is called "the free will defense." God is not responsible for evil because humans have free will, and having misused that free will have brought evil upon themselves. Augustine thus uses an argument that has been at the forefront of a long line of defenses of God's justice. But Augustine is interested not just in exculpating God; he is also very interested in determining what exactly the will is and how it is related to God. For him the problem of evil is more than a logical objection to belief in God; it is a question that arises within the context of the will's relation to God.

In order to launch any kind of free will defense one obviously has to

THE ACT OF FAITH

have a plausibly strong sense of the will's freedom. This would at least involve the ability to choose between doing something and not doing something. Hume notes this freedom in the *Enquiry Concerning Human Understanding* when he defines freedom as: "By liberty, then, we can only mean *a power of acting or not acting, according to the determinations of the will*."[1] Augustine agrees: "The will is moved to action by what can be seen. And while people have no power over what they see or touch, they do have it in their power either to accept or reject.... Hence it is that the rational substance selects from both classes what it wills, and by virtue of its selection achieves misery or blessedness" (De Lib. III.xxv.255). What is glossed over in this apparent agreement, however, are some very deep differences concerning what is at stake in talking about the will's choices. The difference can be seen through a comparison between Stoic understandings of the will, to which Augustine is relatively close, and Hume. For the Stoics what is at stake in the freedom of the will is a question of one's very rationality, and hence humanity. To acquiesce to fate — to will it and desire it for one's own — is nothing more or less than choosing to accept one's own providential role in the world as a whole. To choose one's providential role and honor God by doing so is to be one's true self. For example, Epictetus says: "If, indeed, I were a nightingale, I should be singing as a nightingale; if a swan, as a swan. But as it is, I am a rational being, therefore I must be singing hymns of praise to God. This is my task; I do it, and will not desert this post, as long as it may be given me to fill it...."[2] For Stoicism to will to defy the divine order with respect to one's role may well be to cease having that role at all, and to play another, one belonging to a less than rational nature. It would be seen as becoming something else. This is undoubtedly why Epictetus also warns: "Only consider at what price you sell your freedom of will *(prohairesis)*."[3]

The role of the will here is a moral one that is linked to who one is as a person. Questions of the will for the Stoics are not simply questions about choosing from a range of options, nor is one's freedom simply the ability to choose. Rather, to choose is to be some person within some larger moral context, to have some orientation deeper than mere external choice. Willing is therefore not always of external possibilities or of exercising agency

---

1. 8.73.
2. Arrian's Discourses of Epictetus, Bk. I, chapter XVI.
3. Arrian's Discourses of Epictetus, Bk. I, chapter II.

over some public possibility; at its deepest levels it is a basic orientation, a character. Discussions of the will in this sort of context are far more concerned with a moral evaluation of what we might call the "inner person" than with any specific acts he or she may perform. That this is not so with a Humean conception of liberty is obvious from the very context and content of Hume's own definition of liberty as the freedom to act or not act according to determinations of the will. Anyone who is at all familiar with the *Enquiry Concerning Human Understanding* of course knows Hume's intent. He is seeking to undo the Gordian knot of the metaphysical questions of the will and its causality that one all too quickly encounters in discussions of free will. He cuts the knot by pointing out that the question of freedom is not one of metaphysics, of an inner freedom, but simply a question of the ability to do or not do something. It has nothing to do with the metaphysical status of the will or with moral valuation. This is an impressive move. But at the same time we are impressed we do need to be aware that cutting the Gordian knot that way also does away with the picture of the person that the Stoics and Augustine relied on. For Hume, the person is, and only is, his or her public acts. There is nothing else to be.

The similarity in talking about the freedom of the will thus covers over a deeper question about the will, namely, the question of "freedom for what?" This is a question about whether we take the power of the will to be most importantly an internal power, as the Stoics and Augustine seemed to take it, or an external power, a power to act as Hume took it. The difference lies in whether we put emphasis on the power to accept or reject, to take to heart, say, an argument, or, more important, a worldview, or the power to do or not to do something. Or, put otherwise, it is a difference between understanding the will as an internal activity that lies at the center of our concept of a person, or understanding it as the structure of uncoerced, publicly identifiable activity, which gives us a very different sense of the person.

If Augustine sees the will as a matter of deciding between possibilities, and at one level he does, the most important "choice" of all is the consent and desire that lies behind the particular external choices we make, an acceptance or rejection of who we are and our relation to the world and God. Whether one consents to the world and its creator does matter. What makes that choice crucial for Augustine is that it is this consent that determines the moral quality of the will and person. In fact, it *is* the moral person. Here will goes deeper than choice; it is a deep orientation to the world.

THE ACT OF FAITH

It is an issue of identity and character. Its exercise determines who we are, just as, at the opposite end, Nietzschean *ressentiment* determines a certain kind of character. The interest in who we are morally is a primary interest of Augustine when discussing the question of evil. The question of evil on this account is not just a question of an unhappy state of affairs that can be evaluated neutrally from the outside and for which the will, not God, should be blamed. The question of evil and the role of the will is a matter about willing itself, about our choices and selves within the world. It is a question of how and who we shall be in the world. It is thus a matter of our subjective intentions within a state of affairs. We can now turn to a closer examination of the text of *De Libero Arbitrio* to see how.

1.2. Will, Responsibility, and Identity

In the opening sentence of *De Libero Arbitrio* Evodius asks simply "Is God the cause of evil?" A straightforward question, it is open-ended in a way that Augustine exploits extensively. On the one hand, it is straightforwardly a question about God's justice. That there is evil in the world, no one denies; therefore we ask, "Is God the cause of it?" A chief intent of *De Libero Arbitrio* is to answer this question by arguing that God is in no way to blame for evil, except the sort that one experiences in being punished justly. On the other hand, though, there is another way of taking this question and answering it. That way is to treat it more broadly, more scientifically. In this case asking whether God is the cause of evil or not is not so much asking a question of theodicy *per se* as it is, ingenuously and non-rhetorically, asking the question of "just where *does* evil come from?" That this sort of "scientific" question was also in Augustine's mind is clear from his own description of *De Libero Arbitrio* in the *Retractationes*. There he notes that this book was begun in Rome at a time when "we wanted to explore and discuss the origin of evil." The conclusion of that discussion, he adds, was "that we concluded that the sole cause of evil lay in the free choice of the will" (Retr. I.ix.1), which was why he titled the book "On Free Choice of the Will."

Finding that the origin of evil lies in the free choice of the rational creature exculpates God, a not unimportant conclusion in itself. However, we miss a good deal of Augustine's point in this treatise if we do not take seriously that the book also has another sort of conclusion, namely, a broader one about evil and the will. This other conclusion in turn affects how we understand the exculpation of God with respect to evil. This other conclusion and its importance can be seen by bearing in mind two things: (1) Augustine did at an earlier time have another answer to the origin of evil that also vindicated God, i.e., Manichaeanism; and (2) the reasons why he abandoned that answer. Those reasons were, as he himself makes clear, a newfound ability to think of God as immaterial, but just as important, a realization that evil is not an external thing — an obstacle in one's path, as it were — but a deformation, a privation of some good.

If simply providing an argument that would exonerate God for bringing about a state of affairs were the whole problem, Manichaeanism is not a bad argument. Most people even have a psychological predisposition to it. The problem, though, as Augustine came to see it, is that this argument ultimately is no good because it misrepresents both God and evil. For evil is not simply an unfortunate state of affairs that can be recognized by just anybody; it is not simply external to the thinker as the Manichaeans assumed (i.e., somebody else's fault, as it were). It also has something to do with the person who sees that state of affairs as a problem. So Augustine has an entirely new way (at least for him) of thinking about where evil comes from, and that, in turn, forces him to think about what we call "the problem of evil" in a very different light. This new light above all causes him to locate the site of evil within beings, that which is deformed, and it causes him to locate it at the point of their deficiencies. More existentially, what this must have forced Augustine to realize was that whatever else evil was, it was at least somehow a part of him, and that it was *his own* deficiencies and not some external obstacle that was the problem. Nothing could be farther from Manichaeanism, ancient or modern, which, in effect, denies one's essential moral responsibility for who one is, and blames it on external factors. That he was concerned about this problem can be seen in the *Confessions* when he explicitly contrasts the Christian doctrine of recognizing one's own fault with what the astrologers teach: "It is good to make confession to you, Lord, and to say, 'Have mercy on me; heal my soul, for I have sinned against you.' . . . Astrologers try to destroy this entire saving doctrine when they say: 'The reason for your sinning is determined by heaven,' and 'Venus and Saturn or Mars was responsible for this act'" (Conf. IV.iii.4).

But how is evil rooted in the will? It is two different, although not en-

THE ACT OF FAITH

tirely unrelated things, to say that the deficiency is in the act willed or to say the deficiency is in the willing will itself, i.e., in the character of the will's functioning. For Augustine it is clearly the latter that he is worried about. As he says in discussing the evil of adultery: "Perhaps then lust *(libido)* is the evil element in adultery. As long as you look for evil in the overt act itself, which can be seen, you are in difficulty" (De Lib. I.iii.20). Similarly he argues that Adam's sin was something present in him even before he ate the apple.[4] It is also clear why Augustine is worried about the willing will itself, for not only does it color the external act, but also, if evil is a privation of form, it is the will itself that is deficient. Thus the problem of evil for Augustine is not simply whether evil is logically compatible with God's existence, goodness, and creativity, it is also an existential problem for us. The problem of evil reflects back on the questioner as the possible source of the deficiency. Evil is not simply a matter of choosing bad things; it is also a reason to question the choosers.

To recognize that it is the will itself and its motions that Augustine is most concerned about goes a long way toward explaining certain features that many moderns find unsettling in reading *De Libero Arbitrio*, especially a certain lack of concern Augustine seems to demonstrate toward the problem of suffering. To be sure, he does not ignore it entirely. However, such a thorny problem as that of the suffering of innocent children, which we find terrifically important, is not even brought up until the closing chapters of the final book.[5] Even then the problem is only answered within the larger context of an argument that Augustine has been developing about the just order of the world. Augustine was not an insensitive man; indeed, far from it. Rather, the problem of suffering, which seems to us to be *the* moral problem of evil, is not the one with which Augustine is dealing. His problem is with the will itself.

But why this emphasis on the will itself? Whereas moderns tend to take a "God's-eye view," a stance of complete objectivity, toward knowledge, for Augustine one's knowledge is not simply something one has; it is, as assented to, highly relevant to who we are. The questions of "whence evil?" and the compatibility of evil with God's goodness are also questions that involve self-knowledge. Reflection for Augustine is morally reflexive, and questions of the moral order of the universe are also questions of one's

4. Cf. De Lib. III.XXIV. See also De Gen. ad Litt. Bk. 11.5.
5. De Lib. III.XXIII.

nal one. Thus when the ostensible problem of Book II is solved — that free will is the good gift of God because God only gives good gifts — what the truly free will is, is also established.

Much of the argument of Book III deals with the question of how the will ever turns from God, concluding that movement is *sui generis*. This book also seeks to establish the consistency of the freedom of the will with God's foreknowledge and justice. But an equally important argument is also given, continuing the lines drawn in the earlier two books. That is an argument that depends upon what John Hick has called "the principle of plentitude" and the "aesthetic theme."[10] It argues that good is within the totality of the universe, and within that totality any seeming evils are not only counterbalanced but even contribute to an overall goodness, as seeming imperfections in a painting when viewed too closely contribute to its beauty when viewed from a proper distance. Often mistaken for a theodicy, this is a primary religious intuition, a characteristic and defining belief inherent in Christian faith[11] that no evil is outside God's good providence. Its function within Augustine's argument as a whole is to now introduce the inquiring soul, who, after Book II, sees itself as part of a moral order dependent on God, to an even larger world order. By doing so the will is given the opportunity now to assent to that larger order as ordained by the Creator.

Taken this way, the argument as a whole may be less about God's goodness in creating a universe where certain evils occur and more a question directly posed to the will about its own moral stance toward the creation. It is at least an invitation to disabuse our minds of what Leibniz was later to call our "anthropocentric conceit," the view that our desires are the basis on which the world order is formed. Augustine himself responded to those who cavil about suffering: "They cannot see the highest good — what it is and how great it is — yet they wish everything to be the same as their idea of the highest good" (De Lib. III.xxiii.233). The goodness of the will is integrally tied to its assent, its willingness to play its role within the order of the whole.

Thus for the Augustine of *De Libero Arbitrio* the moral self is deter-

---

10. John Hick, *Evil and the God of Love* (London: Macmillan, 1966), ch. 4.
11. Recognizing, of course, that Augustine did not invent it; it is already present in Plotinus, e.g., *Enneads* III.2. But that doesn't mean that Plotinus did not have it as a religious intuition. Augustine seems to think he did.

THE ACT OF FAITH

mined not so much by its public action or even potentiality for action as it is by the vision of the good to which it assents, with and by which it identifies itself, and to which it is thereby bound. Whether we assent to another as the center and orderer of the world or whether we make ourselves its moral center, that is what determines who we are. That further means that what is morally important about us is our inner willing. It is the attempt to affect and purify that willing that is the ultimate goal and cornerstone of Augustine's own arguments in *De Libero Arbitrio*.

1.4. The Will and Moral Identity

When he began to write *De Libero Arbitrio*[12] Augustine was engaged in a project of establishing an *ordo studiorum* "whereby one can advance from corporeal realities to the incorporeal" (Retrac. I.3). This was a relatively common intellectual project in antiquity, particularly among Platonists. It was also a highly intellectualistic approach to the life of faith, and undoubtedly charted out the path of Augustine's own early aspirations for study in a small community of friends before the call of ecclesiastical duty changed his life once again. Such an approach, of course, threatens to make faith a matter of belief in a cosmic system, the very sort of system that Hume aptly criticizes. Belief here depends upon a dualism of body and soul, as well as positing an inner will,[13] and the value of inner life depends upon belief in a system of the world. Augustine was certainly a metaphysician and remained so throughout his life. But what was at stake for him in that? It is that Augustine is seeking to bring to light certain crucial root concerns of human moral identity and to place them within the larger world in order to understand and live out that identity. "Metaphysics" as an intellectual exercise in this case becomes something like articulating this moral insight about human beings and thinking it through; it is not an intellectual exercise that de-

---

12. *De Libero* was begun in Rome about 387/88, and the first book was largely completed there. The second two were written between his ordination in 391 back in Hippo and 395 when he sent off a copy of the completed work to Paulinus.

13. Gareth Matthews in particular sees this sort of inner/outer dualism operating in Augustine's doctrine of the "inner man" ("The Inner Man," in *Augustine: A Collection of Critical Essays*, ed. R. A. Markus [Garden City, N.Y.: Doubleday, 1972], pp. 176-190). We shall give a much different sort of interpretation of the "inner word" (Augustine's actual concern on this issue) in the third section of this chapter.

signs and proposes a system of belief to the neutral intellect, for there is no such thing for Augustine.

What, therefore, is Augustine's insight that needs to be preserved? First, it is that questions about the will are moral and spiritual questions, and that moral and spiritual questions insofar as they are linked to our sense of self are not always secondary to questions of so-called "objective" knowledge. Indeed, in many instances these moral and spiritual questions often shape and configure questions of fact. The question of who we are *is* a moral question and bespeaks a fundamental moral struggle of the human being. We struggle with ourselves to know about the order of the world in which we live and struggle to put ourselves in some kind of larger order. The order we assent to is crucial to our self-understanding, and hence to a best account of who we are.[14] It has, for example, consequences

---

14. In order to show how it may be, an example can be taken from Simone Weil's discussion of what she calls "the love of the order of the world." This is a love she claims is an "implicit love of God," for in it God is really though secretly present, i.e., in it God has secretly wed the soul to himself. Weil gives us an analogy to help show the difference between having this sort of love and not having it. Morally we are subject to an illusion, she suggests, that is analogous to the one we experience whenever we look up into the sky on a cloudless day and it appears that the sky is a bowl inverted above us, thus making it appear as if we were at the center of a spherical world. In the moral case the illusion is that it appears to us as if we were at the center of the world. We thus appear as terrifically important, and what else is of value can be ranked by its proximity to us. Now there is no problem with this illusion; it is entirely natural. The moral problem, Weil says, is when we assent to this illusion and believe ourselves *actually* to be the center. However, if and when we consent to not being the center, this love of God is born. Weil writes: "To empty ourselves of our false divinity, to deny ourselves, to give up being the center of the world in imagination, to discern that all points in the world are equally centers and that the true center is outside the world, this is to consent to the rule of mechanical necessity in matter and of free choice at the center of each soul. Such consent is love. The face of this love, which is turned toward thinking persons, is love of our neighbor; the face turned toward matter is love of the order of the world, or love of the beauty of the world which is the same thing" (*Waiting for God* [New York: Harper & Row, 1973], p. 160).

For Weil this love of, this assent to the order of the world is clearly something that makes a difference to our moral personhood. But how? Why is it not simply an entertaining image that deserves no special consideration when making moral evaluations? In the first place Weil thinks it is because there are real consequences that come from our deepest assents. She notes that, based on the sort of beauty that we love, we form an image of order that we seek to emulate in our projects; for beauty, or fittingness, is a sort of finality to which we aspire in all our projects. For example, she says: "The love of power amounts

THE ACT OF FAITH

in the world, for we act on the order we understand and aspire to. But most important, it also produces the very quality of our evaluations, and affects what we take to be valuable. We do recognize the goodness of a person who makes one kind of evaluation and not another.

To assent to Augustine's "order of the world" in which we are dependent on God for our being, and for our place in the world God has created as our moral vision, is to evaluate life in a very particular way, and to bind ourselves to a very definite vision of who we are. The internal motions of the will are not otiose explanations of "outer willing," but are of primary importance to our standing as persons; for what is at stake ultimately in the assent of the will is the moral vision of ourselves in relation to the world and God, whether we see ourselves as self-sufficient or dependent upon another. If there is anything morally substantial to us, what we will to think of ourselves is crucial to that substance. This is not self-obsession; it is not a matter of being closed in on oneself. It is a sense of oneself in relation to others. It is, in fact, an openness.

Second, this assent and the moral and spiritual struggle it involves lies at the heart of what faith is. In *De Libero Arbitrio* Augustine focuses on the self's relation to God and the universe as one of will and assent. In conjunction with seeking the order of the universe and trying to provide an alternative to Manichaean determinism and to see the goodness of the creation, he is ultimately trying to bring his identity into conformity with whatever that order is as being God's will. The heart of the ideological argument (if we even want to call it an argument anymore) is precisely this, for in it the particulars of the universe are not at question; it is a question of how one relates oneself to that on which all else depends. That relation for Augustine is the real heart of faith. And *that* relation is at the heart of Augustine's entire project; it is his relation to God that Augustine contin-

---

to a desire to establish order among the men and things around oneself, either on a large or small scale, and this desire for order is the result of a sense of beauty. In this case . . . the question is one of forcing a certain circle into a pattern suggestive of universal beauty." The result in the case of the love of power, though, is that "it is not the universe and it hides it." Thus the order to which we assent and which we seek to emulate affects several, if not all of our projects. It affects what we take to be beauty in another human being, it affects our political institutions and associations, and above all, Weil thinks, it affects the sort of science we have. Loving beauty for itself and not for what it can do for us gives one's projects an entirely different flavor. But not only that; we recognize in time the sort of person who launches these kinds of projects.

ues to ponder and struggle with for the rest of his life. The intellectualistic liberal arts project was soon given up; the struggle to conform with God's will was not. There is, of course, a sense in which Augustine did not change many of his cosmological views, nor given the expectations of his age should he have done so. But he did refocus the terms of that struggle with the will of God. After writing *De Libero Arbitrio* he wrote about assent in the *Confessions* in explicit terms of moral and spiritual struggle. His great final work, *The City of God*, is a vision born of coming to understand himself and his world in the moral and spiritual terms of the Bible — and thus the Bible itself in the terms of a historical human struggle with questions of who and whose we are. Faith is understood in more and more personal terms from here on.

Thus faith for him was not simple belief in what mind could not or did not know, as it appears to be for Hume and much of philosophy of religion after Hume. It was the moral and spiritual struggle of the will, in conjunction with the memory and intellect, to bring himself into conformity with God. That remained constant throughout his writings. Taken in conjunction with Augustine's first insight — that this struggle of the will is at the heart of our very identity — we thus come to see what is at the heart of Augustine's philosophical enterprise. It is a very different vision than the modern one. But it is also very different from what it is often characterized as by modern philosophy. It has an underlying seriousness — a sense that philosophy contributes to who we are — that a good deal of modern philosophy lacks. For the moral order to which we assent makes us who we are, and that may be a far more important question about the freedom of the will than any other.

To be sure, there is also something mysterious about this inner quest, at least insofar as it is something to which public reason and method have no direct access. But it is not, for all that, incomprehensible or unheard of, as Augustine knew quite well. Indeed, it may very well be at the root of the very common enterprise of understanding who we are.

2. FAITH, UNDERSTANDING, AND THE MORAL SELF: AUTHORITY

The importance of the moral self in *De Libero Arbitrio* reveals the larger sorts of questions that Augustine is pursuing generally in his thinking.

THE ACT OF FAITH

More particularly, it sets the context for understanding the particular role of faith within Augustine's thought. For Augustine faith is not a question of whether or not there is a God, but is, at its root, a concept that he uses to move within the space of the soul's deepest relation to God. In one of his earliest treatises, *The Soliloquies,* Augustine says that all he wants to know is God and the soul. The knowledge he seeks goes to the heart of what it means to be fully human. Faith is to be understood within that context, for faith is the way by which the soul responds to and comes to know and live in God. It is the way that God has prepared for the soul to be reformed and to have life in him. Here Augustine does not diverge from either John or Paul.

Augustine's thought world, though, is different from either of those apostles, and it is certainly more complex. This is especially true with respect to his anthropology. In order then to best present his understanding of faith and its relation to the self, I intend to break that presentation into two parts. The first will largely deal with Augustine's earlier works in which he talks about faith as a matter of believing on authority. The second will deal with later works, especially the *Sermons on the Gospel of John* and *De Trinitate.* The division need not be airtight, for the lines of the latter are clearly discernible in the former. The latter does, though, spell out in much more systematic and clearer detail an understanding of the self in relation to God toward which the former seems to be working. But the early works also draw lines that shape the later ones, and if for that reason alone, separate treatment allows the overall character of Augustine's theology of faith and the self to emerge much more clearly.

2.1. Faith and the Will

Augustine's thought is deeply Platonic and there are certain aspects to it that are not fully original, nor would we expect them to be, even though Augustine experiences and relates them not simply as philosophical doctrine but also as deeply personal biographical matters. Augustine works within a framework that involves certain features about the self and its relation to God. These include, first, a sense of the loss of the true self, a sense of alienation from oneself, a division of one's will, as it desires one thing and continually keeps willing others. It is also a sense of alienation from others, as one remains unknown and not understood by them, and unable to know them. And insofar as one does not will the perfect happiness of life in God, insofar as one is unable to live fully in the image of God, it is a matter of alienation from God as well. Second, there is a need to return to oneself to find oneself, others, and God. For Augustine, there is a haunting sense of perfection and of a happy life from which we have not only fallen, but which continually beckons us to return. Both of these features Augustine shares with the neo-Platonic philosophers of his age, and he knows it.

Where Augustine is at his most Platonic, however, is his belief that knowledge and wisdom, in which consists the return to the self, come from the mind's conformity with eternal realities, but most specifically, of course, from conformity with God, the source of all truth.

> Some things are made conformable to that first form such as rational and intellectual creatures, among whom man is rightly said to be made in the image and likeness of God. Not otherwise could he behold unchangeable truth. (De Ver. 82)[15]

It is not that the mind should perfectly *reflect* reality. (Ancient mirrors were notoriously poor at such reflecting, which is why images in mirrors were a metaphor for *lack* of clarity.) It is that the mind be *conformed* to God and identified with God, and that it let itself be shaped by that reality, making room for it; or, more accurately, the soul needs to find its room within God. It is to bear the impress of God and to become like him. For this reason, the mind's knowledge is always a matter of *being* good. Although Augustine carefully distinguished between the moral virtues and contemplation of God, the knowledge of God in which the self returned to itself required virtue. He points out that "virtue is nothing else than perfect love of God," in which "temperance is love keeping itself entire and incorrupt for God; fortitude is love bearing everything readily for the sake of God; justice is love serving God only . . . ; prudence is love making a right distinction between what helps it towards God and what might hinder it" (De Mor. 25). The knowledge of God is never a spectator's knowledge; it involves a change in

---

15. Also: "The wise man is so closely united with God in his mind that nothing can come between to separate them. God is truth, and no one is wise if he have not truth in his mind" (De Util. 33). And: "For the mind becomes like God, to the extent vouchsafed by its subjection of itself to Him for information and enlightenment. And if it obtains the greatest nearness by that subjection which produces likeness, it must be far removed from Him by that presumption which leads the mind to refuse obedience to the law of God, in the desire to be sovereign as God is" (De Mor. xii.20).

THE ACT OF FAITH

the thinker, and for this reason, thinking for Augustine really was a sort of *itinerarium mentis ad Deum*. This holds both in Augustine's early thinking, such as *On Freedom of the Will*, and his later thought, such as in *De Trinitate* and his sermons and scriptural commentaries. Thinking at its deepest levels is allowing the indwelling of the truth, which is God.

The moral and spiritual elements inherent in the knowledge of God are ones that Augustine stresses, although he is not unique in doing so in the ancient world.[16] However, they are prominent in a way that is perhaps unheralded elsewhere because of his sharpening of the concept of the will as a distinct element in the human self. But it is not just his recognition of the will as such that distinguishes Augustine's thought, it is his recognition of it as the wild and uncontrollable element in human thought and action. It is the roving and greedy will as something that is essentially me, and not just ignorance or forgetfulness of life's true goal, that creates the most insuperable gap between aspiration and fulfillment. The best of the ancient philosophers, Augustine thought, recognized the fatuity of the gods of paganism, and had genuine insights into the one God who made heaven and earth.[17] Yet not only were they unable to convert their fellows, they themselves also fell back in practice to lesser lives. What their minds intuited they betrayed religiously, and their way to the goal was incommensurate with the goal.[18] From his own experience Augustine recognized that it is one thing to intuit that there is a happy life and a God to which one ought to be conformed, and quite another to be so conformed.

Where the will presented a truly important problem to Augustine was the fact that it is something that is essentially us, although not more so than our understanding and memory. But the quick and eager will affects both understanding and memory. To will improperly is not just a matter of a bad choice; the whole person is affected. The fall — alienation from self, others, and God — for Augustine is the result of an undue and improper love of physical things. Yet, the problem is not physical things as such. The problem is when they are *loved* as if they were eternal.[19] This for Augustine

16. Cf. Pierre Hadot, *Philosophy as a Way of Life*, ed. A. I. Davidson (Oxford: Blackwell, 1995).
17. Cf. De Ver. 1.
18. Cf. De Ver. 8.
19. In Augustine's *Rule* he gives a very commonsensical illustration of what he means. There he instructs the monks that it is not evil to look at a woman; the problem comes when you *stare*.

is not a simple mistake of ignorance; mistaking is at the level of mere pondering. The problem is one of commitment, for to love them and use them is a matter of self-image and often involves a desire to control; it is a matter of pride. For example, desiring a good and happy life, but thinking that the freedom from fear that such a life entails involves the possession and wielding of temporal power, one loves that power as one's own and not as under God's order. In time one comes to think that temporal power is divine. So not only is the problem that sensual things are loved, but in loving them the memory and understanding come to be unable to free themselves from thinking about the eternal in any other terms. The immorality of seeking to possess the whole in a controllable self-image leads to a breakdown of the reason itself. To heal the fragmented self is then a complex matter, for it is a matter of harmonizing all the aspects of the self, not only with each other, but also with their proper objects, things to which they have not been habitually directed.

Faith, for Augustine, is the way to heal this fragmentation and to reform the deformed soul and to recover God's image. It effects this healing by reversing the order of the fall. So if the will has attached the soul to temporal things in an improper way, and thus has damaged memory and understanding, faith is not a matter of appealing directly to the understanding, but of attaching the will to temporal things in such a way that the understanding can be recovered. It is a matter of purifying the soul so that it may come to understand and in understanding have life in God. A fascinating exegesis of the story of the Samaritan woman at the well illustrates the point. In commenting on this story, Augustine suggests that when Jesus asked the woman for a drink, he "was thirsting for the faith of the woman herself" (Tr. in Io. 15.11). But he also called for her husband, a call that Augustine says is a call for her to bring forth her understanding, by which she could be taught. And having been taught, she came to understand and confess who Jesus was. "That was the reason," Augustine says, "why He said, 'I thirst, give me to drink'; namely, to work faith in her, and to drink of her faith, and to transplant her into His own body, for His body is the Church" (Tr. in Io. 15.31).

2.2. Faith and the Way of Authority

In Augustine's earlier works, faith is chiefly discussed as a matter of following authority. *The* faith is what the church and Scripture teach; to have faith is to assent to that and follow it. But it is not blind assent. The problem is that we have lost our way, although we have retained some sense of the goal. Given the goal, we need a guide in order to reach it. That is what God has provided in Christ and what is enshrined in the faith.

> As eyes which are scarcely opened after a long period of darkness and blindness turn away and refuse the light which, nevertheless, they desire, especially if one try to point them to the sun, so, in my case, I do not deny that there is an ineffable and unique spiritual good visible to the mind, but I confess with weeping and groaning that I am not yet fitted to contemplate it. Nevertheless, he will not leave me if I make no pretence, if I follow the path of duty, if I love truth and friendship, if I am filled with anxiety lest you be deceived. (De Util. 4, also 20)

The grace of revelation is not a matter of providing direct knowledge of God that, if believed, is the object of *contemplation* itself. Faith is not a form of contemplation. Nor is faith the end of thinking, but its beginning. The grace of revelation, if we submit to it in faith, is to set the soul free from its "second nature," the mortality that is acquired by loving temporal things as if they were eternal.[20] Set free, the mind can begin to be healed and move from understanding temporal things aright to being conformed in the fullest knowledge of God, although Augustine emphasizes time and time again, this is not achieved on this side of death. But what then becomes the crucial defining moment in faith is that humble submission, the willingness to be guided. That is a transformation effected by God's admonition and call to the soul in revelation and administered through "temporal junctures and sacramental rites" (Ad Simp. II.2). As such, faith is fully a personal and moral matter. But so too is the knowledge of God. The full knowledge of God, the contemplation of God, only comes by shifting the center of moral gravity from oneself to God. One comes to know God by willing to be taught and led by God.

To put things in this way goes some considerable way toward under-

---

20. Cf. Ad Simp. I.11.

standing just what is at stake for Augustine when he sets off the way of faith from the way of reason. Faith and reason are not entirely distinct things; faith is for the reason, and without it, Augustine believes, reason fails of its own end. But the ways are different, and here he is mainly concerned with ways of seeking. "For him faith and reason operate in the same sphere of seeking to understand; and if reason attempts this without faith, it gets lost."[21] In *De Moribus* he contrasts the Manichaean way of "reason" with the Catholic way of faith. Manichaean "knowledge" fails in important respects beyond those of its more bizarre qualities that hardly qualify it as knowledge anyhow. Augustine argues that eternal life *is* the knowledge of the truth (the Manichaeans would not have argued with him here). To claim to have a way of knowledge *to* eternal life, a way of knowledge to perfection when knowledge is perfection, is simply confused.[22] Augustine is claiming something like a distinction between reasoning and knowing. Reasoning as thinking to reach knowledge is not the same thing as knowing. Reasoning without direction can have the effect of simply spinning within itself, especially when it shows no signs of participating in its goal of knowledge. But more important, knowing, if it is the "*reward* of those made perfect," requires that we first love with full affection him whom we desire to know.[23] It is from that principle of love leading to perfection, that Augustine sees the point of using authority before argument and using it to purify the mind.

What underlies this argument is a distinction between the way of authority and that of reason. As Augustine describes matters, often in biographical terms, in *De Utilitate Credendi,* the way of "reason" as the Manichaeans practiced it really was a way of self-assertion and individual autonomy. His own attraction to the Manichaeans stemmed mainly from the surface impression that they were more sophisticated than the Catholics, and that he felt himself to be more clever and sophisticated by following them. This was part and parcel with his own worldly ambitions, although, he admits in a show of fairness, they did not encourage him in those ambitions and it was because of those ambitions that he chose not to advance beyond the rank of "hearer."[24] But their appeal *was* to his vanity

---

21. Edmund Hill, O.P., "Unless You Believe, You Shall Not Understand," *Augustinian Studies* 25 (1994): 54.
22. De Mor. 47.
23. De Mor. 47.
24. Cf. De Util. 2, 3.

THE ACT OF FAITH

and sense of self-assertion. Nowhere was this more evident, he thought, than in *their* opposition of reason to faith. Their reasons did not make him wiser or better. They did, however, encourage him in a contempt for the Scriptures, and a sense that he could stand alone and judge the truth of divine matters by his reason alone. The ridiculousness of judging the Catholic faith from the Manichaean standpoint of reason (but it was really simply accepting their uninformed opinions about the Catholic faith) was similar to having "the recondite books of Aristotle expounded to him by an enemy of Aristotle" (De Util. 13). From his later position of having seen that there was a great deal in Scripture, something he saw because he was finally willing to be taught by people who understood it, Augustine recognized that there was in the Manichaean way of reason an overweening spirit of pride and a lot of presumption.

> But we, intelligent youths forsooth, marvellous explorers of reason, without seeking teachers, without the slightest suspicion of our own slowness of comprehension, without the slightest heed paid to those whose care it has been that these books should be read, guarded and studied throughout the world and for so long a time — *we* had the temerity to suppose that nothing such men said was to be believed, influenced as we were by their bitter enemies, among whom, because of their false promise of reason, we were compelled to believe and cherish an unheard of number of fables. (De Util. 13)

So while reason promised to be the key to perfection, morally it was no way back to God. It led to self-assertion, smugness, and arrogance.

The way of authority, on the other hand, for Augustine has a markedly different quality. It involves the humility needed to learn from a teacher, which, Augustine notes, he finally had to accept when, despairing of finding the truth himself, he sought out Ambrose in Milan.[25] But ultimately authority is a matter of trusting God, especially trusting that God will help. Quoting Hebrews 11, he notes: "When religion is the object of our quest God alone can provide a solution for this great difficulty. We ought not to be seeking true religion unless 'we believe that God is, and that he brings help to human minds'" (De Util. 29). Trust is as crucial a quality of faith for Augustine as it is for Paul, and indeed for the Old Testament writers.

---

25. Cf. De Util. 20.

Without it, conformity to God as a matter of being a self is simply contradictory.

It now becomes possible to understand what the relation of faith to reason is in these earlier works. For much of ancient philosophy, there were, as there are for many modern philosophers, two epistemological options: knowledge and opinion, with opinion, if it is not simply uncommitted musing but the assumed basis of any further thinking, carrying heavy connotations of credulity. On these grounds, the Manichaeans, of course, could easily characterize the Catholic way of faith and authority as credulousness and authoritarianism, a clear moral fault even then. Augustine, however, saw faith as something quite different from opinion. It was not knowledge (Augustine has very high standards for what is to count as knowledge, especially with respect to divine things), and did involve belief of what was not known by reason alone. But this belief he likens to the sort of application that a studious person has to her subject matter. It is not something she knows, but because it is important to her that she know it, she applies herself to it. Authority's appeal is not to credulity; authority comes into play because one is deeply concerned to know, and seeks the most likely place to learn.[26] For Augustine, particularly at this point in his thinking, the way of authority does not preclude knowing God by reason. But since even advance by reason to the knowledge of God depends upon God, and God has given a way that is practiced in the ongoing life of the church, to disdain this human society is to turn one's back on God. Faith is not an individual achievement, but something learned and practiced within community, and true religion cannot bypass that.

> This [way of not bypassing belief by reason] has been divinely commanded and preserved to our own day. To want to disturb or pervert this practice is nothing but to seek a sacrilegious way to true religion. Those who do so, even if they are allowed to, cannot reach their goal. However they may excel in genius, unless God be with them, they merely crawl along the ground. But God is only with those who, seeking him, have also a care for human society. (De Util. 24)

Faith is then not so much an intermediary intellectual option between knowledge and opinion, although there is a point in so describing it as

---

26. Cf. De Util. 22.

THE ACT OF FAITH

Aquinas later does, but a moral and interpersonal way of exercising our reason. There are similarities here to Newman's illative sense. What knowledge the unperfected mind has is gained by the mind's reaching out towards perfection and making judgments based on earlier moral certainties, e.g., that God is and that he provides help for the mind. Whatever knowledge one has in faith, it is a knowledge that is akin to that of virtue. But that is also the presence of God, the truth itself.

> I need say no more about right conduct. For if God is man's chief good, which you cannot deny, it clearly follows, since to seek the chief good is to live well, that to live well is nothing else but to love God with all the heart, with all the soul, with all the mind; and as arising from this, that this love must be preserved entire and incorrupt.... This is the one perfection of man, by which alone he can succeed in attaining to the purity of truth. (De Mor. 46)

2.3. Faith in What Is Revealed

All this can be put another way. The distinction between the way of faith and the way of reason is *not* a distinction between the *truths* of reason and those of faith. Augustine is firmly convinced they do not conflict, and it is not in any supposed conflict between them that he derives the distinction between the two ways. Rather, the distinction comes from the supposition that fallen human beings in whatever truths they think are not thinking *the* Truth, are not thinking God himself, at least not very well, but are dealing with God and Truth at one or greater remove. Locked into the sensibility of the "outer man," the truths they think are for the most part truths known through an image. Now, for Augustine it is not logically impossible to reason with images in such a way that one can discern their true order, live by it, and purify the mind so that it can behold God, the Orderer. But, as he makes clear in *De Libero*, because our love is disordered, because we love things out of place and order, and tailor them to fit our preferred self-image, we tend — inevitably, Augustine thinks — to fail to get the order right and hence to find the Orderer. The faith given by God's revelation, on the other hand, provides an image of the right order, at least in personal and interpersonal life, which, if we follow it with the humility of love, can lead us back, and purify the mind. Reason is not absent or confounded in such a way back; it receives a focus and form in faith that it had lacked before. Faith is a temporal medicine for the questing mind.[27]

Faith is, then, not a substitute for the deepest sort of knowledge of God. It is a moral stance toward God, born of love, that allows the mind to be taught. But it also involves belief, belief of what God has revealed. And indeed since what God has revealed in the history of Israel and in Christ is a historical matter, belief is necessarily required, for these historical truths are not truths of reason but contingent matters, and need to be believed on the personal authority of witnesses.[28] These witnesses are not to be believed blindly; their credibility is something we have to think about. For example, one has to think about whether they are trustworthy and whether what they are saying bears any marks of the goal we seek. However, *nota bene*, it is not simply a matter of believing the facts they tell us; there is also a shape to their narrative that is important. Thus if faith does involve belief, and it surely does for Augustine, its role in leading the soul back to God is chiefly that of reading what it believes in a certain way, for in revelation God has not simply provided information about the right order of the world, but a way of approaching the world that reads the world rightly. Augustine distinguishes between those things that are to be used for the sake of other things, and those that are to be loved for their own sakes. God the Trinity is alone to be loved for his own sake.[29] If we love in this way, revelation teaches faith how to focus our love so that we know how to use things to lead us back to God.

How does this happen? It occurs by a reorientation of the will that God effects in providence and revelation. In the *Confessions*, Augustine claims, "My weight is my love" (Conf. XIII.9). The will, like weight, has a natural center toward which it tends to carry the soul along. In a fallen state, it loves for themselves things that are to be used, taking the image for the reality. Revelation, on the other hand, provides images of beauty that reorient the will and attract it toward its proper end until the mind is confronted by and conformed to God himself.[30] Confronted by both the beauty of the world and by the examples and teachings of the prophets and

27. De Ver. 45.
28. Cf. De Ver. 46.
29. De Doct. I.3-5.
30. For a full discussion of the role of beauty in Augustine, cf. Carol Harrison, *Beauty and Revelation in the Thought of Saint Augustine* (Oxford: Oxford University Press, 1992).

THE ACT OF FAITH

apostles, those witnesses to God, and by Christ's own teachings and examples, the soul is not only awakened to an awareness of God as the soul's real life, but learns by beauty the way to that life. By loving beauty, it learns to love properly.

While we shall examine in greater detail below Augustine's doctrine of the "inner word" as the way by which he grounds this theological aesthetics, it suffices here to note that what lies behind beauty's ability to awaken and purify the soul is a sacramental theory of signs that is patterned on the incarnation of the eternal Word. The mind in its fallen state thinks mainly in images; by images and temporal realities that signify, and are sacramentally linked to God's own life, one comes to participate in that life. Unable to see God's Wisdom directly, that Wisdom becomes incarnate, accommodating itself to our present understanding in order to heal our understanding. "She is present everywhere, indeed, to inner eyes that are healthy and pure; but to those whose inner eyes are weak and unclean, she was prepared to be seen by their eyes of flesh as well" (De Doct. I.12). By then directing one's love to that which God has providentially caused to be seen, one comes to participate more and more in God's life, for the inner man is reformed and the mind healed until vision replaces faith.

For Augustine, then, by means of outer signs the soul can be healed. This can come from loving God's beauty which is evident in creation:

> We see the ample fabric of the world consisting of heaven and earth, and of all things which are in them; and from the magnitude and beauty of this fabric, we already love even though we do not as yet see the inestimable magnitude and beauty of Him who made it. For He, who cannot as yet be seen in the purity of our heart, has not ceased to place His works before our eyes, that seeing what we are able, we may love Him whom we are not able to see, that by the merit of that love we might at length be enabled to see. (En. in Ps. 103.1)

Beauty most especially is in Christ's teachings and actions. Augustine says in *De Trinitate* that Christ's incarnation was directed to the outer man, so that by the example of the Word in the flesh, one might proceed from the flesh to the Word.[31] "It is he who plants faith in us about temporal things, he who presents us with the truth about eternal things. Through

---

31. De Trin., XIII.24-26

him we go straight toward him, through knowledge toward wisdom, without ever turning aside from one and the same Christ, 'in whom are hidden all the treasures of wisdom and knowledge'" (De Trin. XIII.17). This Christ does particularly by his example of humility, his seeking "to deliver man from the devil's authority by beating him at the justice game, not the power game, so that men too might imitate Christ by seeking to beat the devil at the justice game, not the power game. Not that power is to be shunned as something bad, but that the right order must be preserved which puts justice first" (De Trin. XIII.17). The example of Christ excites in the faithful a love of true justice; the love of justice that is inherent in faith is already Christ's form in the one who is faithful.

It is the incarnation of the Word that stands behind the importance of the words of Scripture, for Scripture, by using the signs of words, directs the mind to meditate on spiritual truths. But these truths are ones that cannot be separated from the love with which they are read, for they reflect back on the reader, putting his or her own narrative into their context. For Augustine, the very act of reading itself, but especially the reading of Scripture, is a matter of deep personal meditation.[32] Thus the faithful reader is obliged to recognize that the words of Scripture contain more than a historical sense; they also contain aetiological, analogical, and allegorical senses.[33] Although Augustine is frequently criticized, and even sometimes rightly so, for the fanciful meaning he imputes to Scripture by his use of allegory, allegory is not a fantastic and willful exegetical tool in his hands. In using allegory, he consistently interprets Scripture as a whole as pointing to what Christ has done for humanity,[34] and reads Scripture as a consistent

---

32. On these issues, cf. Brian Stock, *Augustine the Reader: Meditation, Self Knowledge, and the Ethics of Interpretation* (Cambridge, Mass.: Harvard University Press, 1996).

33. De Util. 5.

34. Cf. Harrison, *Beauty and Revelation,* pp. 85ff. "Augustine's emphasis on figurative, 'spiritual' exegesis is not least due to his belief in its Christocentricity. It is this, above all, which determines his exegesis of the Old Testament. He writes 'our whole design, when we hear a Psalm, a Prophet or the Law, all of which was written before our Lord Jesus came in the flesh, is to see Christ there, to understand Christ there.' Each detail of the Old Testament therefore becomes for Augustine a 'sacrament,' *sacramentum,* or symbol, *signum,* that is, a visible representation and bearer of spiritual reality and truth. . . . But this is not only true of the Old Testament, but of Christ's words and action in the New Testament, which conceal and yet reveal his divinity, and also of the rites and mysteries of the Church which are symbolical, communal actions which transmit divine grace."

THE ACT OF FAITH

witness to the story of salvation. He can do this confidently because Christ is the eternal Word behind all words. But just as important is that through these words — through the story of God's action among human beings that climaxes in the incarnation, crucifixion, and resurrection — the Word addresses itself to the reader, and makes the reader understand his life in the light of the Word. The interpretation of Scripture is self-involving, and the truth that Scripture conveys is the truth that results in the love of God and neighbor. The first rule of Scriptural interpretation remains for Augustine the love of God.[35]

Taken by themselves, these aspects of revelation may still seem too literary, too aesthetic and intellectual. But for Augustine they are ultimately rooted in the concrete practice and lived-out historical tradition of the church. The Scriptures are learned within the community of the church, which takes the inquiring soul on faith and endeavors to transmit through its tradition — through its life and words — what the soul needs.[36] That is the sort of authority Augustine found lacking in the Manichaeans.[37] Moreover, it is in the interpersonal interaction within the church that is contained "love and charity to our neighbor in such a way, that for all kinds of diseases with which souls are for their sins afflicted, there is found a medicine of prevailing efficacy" (De Mor. 62). In the hands-on intellectual and moral training of the church, the love necessary to know God is excited and nourished. In its example, Augustine finds the moral basis of its authority and his own personal reasons for submitting himself to it.[38] For as the soul is nourished by God's word and lives it within the church, the soul becomes more and more like God, something that is always reflected in her concern for others, and in her overcoming the alienation that had separated her from others.[39] The community of faith is where the love of God

---

35. De Doct. I.
36. De Util. 31.
37. C. Ep. Man. 5.
38. "In You it is seen, as is fit, how vain is effort under the law, when lust lays waste the mind, and is held in check by fear of punishment, instead of being overborne by the love of virtue. Yours, as is fit, are the many hospitable, the many compassionate, the many learned, the many chaste, the many saints, the many so ardent in their love to God, that in perfect continence and amazing indifference to this world they find happiness even in solitude" (De Mor. 64).
39. "He loves what many have come to know and love, thereby deserving to be congratulated. For he loves God with all his heart and with all his soul and with all his mind,

is taught, learned, and experienced, and where the relationship with God is healed in the healing of the relationships that bind human beings together.[40]

3. THE WORD AND THE INNER WORD

Augustine understood from early on that the healing effected by faith is something that is ultimately the work of God. It is so, of course, because God is responsible for providing that which will delight and inspire the mind, and provides it at a propitious time.[41] It is also because God is the one who is calling and moving the soul.[42] Faith is thus a response to the Word, evoked by the Word, and made effective by the Word itself. It is a gift at both ends.

Faith was *not* for Augustine, as it was not for Paul or John, something that signaled the willed intellectual transition from disbelief to belief; it was that by which he could talk about life in God. For Augustine, faith is thinking with assent (De Praed. II.5), not a thinking to assent. It is a habit of the heart and mind, not an ideology; it is a practice that is at its root a form of interpersonal activity. It is directed to knowing God, but, as Augustine makes clear, this knowledge comes from dealing with God, a dealing that is initiated by God's revelation of beauty to the soul and that culminates in life in God. It is a movement from using words, which both obscure and hide selves as well as attract and guide them, to life in the Word behind the words. Augustine tells us that immediately after his conversion he decided to retire from his "post as a salesman in the markets of rhetoric . . . ," not wishing his students, bound for law courts as their profession, "to buy from my mouth weapons for their madness" (Conf. IX.2). But he did not give up

---

and his neighbor as himself. God does not begrudge his becoming as he is himself. Rather he even helps him as much as possible. He cannot lose his neighbor whom he loves as himself, for he does not love even in himself the things that appear to the eyes or to any other bodily sense. So he has inward fellowship with him whom he loves as himself" (De Ver. 86).

40. "But the relationship which binds all together is the most important of all. He is not made sorrowful by the death of anyone, for he who loves God with all his mind knows that nothing can perish for him unless it perish in the sight of God" (De Ver. 91).

41. Ad. Simp. II.2, 21, 22.

42. Ad. Simp. II.12.

THE ACT OF FAITH

words entirely. Rather, "You pierced my heart with the arrow of your love, and we carried your words transfixing my innermost being" (Conf. IX.3). It was in these transfixing words that Augustine saw the healing of his own "inner word," and its conformation to the Word.

3.1. Words and the Word: The Sermons on the Gospel of John

Augustine's great commentary on the Gospel of John is in important respects an extended meditation on the prologue to that Gospel. In the vast majority of the 144 sermons that comprise the commentary, Augustine either directly quotes or alludes to the prologue, most frequently invoking "the Word was with God, and was God," or "the Word became flesh." In these words about the eternal Word was the heart and dynamics of the Christian faith and the life of the faithful soul for Augustine.

The importance of the Word in Augustine's later theology comes from an analogy he draws between the Word of God and what he calls "the inner word" that lies behind all humanly spoken words.[43] When a human speaks, she utters words, breaths of air that strike a sound upon the ear and quickly pass away. In these puffs of air and tintinnabulations, communication is effected. They carry meaning, which comes from one mind and is received by other minds. This meaning lies in the "inner word," an understanding and intent that one holds in the mind and expresses in words or works of artifice.[44] Because the inner word is the mind's understanding of

---

43. On the development of Augustine's use of the "inner word" as an analogy between the shape of our inner soul and the Word of God, cf. Olivier du Roy, *L'Intelligence de la foi en la Trinité selon S. Augustin* (Paris: Etudes Augustiniennes, 1966), esp. pp. 428ff. Du Roy makes the analogy far more Plotinian than I do in this exposition.

44. "You can have a word in thy heart, as it were a design born in your mind, so that your mind brings forth the design; and the design is, so to speak the offspring of the mind, the child of your heart. For first your heart brings forth a design to construct some fabric, to set up something great on earth; already the design is conceived, and the work is not yet finished: you see what you will make; but others do not admire it, until you have made and constructed it, and brought that fabric into shape and to completion; then others regard the admirable fabric, and admire the design of the architect; they are astonished at what they see, and are pleased with what they do not see; who is there that can see a design?" (Tr. in Io. 1.9).

something, one's outer words have the sense they do by being the means of communicating this understanding. But it is not just the words themselves that carry the meaning. They are spoken with an intention to communicate. Because they are, they carry not simply bare "objective" meaning, but something of the speaker with them. They are both "the offspring of the mind" and "the child of the heart." They bear the speaker's understanding, not understanding in general. They, therefore, also bear something of the speaker's character. Coming from the truly knowledgeable and wise speaker, they are words well worth listening to, for to take them to heart and use them to understand, one not only comes to know the wise, but to be wise.

How are we now to understand John's Prologue? The Word of God is the eternal, ungenerated, inner word of God who is God's own heart. The world that is created by him is his intention, and its meaning and order lie in that Word that is present in the creation.[45] Thus God can be understood through the creation as one can understand another person from what he says to us. But more specifically, the Incarnate Word in the man Jesus is the word spoken to human beings, whose sense and meaning lie in God's own inner word. He is the outer word spoken by God so that God might be known by human beings, especially since by the fall they can no longer understand well enough God's other words in order to find God. "That there might be a way by which we could go, He has come from Him to whom we wished to go" (Tr. in Io. 2.2). Analogously, the words and actions (signs) of the Incarnate Word can trace their intention and meaning back to their personal source.

Thus to believe in Christ or to believe his words and those words he has inspired is to believe in God.[46] But if this communication is from God, albeit indirect and veiled in transient flesh and symbols, and is directed to the reformation of the human soul, to be reformed one must be willing to be communicated with. That requires the engagement of both the understanding and will. First, the understanding has to be brought forward and opened. That is the activity of faith, and in opening the understanding, the understanding comes to be healed.[47] "For we, by turning away to sin, lose enlightenment; and by turning to God we receive enlightenment" (Tr. in

---

45. Tr. in Io. 2.10.
46. Tr. in Io. 54.3.
47. Tr. in Io. 9.5; 15.

THE ACT OF FAITH

Io. 21.4). The purpose of faith is to quicken the understanding; without the engagement of the understanding, without its being brought forth, however, there is no communication. So the understanding is engaged in faith. But, second, so is the will, for if one needs *to want* to be communicated with and to understand, then faith also depends on love and desire for that which is intimated in flesh and symbol. Faith, if it is desire for fulfillment, i.e., for the Word itself, and not just a desire and longing for the beauty of the outer words, as happens with those who are delighted by rhetoricians, is then a matter of having faith *in* or *on* God *(credere in Deum)*, a matter of loving God.

> [H]e that believes Him does not necessarily believe *in* Him. For even the devils believed Him, but they did not believe in Him. . . . What then does it mean "to believe in Him"? To love Him by believing, to go into Him and to be incorporated in His members by believing. It is faith itself that God exacts from us: and He does not find that which He exacts, unless He has bestowed what He may find. . . . Not faith of any kind whatsoever, but "faith that works by love": let this faith be in you and you shall understand concerning the teaching. That "this teaching is not mine, but His who sent me"; that is, you shalt understand that Christ, the Son of God, who is the teaching of the Father, but is the Son of the Father. (Tr. in Io. 29.6)

Faith is not simply believing something to be the case, but a willingness to learn and to be reformed. This willingness, however, is itself the beginning of a new understanding and the process of reformation. It is the regeneration of the inner person, a process that takes place by an ever increasing grasp and participation in its goal. By reforming the "outer man," the inner man is reached and affected. "I would move a longing desire in your heart. Good character leads to right understanding; the kind of life leads to another kind of life. . . . You have, by the very desire, begun the life of the angels. May it grow in you, and be perfected in you; and may you receive this, not of me, but of Him who made both me and you!" (Tr. in Io. 18.7).

This reformation of the understanding and its growth through faith is the growth of the Word within the hearer.[48] The decrease of self-assertion and direction is the increase of God within the soul, and ultimately, there-

---

48. Tr. in Io. 75.5.

Augustine

fore, the increase of us as persons in the image of God.[49] One comes to Christ the Word through Christ the man.[50] Faith is thus ultimately participation in the Word through the Word's own freely given communication; it is life within God given by God, the being ingrafted into his body.[51] This is not a reformation *ex opere operato,* but, if a reformation of the image of God in the mind, then a reformation of the mind's inner word that comes by listening to the words of the Word.[52] What we are, do, and know is our inner word; in learning to know God, that inner word in what it knows becomes conformed to God. It becomes like what it knows. It is in this way that one becomes united to God by Christ the Incarnate Word.

But what does it mean to be united to God in such a way? For Augustine it means that one's understanding is informed by God, taught by the Holy Spirit,[53] although he is careful to note that this is not direct, but still through an image in this life. But if so, Augustine focuses neither on what it is to know the inner life of God nor on generating pronouncements of eternal truths from that teaching. To know God through faith and to be united to him is to be like God in what we say and do. The inner word for the faithful is still known by the outer word and the communication it intends to effect. Simone Weil once suggested that one cannot verify the inner life of a soul but that "one can only verify whether the behavior of a soul bears the mark of an experience of God." For Weil this meant that it is not so much the way that one talks about God, but the way that he talks about the things of this world that "best shows whether his soul has passed through the fire of the love of God." Thus "there is no fire in a cooked dish, but one knows that it has been on the fire" (SW 108). In a strikingly similar

49. Tr. in Io. 14.5.
50. Tr. in Io. 13.4. "If you seek truth, keep the way, for the way and the truth are the same. The way that you are going is the same as the *whither* thou art going; you are not going by a way as one thing, to an object as another thing; not coming to Christ by something else as a way, you come to Christ by Christ. How by Christ to Christ? By Christ the man, to Christ God; by the Word made flesh, to the Word which was in the beginning with God; from that which man ate, to that which the angels eat daily."
51. Cf. e.g., Tr. in Io. 21.8; 22.9, 10; 23.5; 25.18; 26.10.
52. Tr. in Io. 20.2; 37.4; 57.3; but especially 97.1: "In the very mind, therefore, that is to say in the inner man, there is a kind of growth, not only to the transition from milk to solid food, but also to the taking of food itself in still larger and larger measure. But such growth is not in the way of a space-covering mass of matter, but in that of an illuminated understanding; because that food is itself the light of the understanding."
53. Tr. in Io. 32.5; 40.5; 96.4.

image, Augustine argues that one's righteousness is the mark of the reformation of the inner word.

> By forsaking God, the soul becomes unrighteous; by coming to Him, it becomes righteous. Does it not seem to you as it were something cold, which, when brought near the fire, grows warm; when removed from the fire grows cold? A something dark, which when brought near the light, grows bright; when removed from the light, grows dark? (Tr. in Io. 19.11)

Thus the reformation of the inner word *is* the gifts of wisdom, godliness, righteousness, and charity, all active virtues.[54] It is the ability to give the quality of justice to what one says and sees and points out. This is not an isolated gift, but one that is exercised within the unity and community of those who also are similarly formed; indeed, the unity of the body of Christ comes from the Word itself, formed by and the result of faith.[55] The community of faith is that which receives and lives by just words.

In the first of the *Sermons on the Gospel of John* Augustine gives an illustration of the Word's communication that underlines the reformation of the speaker that faith effects. In the first part of that sermon Augustine concentrates at some length on John the Baptist and his preaching, which witnesses to the Incarnate Word. John is in no sense the Word, the one that is to come, Augustine recognizes. But in the words that he speaks, he is able to effect faith and peace and righteousness in his hearers, something that makes him one of "the mountains of God." If he is able to do so, Augustine points out, it is because he himself has received peace and contemplated "the divinity of the Word." But that peace that has been communicated to him makes him a communicator of peace to others. "Those who have received peace to proclaim it to the people have made Wisdom herself an object of contemplation" (Tr. in Io. 1.4). *That* is the evidence of his having received the Word, for that is the work of the regenerating Word in the world of flesh and symbols. John's words have authority, Augustine wants to say, because of the Word's indwelling in him and his words. But Augustine never looks into John's soul to see how that comes about, nor does he think that looking into John's soul is possible. It is because John is able to teach that Augustine wants to say that the Word is involved. That is less a deduc-

54. Tr. in Io. 19.12.
55. Tr. in Io. 13.18; 18.4; 26.13; 32.8; 39.5; 106.2.

tion, and more a part of a life lived well as a result of having been taught well, a life of seeing clearly because one has been taught by one who has seen. John's teaching is not an invitation to look at John, but to refocus one's sight.

3.3. The Inner Word in *De Trinitate*

Augustine's doctrine of the "inner word" can at first blush appear to be a quaint and antiquated philosophical doctrine that no longer has much epistemological or anthropological force. Consideration of its role in the *Sermons on the Gospel of John* should give some much needed perspective, for within its religious context there it appears far less an explanation, and far more a key descriptive element used to talk about the deeply personal and interpersonal nature of religious faith and understanding. This context is one that needs to be kept in mind while examining Augustine's most carefully worked out exposition of the inner word and its role in human mind in *De Trinitate*. *De Trinitate* is one of the great seminal works on trinitarian theology in the church, especially in the West. But since so much of the exposition depends upon an analogy that Augustine draws between the human mind and the Trinity, based upon the human being as the image of God, it is also the high-water mark of Augustine's thinking about the nature of the mind and self. This dual nature of the work, however, lends a certain interpretive ambiguity to the work: Is the discussion of the human mind as the image of God using the mind as an analogy in order to understand God as Trinity? Or, is the presumed unity of the three-personed Trinity in its operations a way to understand the image, the mind itself, a teaching of the church that provides an image by which the fragmented self may recover *its* unity? Consistent with the discussions of faith above I take it to be the latter.[56]

For Augustine, the mind's operations are unified, but they can be analyzed into three functional aspects: memory, understanding, and will. To know something, to render a true judgment of it, on the basis of this analysis then looks something like this: Suppose one is trying to say something

---

56. For a discussion of the relevant literature on this issue, see Ellen Charry, *By the Renewing of Your Minds: The Pastoral Function of Christian Doctrine* (New York: Oxford University Press, 1997), ch. 6.

about an arch he has seen in Carthage. To do so, he needs to produce an image derived from having seen the arch. That is stored in the memory. But to make a judgment about it, he needs to do so using a certain form and standard. That, too, comes from memory. Understanding, then, is the resultant judgment that comes from reflection upon the particular image by the standard. But the will comes into play by virtue of the fact that one affirms the judgment as true. For Augustine, these are not operations separated and carried out *seriatim*. They are just factors that are involved in a human being's saying something like "this arch in Carthage is beautiful." The inner word arises when in true judgments by the eternal form and standard we "conceive true knowledge of things," i.e., fit them appropriately to the standard, and then "we have with us a kind of word that we beget inwardly, and that does not depart from us when it is born" (De Trin. IX.12). It is the responsibility for the judgment as ours when it is born, or spoken outwardly. But it is also, therefore, the personal intention involved in the judgment. There is not any inner word conceived when one is just repeating facts, as one might do by simply defining moral acts or grammatical terms. But to commit oneself to be moderate or not to speak ungrammatically does involve such a word, for knowledge here is "knowledge with love" (De Trin. IX.15). This is to say, knowledge when loved is taken by the mind to apply to the mind and binds it to itself. To use a more contemporary way of speaking, judgments involve an inner word when they are intentional and self-involving performative utterances.

What Augustine describes is a summary of the grammar of the self-reflexive pronoun "I." In understanding something, for example, one says, without a separate act of deliberate reflection, "I understand," and never "there is understanding going on in this room." But Augustine thinks that the fact that one doesn't make this kind of mistake is because when speaking we always have a sense of self; that is a matter of engaging the memory. Would this then mean that the memory alone is the self? Not at all, for my memory, my use of "I," comes into play only when the mind is understanding and when the will is involved by my meaning what I say, when in the latter case, for example, I have to take credit or blame for my statements and see them as mine. What then I say as *my* saying is born of the inner word that is the linking of my understanding, my memory in my self-image as it were, and my self-involvement in what is being said.

The will in all this is the variable element. When the will rests in the act of knowing, i.e., affirms a judgment made according to a standard, "the conceived word and the born word are the same thing" (De Trin. IX.14). In this case, and Augustine has here in mind the knowing of spiritual things such as justice, one *is* just, one has the character of the just person, for the mind is unified and conformed to what it knows. The inner word is conceived by a love and desire for justice and born by an act of affirming that justice as right and good. Thus he observes, "All positive quality of mind is like the thing it knows" (De Trin. IX.16), for the will approves and affirms that knowledge as true and right in itself, but as it does so its own act as a self is constituted. In the case of justice, then, to desire and to affirm and love this knowledge is to have one's inner word formed by it, and is to have the character of a just person. On the other hand, the inner word can be conceived and born in a quite different way. It, for example, can be conceived not out of love for justice or to see a thing as it is in the eternal order, but for self-seeking ends; that word is born in the world in acquisitiveness. The thief is responsible both for his desires and for acting on them, and is rightly understood and negatively evaluated as a thief because of both, because he is morally, as a self, a thief.

This analysis allows Augustine to describe the nature of the fallen self. When one loves and desires temporal things and strives to acquire them, the problem is not so much the act as it is the injustice of thinking about things through a self-imposed and self-centered understanding of the order of the world. It is unjust to impose a role on things that they must play in a false order; the resulting deformation of the memory and understanding of one's own self makes one unjust. When the will marries the form of justice to a limited image, the image has to serve as the form.[57] The self is not unaffected, for in such cases "I" is now said in reference to an image of the self that is constituted not by a desire and affirmation of justice in itself, but by a limited image of justice that has been tailored to one's own temporal ends. By thinking oneself to be the center of the world, which occurs simply in our willingness to think about justice in a way that serves our own limited ends, we not only degrade justice and fail to see others justly, but our own ability to see and know is degraded. One is a different sort of self.

The fallen self is an alienated self. In its self-assertion it identifies itself with an image that is outside and adventitious. (This is inevitably, if not necessarily, the case in Lockean radical reflexivity.) At the same time that it

57. De Trin. XI.9ff.

THE ACT OF FAITH

seeks its unity and completeness, by seeking it in an image — worldly success, power, control, etc. — it depends upon another. But in seeking itself in another, it is also unjust to that other, making it an extension of the self. Denying space to others, it fails to find its own space. The inner word intends the soul's happiness, but intends it in a way that ultimately effaces memory and understanding.

For Augustine one of the consequences of the fall is that the soul invariably thinks in images, including thinking about God, and can only with great difficulty get beyond them. This was Augustine's own experience in trying get free of Manichaean anthropomorphism. The real problem for him, however, is not thinking by using physical images as such. As he makes clear, there is in moral virtue, for example, a genuine knowledge *(scientia)* that has to do with physical life, the life of the "outer man."[58] Similarly, empirical judgments can also be *scientia*. The problem is when the will finds its gravitational center in those images of God or justice, and not in God or justice. Even in leading a virtuous life, the soul is still dependent on externals to know itself. Now, the point of the criticism here, if criticism it is, is not that the soul should be rendered isolated and unassailable from life in the body or interaction with others. Augustine's point is that even when life is lived well and in truth, if lived entirely in the "outer man," even virtuously, the mind is still at one remove from affirming consciously and as its own, its own self. It is present to itself, but not fully as itself, for its springs still lie hidden. As Plotinus would similarly suggest, the soul does not possess itself. More theologically to the point, and this surely is Augustine's chief concern, while the mind judges according to the truth and one's inner word is formed accordingly in virtuous life, it cannot for all that make itself aware of the Truth as Truth. In short, its life is led by God's Truth, and hence by God, but still does not have the knowledge or wisdom *(sapientia)* that comes from that perfect awareness.[59] But if this is the case with virtue, the soul that lacks even the virtue of the outer man is doubly estranged from itself.

Augustine's positing of — and aiming toward — a perfect, contemplative wisdom in which the mind is constituted by a self-aware understanding of the eternal truths that underlie its own operations seems to smack strongly of the ancient world's preference for the intellectual, con-

---

58. De Trin. XIII.1.
59. On the distinction between *scientia* and *sapientia*, cf. De Trin, XIV.3.

templative, and theoretical over practical knowledge.[60] But Augustine's theology is no mere gloss on this tradition, if tradition it is, nor in the end is his view of the self one of an isolated thinker.[61] In his discussion his point is not to underplay the value of virtue and the outer man, but to emphasize it, for virtue is the way back to the inner man.[62] By healing the outer man in virtue, by ordering his desires in the temporal world where he seems to be fixed, order can be restored to the soul, and the inner self can be reached. (This, of course, was Pascal's point in giving the gambler the advice he did to take holy water, etc., if he couldn't bring his heart to faith.) But that is to reach a relationship with God through God's own gift. If the inner word of the fallen self is formed around images, Augustine thinks that certain images can have the salutary effect of forming the inner word in such a way that the will, and hence in time, the memory and understanding, can be redirected to form an inner word that is conformed to God.

This is the point of the Incarnation, and of faith. Faith is directed to the outer life, toward *scientia;* it is not a description of the inner life of God that is to be believed, nor is it itself the recovery of the inner self. It is an active inner word formed by the revealed image of the Word made flesh, being received from hearing its words and the words generated by that reve-

---

60. Du Roy sees this vestigial Platonism even in De Trin. (Cf. du Roy, *L'Intelligence de la Foi*, pp. 442ff.) The degree to which this split was radical in ancient philosophy is questionable, however. Cf. Joseph Dunne, *Back to the Rough Ground: 'Phronesis' and 'Techne' in Modern Philosophy and in Aristotle* (Notre Dame: University of Notre Dame Press, 1993), who suggests that it is not so radical, except in the modern world, and that thinkers such as Gadamer, Arendt, Collingwood, and Newman were trying to recover something of the importance of practical, interactive knowledge as being at the root of all knowing.

61. Cf. Mary T. Clark, R.S.C.J. "The insight into interiority as essential to human personhood was a valuable gift from Plotinus. But Augustine did not leave it as he found it. He viewed it not as a proof of affinity to God but as corroboration of the revelation that the human being was made to the image of God. The very notion of image entails a relationship of origin. In choosing image as the most fundamental aspect of human persons, Augustine accented their relationship to the Trinitarian God as fundamentally a call to a growing union with divine Persons by a continual growth in the relationship of love. His preferred image and the likeness of God within the soul was the action of remembering, understanding, loving God" ("Augustine on Person: Divine and Human," in *Augustine: Presbyter Factus Sum,* ed. Lienhard, Muller, and Teske [New York: Peter Lang, 1993], p. 107).

62. A point that he thinks Plato is in agreement with him on. Cf. Civ. Dei. VIII.8.

THE ACT OF FAITH

lation and lived out in the active life of the soul. How the Incarnate Word effects this is less a matter of teaching rules for a well-ordered life and more a matter of demonstrating what a well-ordered life is like. Augustine's chief example is his description of the atoning death of Christ. Whereas humans desire both to will rightly and to be able to do what they will, to have a good will and the power to realize that will, they invert power and knowledge: "It is right to desire power to be given to you now, but against your faults; men hardly ever want to be powerful in order to overpower these, they want it in order to overpower men" (De Trin. XIII.17). Christ, on the other hand, defeats the devil not by power, but by justice, and so teaches humanity the proper relation between power and justice and humility. Thus if we imitate the Word's incarnate example faithfully there is a training in virtue.[63] Moreover, Augustine adds, Christ in his incarnation and death shows the grace of God toward humanity, and by his humility overcomes human pride.[64] As then faith, by loving this image of God in the flesh, forms its understanding around that image, the self is purified by faith in order to contemplate God eternally.

> Our knowledge therefore is Christ, and our wisdom is the same Christ. It is he who plants faith in us about temporal things, he who presents us with the truth about eternal things. Through him we go straight toward him, through knowledge *(scientia)* toward wisdom *(sapientia),* without ever turning aside from one and the same Christ, "in whom are hidden all the treasures of wisdom and knowledge" (Col. 2:3). (De Trin. XIII.24)

The inner word as formed by the given image of God is hearing and loving that life. But in that the Word, in its own image, is conceived and born, and the faithful have a life in God that will bloom in full vision in the resurrection. Faith then is life in God, given by God that moves to God. From our alienation from self, God, and others, we move to full society within the unity of our selves, and to society with others and God.

---

63. De Trin. XIII.20.
64. De Trin. XIII.22.

3.4. Conclusion: Faith and the Personal Dimensions of Knowing

What is the significance of Augustine's concept of the inner word? The inner word is not an inner explanation for what we say; talking is not a matter of translating from "mentalese" to Latin or English. Rather, Augustine recognized, what we say is not just out there, and it is not just neutral. There is a sort of shape or form to what we say that involves us, and gives us away in what is thought and said. What knowledge is, therefore, is not simply a fact in the mind, but the mind of the thinker as well. And what is known, insofar as it is known, is in an important sense the shape of the thing itself, consented to and entertained by the mind, shaping the mind in relation to it.

There are, of course, huge philosophical issues about this conception of knowledge and the self that can be raised. Augustine does subscribe to a view of knowledge that involves universals, and to a view of the self that is arguably described as a substantial self, not a fully relational one.[65] These issues, however, may not be the most important ones at all. What may be more important to think about, and what may have been most important to Augustine, is what the personal and moral dimensions of knowing and being a self are within this sort of view of knowledge. Or, even more simply, what may be most important to note is that there *are* personal and

---

65. Paul Henry, S.J. (*St. Augustine on Personality* [New York: Macmillan, 1960]) suggested early on that Augustine in his emphasis on subjectivity had made a break with the traditional view of the person as substance. A. C. Lloyd ("On Augustine's Concept of the Person," in *Augustine: A Collection of Critical Essays,* ed. R. A. Markus [Garden City, N.Y.: Doubleday, 1972], pp. 191-205) suggested quite the opposite. According to Lloyd "the only object to which these persons have a necessary relation is God himself, who, of course is to be found within us" (p. 204). In a mediating position, William Riordan O'Connor ("The Concept of the Person in St. Augustine's *De Trinitate*," *Augustinian Studies* 13 [1982]: 133-43) suggests that while there is no reason to think that Augustine fully broke with the traditional doctrine of the self as substance, nevertheless "we do find in *De Trinitate* a theory of the human being as the image of God according to which the human being is constituted as a personality by his relations to others" (p. 143). Mary T. Clark, R.S.C.J., in "Augustine on Person," adds that Lloyd's criticism "fails to see that the interior faculties chosen as analogies by Augustine are not merely mutually related but are the source for all human relating. Moreover, Augustine explicitly exhorted human persons to image the relational character of God by individually relating by love to the Trinity and to one another" (p. 114).

THE ACT OF FAITH

moral dimensions to knowing, and that is what Augustine is after. And to the degree that there are such dimensions, knowing becomes a task not simply of knowing what is the case, but of forming a personal inner word that is just to what is known, and that thereby makes us just. The task of knowing in the fullest sense for Augustine is always a matter of becoming something ourselves, a matter of unifying our understanding, remembering, and willing. For often, Augustine recognized, the inner word we express is conceived and born out of our inner fragmentation, and what is known is shaped by selfish self-willing.

In the case of "spiritual things" — the moral virtues and God — the formation of that inner word is to become like that very thing that we know, for to know these things is not simply to know something, it is to have a certain shape to what else we know and say; it is to be a certain way ourselves. Thus Augustine explains: "The word conceived and the word born are the very same when the will finds rest in knowledge itself, as is the case in the love of spiritual things. For instance, he who knows righteousness perfectly, and loves it perfectly, is already righteous . . ." (De Trin. IX.9). To know God is to know God's Word and to love it, and in so doing, it is to make that Word our inner word, the very shape of our lives; the Word gives shape to all the words that we speak. To know God as the Selfsame, to know the Selfsame, "that which always exists in the same way; that which is not now one thing and again a different thing" (En. in Ps. 121, 3, 5), *is* to be healed of our own fragmentation of spirit.

By the time he wrote the *Sermons on the Gospel of John, De Trinitate,* and the *Commentary on the Psalms,* Augustine had traveled a long way from his more intellectualistic attempts to understand the soul's relation to God in the early liberal arts project. He now understood that thought alone did not make for participation, although even in the beginning he well understood that thought is morally reflexive. Although "participation" is a Platonic category, and Augustine uses Platonic imagery to describe the "inner word," it is under the personal categories of virtue, and Word and words, that he develops his understanding of faith. And it is through commentaries on the Bible, through words exercised on its words, that this understanding comes. If Augustine is a Platonist, and he is, he has surely transformed Platonism itself through the Bible, just as his own mind was transformed by the biblical words. If Platonism wasn't personal before, it surely is now. Plato had de-anthropomorphized the ancient gods. Within Augustine there is now a mind that thinks the Ideas and a face by which to behold the mind, and a mouth that speaks the Word to persons he wishes to draw into his Life. This is what it is to know the Truth. Thus faith for Augustine is a personal transformation by the Word through the words heard and spoken. To have faith is not just to think something, as "thinking with assent"; it is to think actively by listening to and learning from the Word, which is ever personal both in intent and in delivery. It is to take that Word to heart and live by it. That is what it is to participate in God, to be taken up into God's own life.

CHAPTER V

Aquinas and Calvin

1. CATHOLICS AND PROTESTANTS: ANCIENT AND MODERN

Augustine's influence on the West during the following millennium and beyond was formative, abiding, and wide ranging. At its heart lay a conception of life as a space and time set out by God and by one's responsibility to God, and since the advent of the gospel, the *interregnum* in which the outer man could be led inward to a deeper knowledge of and union with God through God's personal revelation. To conceive the moral space of humanity in this way was to conceive of human and divine institutions in importantly linked ways. It was also to think about thinking, about philosophy and theology, in similarly linked ways as all was embraced under a single divine end. Ironically, the figures in Christian theology who come after Augustine and loom largest in its later development, and who would set the theological issues of faith for later years, Aquinas, and Luther and Calvin, seem to diverge far from each other in spite of their reliance on Augustine.

Where they diverge, however, and where they are called on to support divergences of later generations may be two very different things. For *they,* especially in their understandings of the nature of faith, broadly share a concept of the life of faith in which love and understanding are tightly linked, and in which faith is participation in God, enlivened by God's Word. They differ on specific criteria of what is to count as knowledge, and

THE ACT OF FAITH

in their formal definitions of faith, but they do share a world in which knowledge and faith are still a matter of personal knowledge and moral identity, a world in which faith involves personal interaction with God, and interaction with neighbors within a space defined by the possibility of knowing God. That is not often the case with their later adherents. This can be considered historically by first considering the issues that divided Protestants and Catholics over faith at the time of the Reformation, and then by considering the very different issues that emerged in discussions of faith after the Enlightenment.

First is the disagreement between Catholics and Protestants within the sixteenth century. Luther and Calvin, relying on Paul and drawing on Augustine, insisted that human righteousness came by grace alone, revealed by the gospel, and not by any act of human will. This was received by faith, which itself was a gift. Salvation was therefore by faith alone, as defined by Scripture. Thus, for Luther, "the righteousness of God is revealed by the gospel, namely, the passive righteousness with which merciful God justifies us by faith."[1] They were also particularly concerned to emphasize that faith was not mere belief. Faith was the personally enlivening reception of God's grace, a knowing confidence in God's promises. Melanchthon claimed, "It is a confidence in God and in the fulfillment of his promises. Augustine also reminds us that we should understand the word faith in the scriptures to mean confidence in God, assurance that God is gracious to us, and not merely knowledge of historical events as the devil also possesses."[2] Calvin, for his part, defined faith as "a firm and certain knowledge of God's benevolence toward us, founded upon the truth of the freely given promise in Christ, both revealed to our minds and sealed upon our hearts through the Holy Spirit" (Instit. III.II.7). He also spent considerable effort in attacking any suggestion that Christian faith was "implicit faith" or "unformed faith," that is, faith that was mere belief, especially in authority, and that did not sanctify.

The Catholic opposition at the Council of Trent on the issue of faith was extensive, covering a range of issues such as the role of the human will in justification, and countering the suggestion that faith was merely pas-

---

1. John Dillenberger, ed., *Martin Luther: Selections from His Writings* (Garden City, N.Y.: Doubleday, 1961), p. 11.
2. The Augsburg Confession, XX, "Faith and Good Works," in John Leith, ed., *Creeds of the Churches,* 3rd edition (Louisville: John Knox Press, 1982), p. 77.

sive, claiming that faith was a movement toward God. Yet they did not deny that it is a gift of God. They were concerned, however, to rebut the suggestion that faith *alone,* as they thought the Protestants were proposing, sufficed for righteousness. Rather, as stated in the Sixth Session: "Faith, unless hope and charity be added to it, neither unites man perfectly with Christ, nor makes him a living member of his body. For which reason it is most truly said that faith without works is dead and of no profit."[3] Canon 14 went on to condemn the error of saying that just "because one firmly believes that he is absolved and justified."[4] But there is an additional reason that is related to the Protestant attack on "historical faith" for saying this. The Council was also concerned to rebut any suggestion that what was to be believed was a matter indifferent. The Council was not reacting to an implicit or even explicit Protestant "subjectivism," but to the very real Protestant attack on dogmas that the Catholics declared to be revealed. Faith, for them, even if it was *fiducia,* was a matter of assent to what God had revealed. Confidence in God's promises and in God without trusting his material revelation seemed contradictory. The content of faith mattered very much. But the Council was also concerned to argue that the proper character of faith, which it sought to distinguish from Protestant *fiducia,* is that it is "not an act of confidence in the divine mercy, but an act of the intelligence which submits itself to God and recognizes the truth of what he has revealed."[5]

The issue on this count was one of the authority of testimony. Catholics took faith to be based on the authority of personal testimony, rooted in God himself, and preserved in the church as the *depositum fidei.* Protestant attacks on specific Catholic doctrines *were* an attack on the personal authority of the church. However, in a less polemical situation, Protestants themselves might not have disagreed that in faith the intelligence submits itself to God and recognizes the truth of what God has revealed. Protestant attacks themselves were consciously based in authority and personal testimony, namely, the biblical witness, with a generous acceptance of the patristic *traditio.* Luther and Calvin never sought to rework the basic teach-

---

3. Leith, *Creeds of the Churches,* p. 421.
4. Leith, *Creeds of the Churches,* p. 422.
5. Roger Aubert, *Le Probleme de l'Acte de Foi,* 3rd edition (Louvain: Publications Universitaires de Louvain, 1950), p. 78. Aubert notes, however, that many of these truths are, to be sure, promises, capable of exciting the confidence and recognition of the believer.

ings or creedal formulations of Nicaea or Chalcedon, and regularly drew on patristic authorities such as Augustine. The Reformation cry of *"sola Scriptura,"* if not naïve, was at least rhetorically excessive. From the Protestant end, the issue was that the late medieval church had not only lost its moral credibility, but it also did not have the authority it claimed to have to promulgate the doctrines it did. Their concern, therefore, was not to bypass authority in matters of faith, but to re-establish the norms of authority and the means of participating in them. If the attack on "implicit faith" or "mere belief" was an attack on authority, it was because the knowledge of faith — and Calvin claimed that faith is knowledge — has a personal and moral dimension to it that is essential. It claimed the believer, and any blind intellectual subscription to a lineup of doctrines that did not involve being claimed was not faith. Yet the Catholics, or at least Aquinas, who gained considerable authoritative status at Trent, would not have disagreed. Aquinas himself clearly argued that such faith was not saving faith, the faith that lets one participate in Christ.

The sorts of issues that arise within this context, however, take on a very different sort of cast, especially after the Enlightenment. Talking about faith — which Aquinas and Calvin did as a matter of explicating the Christian faith to birth Christians, and with no hard and fast dividing line between nature and supernature — sounds much different in a later age. Intruding Cartesian doubt, for example, does not necessarily create skepticism. It does, however, if one takes it seriously, put one outside the lived religious context to examine independently the grounds of God's existence and veracity. Thus the question of faith easily becomes not one of what faith is, but one about the prior reasonable grounds for faith. In an even later period when epistemological agnosticism gives way to a presumption of atheism, defending and explicating the faith become a matter of arguing for the possibility of faith, and arguing not from any sort of religious context, but in a foreigner's court. Here the internecine argument about the proper relation between will and understanding, and about the proper locus of authority, has its terms changed significantly and is inherited as a problem about the reasonableness of faith.

We can consider the change from the Catholic perspective first. For Trent, as for Augustine and Aquinas, faith is an act of the intellect. This act is not blind, but is in response to credible evidence. But how this "credible evidence" was understood seems to have been different for them than it was for later generations. As G. de Broglie suggests, from the beginning of the fourteenth through the middle of the seventeenth century, faith was conditioned by the evidence in the following way: "Having seen these concrete signs and indicators that invite me, I can and ought to believe that the doctrine of the Catholic church is revealed by God, and therefore also believe, at the same stroke, that it is divinely revealed."[6] This is to say, the fact of revelation itself — what was revealed — made belief in the faith evidently believable. The evidence for faith was the revelation, and there was no attempt to assess the evidence independently. Nor was there any need to do so since the revelation was ordered to the proper end of will and understanding, corresponding to the divine end for which God had graciously made human beings. Faith, as a virtue and *habitus* of the self, by its very nature went out to its proper end and beginning, both of which are given in revelation; it could rest there securely. Faith as a virtue was an act of the self, and needed to be understood in personal, reflexive terms. That was an important aspect of what was meant by faith's "certitude." After the middle of the seventeenth century, this changed, and assessment of the "evidence" was no longer contained *in* faith, in the personal act, but could be conceived as something independent and prior to faith. In good part this was because the very idea of intellectual virtue itself was in decline, and evidence and its rational assessment was now seen to be a direct relation between the universally rational but morally undefined mind, and what presented itself to the mind. So in order to ensure that faith really was an act of the intellect under the new understanding of the intellect, Catholic theologians began to suggest that the role of the "preambles of faith" — what could be proved about God by reason alone — was to prove the existence and veracity of God, to which grace was then added as a separate supernatural gift to the intellect, a sort of elevation of the natural faculty, but psychologically *the same sort of act* as "natural faith." That is to say, faith was strictly an act of the mind conditioned by evidence, and the evidence could be assessed by the mind, albeit sometimes with divine "help." Roger Aubert describes the situation in France at the turn of the twentieth century:

> All our theologians were in accord in conceding, on the one hand, that in practice it is indeed difficult, even impossible in certain cases, to believe in Christianity with a purely natural faith, and therefore grace

---

6. G. de Broglie, "La vrai notion thomiste des 'praembula fidei,'" *Gregorianum* 34 (1953): 348.

THE ACT OF FAITH

> plays a role, sometimes important, in the acquisition of the state of believing.... Dominated by an apologetic point of view and preoccupied with beating rationalism on its own ground, our theologians applied themselves above all in showing how it is theoretically possible to demonstrate all the antecedents of faith, and moreover, for those who are capable of appreciating the motives of the state of credibility, of arriving at a purely natural evidence for the truth of Christianity.... They estimated in fact that one can have, and one ought normally to tend towards having, inasmuch as it is possible in the order of contingent and historic truths, evidence of the fact of revelation, and that in consequence the certitude of faith can attain, even on the natural plane, an infallibility comparable to that of science.[7]

The project was not to dismiss grace. Rather this was a project of explicating the nature of the act of faith and its intellectual certitude, but with "intellect" being understood in a very modern sense. In doing so, it also took "belief" largely in its more modern sense, and tried to show how belief as an intellectual act could have certitude, and was not, as secular opponents charged, mere "blind belief," even though it was belief. Applying the principle that grace does not destroy nature, but perfects it, they could show how divinely given super-added content, which need not be of an intellectually different sort than any object of natural belief, gave belief its "supernatural" character. This gave rise to a "two-story" view of nature and grace. Formally as an object of the intellect, the added content is really no different than what the mind can believe on its own, although its significance is far greater and the human mind is limited in its capacity to comprehend it. If the mind can then have certitude in believing that God exists and that God acts in certain ways, it can have certitude in the divine truths proposed by God such as that God is a Trinity and that the Son became a man. This was a much more intellectualistic enterprise than Aquinas's, or at least had a very different sense of what the intellect is. As Gabriel Marcel insisted in reaction to this enterprise, God had become an intellectual problem or puzzle.

What this looks like in practice can be seen in the way that Aquinas, who after the First Vatican Council became the *magister* of Catholic theology, came to be read. Rather than being read as a theologian who assumes

---

7. Aubert, *Le Probleme de l'Acte de Foi*, pp. 229-30.

faith and is speaking to the faithful, he appears something more like a Cartesian philosopher who, starting from a neutral point, proves as much as he can by natural reason, and then, having shown the credibility of God's existence and veracity, drops in additional revealed items. On this reading the *Summa Theologiae* begins to look a lot like the first book of Euclid's *Elements of Geometry*, where Euclid proves as much as he can with provable or undisputed axioms and postulates, and then drops in the unprovable fifth postulate concerning parallels in order to go on to prove higher truths concerning triangles. What it takes for the mind to demonstrate is not changed, although it certainly could not have knowledge of Propositions 33 and following without the fifth postulate. It is hardly surprising in this context that Aquinas starts to look like Locke.

Although the issue of the *depositum fidei* never dropped out of sight, from this perspective, Protestant theology, on the other hand, begins to look more and more subjective to Catholics, an attempt to base knowledge on experience.[8] It was now not only *what* Protestants failed to believe that was at stake; it was the *way* that they believed that disturbed Catholics. Starting out from uncertain foundations in private experience, it was no surprise to Catholic minds that Protestants would end up where they did on doctrinal issues.

Protestant theology hardly escaped the Enlightenment without changing its terms and focus on the issue of faith, either. Having arisen in a time of nominalism, and not having a historical *magister* such as Aquinas who had defended anything like natural theology, Protestants, of course, had fewer motivations to approach the issue of the certainty of faith in the way that Catholics did, although they went through their own form of scholasticism. Indeed, they had a certain continuing suspicion of natural theology from the very beginning, and after Kant they felt especially confirmed in it, arguing that it did not go to the moral heart of faith. But in circumscribing the bounds of reason to make room for faith, they simply adapted the terms of modernity in a different way. They no less than the Catholics effectively replaced a unified view of the relation of nature and grace. If the Catholics had allowed nature in the modern sense to be the normative base for grace to add to, the Protestants gave up nature to science, and sought faith elsewhere.[9]

---

8. Cf., e.g., Martin D'Arcy, *The Nature of Belief* (St. Louis: B. Herder, 1958), ch. 8.

9. Dupré argues that two conflicting doctrines of nature and grace were interpolated from Augustine's anti-Pelagian writings that bloomed in the Reformation and after, and

THE ACT OF FAITH

Schleiermacher's attempt to work out systematically the articles of Christian teaching beginning from an unconditional feeling of dependence not only proposed serious alterations in the church's historical teaching, such as his dismissal of the Trinity, but inverted the Reformers' own stance on the issue, a stance that took the experience of faith to be properly shaped by Scripture and doctrine and the concrete historical workings out of Providence in the Christian communion.

This brief history is, of course, too sketchy to convey a nuanced development of the understanding of the act of faith in the theologies of the West in the modern period. It, however, should suffice to draw our attention to an important fact. Despite the differences between theologians such as Aquinas and Calvin, differences that are large enough to be sure, the greater difference that may need recognition is the one between what they may hold in common concerning the act of faith and what modern philosophy and theology hold concerning faith.

It is not entirely original at this point in theology and philosophy to suggest that Aquinas has often been misread since the seventeenth century, even by theologians who have professed to follow him, and that it can therefore be salutary to take note of that fact as a way of understanding something about how theology has been thought since the Enlightenment. Nor is it entirely original to note, as the polemical situation has cooled since the Second Vatican Council, that the Reformers and the great *magister* of the Roman Catholic Church may have more in common than the shouting would have let us previously believe.[10] Although, of course, it does not hurt to underline both those points, either. Nor, finally, is it origi-

---

that characterized later theology. "According to one doctrine — the one that emerged in late medieval theology — grace superimposes a different reality on nature. The other, which was prevalent in the Reformation and to some extent in Jansenism, reacted against the worldliness implied in a theory that conceived of nature as independent and self-sufficient. It stressed the corruption of nature to a point where grace, no longer able to transform it, merely covered its sinfulness or, as in Jansenius' theology, replaces it altogether. Thus grace in one case is added to nature; in the other, substituted for or extrinsically imputed to nature" (*Passage to Modernity: An Essay in the Hermeneutics of Nature and Culture* [New Haven: Yale University Press, 1993], p. 170).

10. On the issue of faith, see especially the ground-breaking and ingenuously eye-opening book of Arvin Vos, *Aquinas, Calvin, and Contemporary Protestant Thought: A Critique of Protestant Views on the Thought of Thomas Aquinas* (Washington: Christian University Press, 1985).

nal to suggest that the understanding of Christian faith since the Enlightenment, especially by many of its philosophical opponents, is seriously flawed. Alvin Plantinga's proposed "Reformed Epistemology," which he claims is based on Calvin, for example, signals an important attempt to recover Christian faith and philosophy in the contemporary context, to find a Christian faith and philosophy that avoids the reductionism of modern naturalism and foundationalism. But it may well be important to draw these various strands together, at least in some loose way. For what seems missing in many contemporary apologetics, right as they may be in intention, is a sense that they are shaped by or helpful to the same sorts of *religious* concerns that shape either Calvin's or Aquinas's work. At stake is at least an understanding of the range of what it means to know. And if faith's knowledge is something more like a moral knowledge, its explication and apology will need to be firmly ensconced within a form of life. Without that understanding, the problem may well be recognized but the solution does not extricate us. In that respect there is still much to learn from both Aquinas and Calvin.

2. AQUINAS ON FAITH

2.1. The Intellectualistic Interpretation of Aquinas: The Reformed Objection

Trent accused the Protestants of making faith into a matter of mere belief that alone would save them. Ironically, that is precisely what many Protestants think Catholics do, i.e., accept doctrinal propositions proposed by the church. Faith for the *rudes* is a matter of accepting church authority; for those who are capable, it is based on rational evidence discoverable by the unaided intellect. In making these charges, Protestants have pointed to Aquinas himself. The case is broad.[11] Aquinas distinguishes the three theological virtues of faith, hope, and love, and while he argues that they interpenetrate each other, it would seem that faith can stand alone. This is corroborated by Aquinas's claims that "unformed faith" (faith without love) is

---

11. For a particularly clear and cogent recent presentation see Terence Penelhum, "The Analysis of Faith in St. Thomas Aquinas," in *Faith*, ed. T. Penelhum (New York: Macmillan, 1989), pp. 113-33, esp. p. 117.

faith. Since Aquinas also understands faith to be primarily an act of the intellect, in its naked essence faith then would be primarily the intellect's submission to propositions it probably does not understand.

This, of course, is a rather Lockean view. It also creates a problem. If one cannot believe in God unless one believes certain propositions about him and, in believing these propositions one does so because they come from God, then it would appear that there is a vicious circularity. "One cannot believe a given proposition as coming from God unless one believes that God exists and has spoken; but one cannot (can one?) believe that God exists and has spoken *because* these propositions come from God. Surely at some stage one's assent has to be based on something less explicitly part of the faith than this, or how could it all begin?"[12] Usually it is held that Aquinas resolves this problem by making the authority on which the believer accepts propositions about God rest on prior epistemological credentials, i.e., the preambles of faith in which the existence and goodness of God are demonstrated, and the miracles and other evidences that favor the Christian proclamation.[13]

Calvin says why this reading of Aquinas is troubling. Calvin deeply objected to at least two of the received Catholic teachings of his day on faith[14]

---

12. Penelhum, "The Analysis of Faith in St. Thomas Aquinas," p. 122.

13. Penelhum's view is given further voice by Alvin Plantinga: "What he means to say, I think, is that to believe in the mysteries of the faith is not to be foolish or to believe with undue levity, because we have *evidence for* the conclusion that God has proposed them for our belief.... I think he means to suggest, furthermore, that if we did *not* have this evidence, or some other evidence, we would be foolish or irrational in accepting the mysteries of faith. It is just because we have evidence for these things that we are not irrational in accepting them" ("Reason and Belief in God," in *Faith and Rationality*, ed. A. Plantinga and N. Wolterstorff [Notre Dame: University of Notre Dame Press, 1983], p. 46).

14. Teachings that may not have been Aquinas's at all. Indeed, Calvin may never have read Aquinas. As Vos points out, Aquinas himself is actually only quoted twice in the *Institutes,* and these could have simply been gleaned from manuals or knowledge of what was in the air. Although the standard American edition of the *Institutes* regularly cites Aquinas when Calvin is talking about a position of the "Schoolmen" as the locus for the position, this seems to be largely the result of taking Catholics at their word that Aquinas is the *magister* of all Catholic doctrine and therefore pinning every "Catholic" opinion on him. There is no reason to think that Calvin actually had Aquinas in mind, or that he had any firsthand, in-depth knowledge of him, and very good reasons to think that the "Schoolmen" of his day had differences from Aquinas, who wrote nearly three hundred years before. Cf. Vos, *Aquinas, Calvin, and Contemporary Protestant Thought,* pp. 38-40.

that go to the heart of Aquinas's position as described. These were, first, the idea of "implicit faith," an assent to doctrines held by the church, most of which the believer may have been unaware of, and yet was held to assent to by virtue of his assent to the revealed authority of the church itself. The second was "unformed faith." The issues are not exactly the same, but for Calvin there seems to be a common root to his response. Although he sees faith as a matter of knowledge, and sees it confessing to the proper doctrines of the church, as an act of knowledge he contended that it was a "knowledge not only of God, but of the divine will" (Instit. III.2.3). He explains: "Faith is not merely a question of knowing that God exists, but also — and this especially — of knowing what is his will toward us. For it is not so much our concern to know who he is in himself, as what he wills to be toward us" (Instit. III.2.6). Assent is "more of the heart than the brain, and more of the disposition than of the understanding" (Instit. III.2.8). The knowledge of faith is formed by the apprehension of the *pro nobis* character of what is revealed. This leads to conclusions that are at odds with the idea of unformed faith and implicit belief being anything like faith. On the one hand, since the knowledge of God in faith is always self-involving and existential,[15] it is transforming knowledge. There is no knowledge of God that is not at the same time the beginning of sanctification[16] — the mortification of the proud egocentric self, and vivification of the new person in Christ.[17] So unformed faith is not faith at all. On the other hand, since faith is *knowledge* of God's will toward us, what is essential to faith cannot be hidden or implicit, even if we do not know all that it may involve at any given point in our lives. To locate faith in doctrinal assent before locating it in the transforming knowledge of God's intentions is to mislocate faith because we have sure knowledge of God's intentions to us. And because we have this knowledge we can and do remain confident even when we don't comprehend the full extent of doctrine; we can therefore afford, without peril to our souls, to make mistakes in theological reasoning.[18] The confidence of faith in God's will can lead us to explore further his revelation in order to grasp it fully without fearing any unseen conclusions.

---

15. Cf. Edward A. Dowey, *The Knowledge of God in Calvin's Theology*, 3rd edition (Grand Rapids: Eerdmans, 1994), p. 24.
16. Instit. III.2.8.
17. Instit. III.3.3, 8.
18. Instit. III.2.2-4.

THE ACT OF FAITH

Calvin simply seems to wed what Aquinas keeps separate or separable. Faith is love *and* knowledge in Calvin; in Aquinas, faith is defined by its adherence to propositions, and thus needs to be completed by hope and love, as the Council of Trent asserted. This would be a matter of semantics were it not that the two seem to differ so fundamentally on the way in which the act of understanding is gained and completed. This is the key to Calvin's criticism. For Calvin, the knowledge of faith is only given by the Spirit, who in giving it begins the process of sanctification; it is held only in moral transformation and in a personal sort of interaction between the Spirit and the believer. In Aquinas, if the definitional key to faith lies in unformed faith and not the virtue of formed faith, then the intellectual act of faith would seem to be separable from religious self-knowledge. This leads to the second issue, that of believing God to be the revealer of what is believed because we have evidence for it. The problem with Aquinas's supposed "evidentialism" is that belief in God is only rationally justified on the basis of other beliefs that we hold.[19] Not only does that make whatever knowledge of God we have in faith epistemologically dependent on other knowledge, and thus derivative; more importantly, faith's assurance ultimately depends not on God or knowing God, but on our confidence in the demonstrations that the natural world provides us, or on our own reason. In short, our knowledge of God, if it rests on demonstrations from things other than God, is not personal knowledge and confidence, but an inferred knowledge that we rest in to a degree no more sure, and usually less sure, than our knowledge of the natural world from which the rest of our knowledge is gained.

Why is this a problem? Calvin intimates the reasons. He argues that "we ought to seek our conviction in a higher place than human reasons, judgements and conjectures, that is in the secret testimony of the Spirit" (Instit. I.7). We need to be certain of that which is most important to human life. More important, however, Calvin is suggesting that the knowledge of God has to be involvement with God, and life in God. *That* theme has been an important part of Protestantism's resistance to natural theology, and has been echoed repeatedly. Kierkegaard, for example, argued — and he thought this was strictly a matter of analysis — that if Christianity is a passion, that is, a personal sort of knowledge that requires absolute, unreserved commitment and taking on a certain moral point of view, it is actually exis-

---

19. Plantinga, "Reason and Belief in God," p. 47.

tentially impossible to prove the existence of God, as a matter of being really convinced so that one takes the proof to heart. Anyone trying to prove the existence of a God he did not understand, in order to come to belief, would be in a state of doubt and hesitation, a state of reservation as long as he depended on reason, something that remains more sure than God's existence for him. Reason, one's own reason, remains the source of one's life, not God. Therefore as long as he directs his attention to the proof he continues to hesitate and not understand. The very worrying over the need for a proof is a reservation that puts one outside the relation. Only commitment can overcome the reservation.[20] Karl Barth similarly saw "natural theology" — the attempt to ground knowledge of God in natural knowledge — as fundamentally irreligious. With real insight into the nature of religion in the modern age, he saw it as an attempt to assert human autonomy over the sovereignty of God, for what we would know of God we would know on our terms and not God's.[21] For this reason, when treating of the act of faith himself, Barth did so by placing it within a carefully defined logical (or theological) space, wherein faith takes place within the Christian community, which is formed by the Word of God, which proceeds from the Trinity. Faith is an act that is only really possible within this space.[22]

---

20. "And how does the existence of the god emerge from the demonstration? Does it happen straightaway? Is it not here as it is with Cartesian dolls? As soon as I let go of the doll, it stands on its head. As soon as I let go of it — consequently, I have to let go of it. So also with the demonstration (that is, continue to be one who is demonstrating), the existence does not emerge, if for no other reason than that I am in the process of demonstrating it, but when I let go of the demonstration, the existence is there. Yet this letting go, even that is surely something; it is, after all my contribution. Does it not have to be taken into account, this diminutive moment, however brief it is — it does not have to be long, because it is a *leap*" (Søren Kierkegaard, *Philosophical Fragments,* trans. H. & E. Hong [Princeton: Princeton University Press, 1985], pp. 42-43).

21. Barth's attacks on natural theology are extensive. Most pointed are those in *No! Answer to Emil Brunner* (in *Natural Theology* [London: G. Bles; The Centenary Press, 1946), and those in *Church Dogmatics,* I.1 (rev. ed., Edinburgh: T. & T. Clark, 1975).

22. *Church Dogmatics,* IV.1 (Edinburgh: T. & T. Clark, 1956), pp. 740-80. Barth's brief treatment of the act of faith is not his strongest work. But there is something very significant within twentieth-century theology about his mere location of that discussion. Christian faith, for Barth, is an act that is possible only within a logical space determined by the Word of God, and as such he illustrates very well how as an act it functions *within* and depends upon a prior theological conceptuality. Faith only arises in response to an opening of a certain space by the Word of God, revealed in Jesus Christ. Yet his own need

2.2. Aquinas's Non-Evidentialism

So is Aquinas guilty of thinking that faith must rest on prior nontheological knowledge? And is he guilty of making faith a matter of simply believing propositions, something to which love had better be added after the fact to make faith even religiously interesting?

The first question can be answered by considering the overall project of the *Summa Theologiae*. The charge of evidentialism assumes that Aquinas conceived of his overall project from a neutral standpoint, and that he himself believed that any other standpoint needed justification. There is little reason to think that he believed anything like this. Even when writing philosophy he did not sharply distinguish it from theology, and by theology he would have understood Christian theology.[23] The *Summa Theologiae* assumes faith from the very beginning, not only in its treatment of its subject matter, but also in the minds of those who would be instructed by it. Whether it was intended as a first instruction in Christian theology or one for much more advanced students, it is designed to shape the mind of the student to its subject matter, not to argue whether or not there is a subject matter. It also has a theological structure that reflects the theological structure of the world and the divine purposes for human life within it. The *Summa* actually exhibits a pattern of *exitus-reditus* — a going out of God into the creation and the subsequent regathering of the creation back into God. So the late placement of the treatise on faith is not something that needs to be argued to, but is meant to say something about the heart of Christian life within the context of God's overall creating and redeeming purposes, much as it is even in Barth.[24]

---

to make dogmatics an objective *Wissenschaft* that depends on God's Word alone, and suspicion of Schleiermacher's rooting of doctrine first in human experience, drives him from ever developing his discussion in terms that we have been calling moral space, which has made his work terrifically difficult to develop in relation to fields such as psychology or the humanities, including philosophy. For rather than using this to reconfigure human knowing and experience more generally, he seemed to assume a distance between theological knowing and other fields, and defended theology precisely on the basis of the distance.

23. Cf. Mark Jordan, "Philosophy and Theology," in *The Cambridge Companion to Aquinas*, ed. N. Kretzmann and E. Stump (Cambridge: Cambridge University Press, 1993), pp. 232-51.

24. As Mark Jordan suggests, "the structure of the *Summa* puts the teaching about

This sort of context suggests that whatever "natural" knowledge of God Aquinas talks about is configured within "supernature," and not vice versa.[25] Indeed, Aquinas explicitly argues that God is graciously the cause of all knowledge;[26] moreover, "to love God above all things is natural to man and to every nature . . . according to the manner of love which can belong to each creature" (ST Ia-IIae 109, 3). Even if it were correct to say that Aquinas bases faith on natural reasoning, natural reasoning and nature itself rest in and are, in Aquinas's view, ordered to God. It is also a mistake to split too deeply nature and the divine;[27] if the divine end for humans is not part of their nature, nevertheless, there is no human being to which the divine end does not apply, and nature is permeated with grace. All this should affect the way Aquinas is read. Nature is not neutral for him, but is morally and religiously charged. To demonstrate the existence of God in this sort of context is not to provide a foundation on which to believe, but the mind's reaching out to its given end in conjunction with the will that delights in that end. For Aquinas there is no nature independent of God, and in *this* sense, it is utterly natural to believe that God exists. But that is because Aquinas does think that God exists and orders nature to him, and that God's action is inherent in nature.

So in the *Summa Theologiae* Aquinas is a Christian theologian throughout whose terms are fixed by their Christian reference.[28] Nature is

---

Christian living right in the middle of a complete pattern of Christian instruction" (Jordan, ed. and trans., *On Faith. Summa Theologiae 2-2. qq. 1-16 of St. Thomas Aquinas* [Notre Dame: University of Notre Dame Press, 1990], p. 9). The spiritual structure of the *Summa* and its assumed standpoint of faith have come to be increasingly recognized. Cf., e.g., M.-D. Chenu, *Toward Understanding Saint Thomas* (Chicago: Henry Regnery, 1964), pp. 310-17; A. N. Williams, "Mystical Theology Redux: The Pattern of Aquinas' *Summa Theologiae*," *Modern Theology* 13, no. 1 (1997): 53-74; John I. Jenkins, *Knowledge and Faith in Thomas Aquinas* (Cambridge: Cambridge University Press, 1997), pp. 219-26.

25. Cf. Eugene Rogers, "Thomas and Barth in Convergence on Romans 1?" *Modern Theology* 12, no. 1: 57-84. Rogers argues that Thomas's sense of "natural knowledge" is a sort of "graced knowledge" and not necessarily at all what Barth was arguing against.

26. ST Ia-IIa. 109.1: "Hence we must say that for the knowledge of any truth whatsoever man needs divine help in order that the intellect may be moved by God to its act"; and rep. obj. 1: "Every truth, by whomsoever spoken, is from the Holy Spirit as bestowing the natural light, and moving us to understand and to speak the truth. . . ."

27. Again cf. de Lubac, *The Mystery of the Supernatural*, trans. R. Sheed (New York: Crossroad, 1998).

28. In "Aquinas as Postliberal Theologian," *Thomist* 53 (1989): 353-402, Bruce Mar-

THE ACT OF FAITH

"Creation." The "natural knowledge of God" that can be gained from the effects of God in nature is not a *base* for faith but, from the perspective of divine faith — and this is Aquinas's perspective — something more like what Newman was later to call "human faith," a movement of the mind towards the Good and True made without being able to conceive its face, and which because of the Fall the mind cannot adequately conceive and delight in. Aquinas does not think that this "human faith" is a divine, saving faith. It might prepare the understanding and will for that faith, but God has made human beings for more than it can give; it remains a longing, still incomplete. The movement from un-faith to Christian faith is then not a movement of the distanced intellect, but of the unsatisfied heart and mind, and it depends on the self-giving presence of its end.

2.3. The Treatise on Faith

Important as these contextual considerations are, the case for Aquinas's understanding of faith must ultimately rest on his full treatment of faith at ST II.II qq. 1-16. At the outset two things need to be kept in mind when discussing the treatise on faith. First is that Aquinas is not particularly interested in issues of credibility or belief in general. His focus is solely the act of Christian faith. Much, therefore, of what he has to say has at best only an analogous application to other sorts of beliefs that we loosely call faith, and even that is rather minimal. He assumes Christian faith as a historical and spiritual fact, and is chiefly interested in explicating its particular nature to students of Christian theology, using the historical resources of Christian theology. Second, even if one should not split the natural and supernatural too widely, there are also important differences with respect

---

shall argues that Aquinas is much more of a "postliberal" theologian than natural philosopher. ". . . [F]or Thomas Christianity is a complex and variegated network or web of belief in which the truth of any one aspect is measured by its coherence with others. The unit of correspondence would not be the isolated proposition, but the whole web of belief . . ." (p. 372). And: "The Person whose discourse does not cohere with the broader norms of Christian belief is not even talking about God, and so cannot possibly know how to refer to him" (p. 379). This article is followed in this issue by a response by George Lindbeck, who agrees with the assessment. There are two further responses by Louis Roy and Frederick Crossan, with a further response by Marshall in *Thomist* 56 (1992): 473-524.

to the natural and theological virtues, most especially that the latter depend on God's gift, and are a distinctive, unique way of participating in the life of God. Even if one can have a natural love of God, full conscious participation in God's life — and this is where Aquinas is going — is a distinct gift of God that transcends natural life. "When one acquires faith, hope and charity, then, one does not move simply from a rudimentary inclination to the steady disposition. New inclinations, new *principia* are needed."[29] This does not mean that what we have called human faith cannot dispose the will and understanding to accept these new inclinations; it is not *opposed* to divine faith. However, the new inclinations depend upon the indwelling of the Holy Spirit, which is a divine gift. Even for us to recognize that we have a supernatural end, much less to be inclined to act on it, depends upon this sort of grace. Furthermore, whereas the natural virtues are principles of action themselves, e.g., to have the virtue of justice is to act justly, the theological virtues are not principles of actions; rather, "the infused virtues are rudimentary inclinations which become steady dispositions through the promptings of the Holy Spirit and the Gifts, each of which is a habit to be moved readily in accord with such promptings."[30] They are not self-moving principles, but principles that allow one to be moved by God, to be indwelt by God in a way that exceeds the capacity of our nature. They are principles of a certain kind of passivity that allow one to accept the gifts of understanding and wisdom of the faith, which then allow one to think by using them.[31]

---

29. Jenkins, *Knowledge and Faith in Thomas Aquinas,* p. 156.
30. Jenkins, *Knowledge and Faith in Thomas Aquinas,* p. 157.
31. It is also perhaps helpful to bear in mind *how* Aquinas makes his presentation, as this is often difficult for contemporary readers to grasp. In the first place, it is generally highly dialectical. Aquinas's discussion of questions in the *Summa* regularly presents a strong thesis and then qualifies it, particularly according to our mode of knowledge. Second, with particular respect to Aquinas's discussion of faith as a virtue he follows a set order for his discussion, starting with a discussion of the virtue itself (qq.1-7), which includes, in order: its object, its inner and outer acts, and its nature as a virtue. He then moves to the corresponding gifts of understanding and knowledge (qq.8-9) that it receives, to the corresponding vices (qq.10-15), and finally to the pertinent precepts (q.16). Within this structure, he also seems to be moving from the outer — the object of faith — to the inner act of the virtue of faith, and then back out to the outer effects of faith; this then comprises his discussion of the relation of the object of faith, God, and the believer. Cf. Mark D. Jordan's introduction to his translation of *On Faith,* pp. 9-14.

THE ACT OF FAITH

2.3.1. The Object of Faith

From the outset, Aquinas takes faith to be an intellectual act, for the formal object of faith's habit of apprehending *(habitus cognoscitivus)* is God, the first truth. While faith would also seem to assent to particular truths and doctrines as well, he argues that all the particulars to which faith assents are ordered to the first truth (Q1.a.1). But if God is the formal object of faith, God, of course, is not directly present to the mind, nor is the human mind in its present state capable of comprehending God; it must think in its customary modes. Therefore while the object of faith is simple, from the point of the believer's believing, faith is directed to, and the object known by, other means, namely propositions (Q1.a.2). Seeing the temporal, it confesses the eternal (Q1.a.4. rep. obj. 1).

Because faith deals with propositions, it has similarities to other intellectual acts and virtues. But it is also distinctive, lying between knowledge and opinion. On the one hand, it is not moved by the intellect's clear sight of its object nor by a demonstration of the object's truth. In this sense it is not knowledge. On the other hand, unlike opinion, which wavers and is doubtful, faith is certain, and nothing false can come under faith. The latter point Aquinas argues is the case because faith is a virtue that completes the understanding, and were it to rest in anything false, it simply would not be a virtue (Q1.a.3). But how can it rest so firmly if there is not direct or demonstrated knowledge? Rather than vision or demonstration moving the intellect to assent, Aquinas argues that in faith it is the will that moves the intellect to rest in its object and fixes it there (Q1.a4). This, of course, would immediately seem to raise the question of whether one can simply will a belief to be true. Aquinas will deal with the question of the will and the intellect in the next question. At this point, though, his chief intention in the first question is to discuss the relation of the *object* of faith to the believing mind, and to argue that while it is God, it is not God as directly perceived. God may be known more directly at some point, as in the beatific vision, but that is not the present case with *faith*. And therefore what is known by demonstration or direct acquaintance cannot be held at the same time by faith (Q1.a.5). But neither is the relation one of mere opinion, either. Rather, the mind is firmly and fixedly related to the unseen in faith, revealing God through holding the articles of the faith in front of the mind by the will.

2.3.2. The Inner Act of Faith: Thinking with Assent

Aquinas now appropriately turns to discuss the act of faith itself, its inward nature. What distinguishes it from other sorts of acts of the intellect is that it is, following Augustine, "thinking with assent." Aquinas's discussion of what he means by this is clear but somewhat compact in the *Summa*. "Thinking" can be taken quite naturally in three different ways. It can simply be any employment of the understanding. Or it can be "the consideration of the understanding that takes place with inquiry before one comes to the completion of the understanding in the certainty of vision" (ST II-II.2.1). This is the process by which we come to know, the "act of the understanding deliberating." Or, finally, it can refer to the cogitative power itself. The thinking Aquinas has in mind is the second sort; he calls it the whole account of the act of believing. Thinking in this sense is not needed when one knows. When one does not know, however, and has to engage in this sort of thinking to get to knowing, there can be different intellectual results. One can reach tentative conclusions, as in the case of one who suspects that such and such is the case; or one can adhere to one alternative, but with hesitation about the other, as in the case of one who simply opines that such and such is the case. In the case of faith, however, one holds firmly to one alternative; in doing so, although without knowledge herself, she agrees with somebody who actually does know and who understands. This firmness of thought is achieved by the will.

So faith holds firmly to a truth that is not manifest to it, but does so precisely in and as the process of coming to apprehend the truth it believes. This, Aquinas claims, significantly distinguishes faith from all other intellectual acts. It is important to take Aquinas at his word here. At first glance it appears that he is suggesting that faith simply wills firmly and doggedly the result of thinking before that result has been achieved. But closer consideration dispels that notion. Both "opinion" and "suspecting that such is the case" are themselves modest affirmations by the will that result from an act of thinking that has not reached its final conclusion. If faith were modeled on the account of "opinion" or "suspecting that," it would be a matter of firmly willing what is not yet known, with the will making up for the evidence, bringing the uncompleted process to a close in a way that opining or suspecting do not (or should not). That would put faith in the same genus as "opinion" or "suspecting that."[32] To the modern mind, all seem to

---

32. This seems to be how Louis Pojman takes Aquinas's "volitionalism" when he as-

THE ACT OF FAITH

be beliefs, with the variable factor being the degree of exercise of the will. But that is not what Aquinas is suggesting at all. Nor is he quite suggesting the opposite, either; that is, that the conclusion is first willed and *then* the mind is set to pondering it. Rather faith is distinctive because the will is firmly fixed *and* the mind is thinking discursively at the same time. It is a unified act of the mind, not a series of acts.

Aquinas is often portrayed as describing the certainty of faith this way: faith does not have the manifest or demonstrative certainty of knowledge, but because of the nature of its object, it is nevertheless certain because its object is certain. That is not an entirely inaccurate way of describing things, but it concentrates on the objective relation, not the inner act, which is what Aquinas is talking about in this question. What is at stake is certainty as an act of mind itself. Knowledge or understanding as an act of mind arises when thinking and will coincide in a true judgment; in the case of what is already known, they simply coexist. In the case of faith, for Aquinas, "the assent and the discursive thought are more or less parallel" (De Ver. 14.1). In the case of opinion or suspecting, however, the process of thinking and the affirmation of the judgment are separable. What Aquinas wants to say about faith is that the act of thinking, while yet incomplete, nevertheless is present with a complete act of will. Thus faith is distinguished as an intellectual act *per se* from both knowledge and opinion, and not just in its formal relation to its object.

Aquinas's earlier treatise on faith in *De Veritate* helpfully discusses the role of the will's assent in the inner act of faith. The will's assent is not a blind or arbitrary choice to believe one thing or another. Rather, it is an assent given to what is revealed because in what is revealed it finds its own proper end; it finds the Good to which it is naturally oriented.[33]

---

cribes to Aquinas the position that: "Although grace enables us to believe when the intellect has not been fully persuaded, the will must overcome natural timidity and temptations to doubt and believe for the sake of eternal life" (*Religious Belief and the Will* [London: Routledge & Kegan Paul, 1986], p. 35).

33. Recent work emphasizing the role of the will in religious belief includes: James Ross, "Rational Reliance," *JAAR* 62, no. 3 (Fall 1994); "Cognitive Finality," in *Rational Faith: Catholic Responses to Reformed Epistemology*, ed. L. Zagzebski (Notre Dame: University of Notre Dame Press, 1993), pp. 226-55; "Aquinas on Belief and Knowledge," in *Essays Honoring Allan B. Wolter*, ed. W. A. Frank and G. J. Etzkorn (St. Bonaventure: The Franciscan Institute, 1985), pp. 245-69; and Eleonore Stump, "Faith and Goodness," in *The Philosophy in Christianity*, ed. G. Vesey (Cambridge: Cambridge University Press, 1989), pp. 167-91.

> In this situation our understanding is determined by the will, which chooses to assent to one side definitely and precisely because of something which is enough to move the will, though not enough to move the understanding, namely since it seems good or fitting to assent to this side. And this is the state of one who believes. This may happen when someone believes what another says because it seems fitting or useful to do so. (De Ver. 14.1)

Thus, Aquinas continues, we believe what God says because of the good that he has promised, that is, eternal life. It is this that moves the will to assent, "although the intellect is not moved by anything which it understands" (De Ver. 14.1). The will assents because of the goodness of the promise, although the understanding does not fully comprehend all that that entails. But it does keep thinking about it in order to reach clarity of vision.

The will and understanding are aspects of a single mind. As such, the self is fully realized when it finds truth, i.e., understands it *and* delights in it. For the human soul the point of knowing is never knowledge for its own sake; the act of knowing is humanly fulfilling. We want to know because we delight in knowing and in what is known. In the case of immediate knowledge, understanding and the delight of the will coincide in full actuality. In the case of faith, delight and love are fixed before the mind comprehends. But the mind is focused in such a way that it now thinks that which will fulfill it. It has received that which it needs to think well, given its divine end. This does not mean that the understanding simply shuts down other options. In fact, Aquinas thinks that "thinking with assent" is a discursive process of comparing and contrasting various options as is necessary for knowledge to occur. So "a movement directly opposite to what the believer holds most firmly can arise in him, although this cannot happen to one who understands or has scientific knowledge" (De Ver. 14.1). The one who *knows,* knows and understands the falsity of other options; they are no longer intellectual options. The one who has faith but does not yet fully understand, while yet firmly holding to the promise, exercises his understanding in the standard way, by comparing and contrasting in order to understand why his believed conclusions are the way they are.

An example will help, one that moves us toward the sort of learning and knowing that Aquinas has in mind when discussing faith. In the process of learning a field such as mathematics a student takes a professor at his word when he puts the answer on the board. Or, similarly, in doing her

THE ACT OF FAITH

homework she might take the answer at the back of the book to be right. But, although she is convinced that this is the answer, she still does not understand why. Nevertheless, because of the good promised to come from understanding mathematics, she is willing to trust the one who knows. It does not stop there. Without changing her assent to the answer, she then either listens to the professor as he works the problem and explains the theory or as he helps her as she works it; or, in the case of an answer in the back of the book, she works the problem herself trying various options until she arrives at the answer and understands it. In time, what she believes, she comes to understand. As Socrates points out in the *Meno* after getting the slave boy to recollect the right answer to the problem of doubling a square, the boy still needs to go over the problem several times himself before he understands why it solves the way it does.

This example is helpful in understanding how assent and thinking can go together, and even how assent can be helpful to understanding. In Aquinas, however, the situation with respect to the will's assent is more religiously pointed than this example suggests and must be pushed further. Belief is not simply an efficient and pragmatic way to understanding. Within religion, the will's commitment to the teacher is essential, and is a good for the self *per se*. The teacher is a good and a delight for the soul, in good part because the knowledge he is willing to impart is not separable from him, as mathematics is separable from a mathematics teacher. The soul's basic commitment neither increases or decreases when understanding is achieved; in the act of faith it is already full and participates in its end. So one does not believe the teacher *simply* because he has the answer; one believes the teacher in order to share the point of view of the teacher. Faith is the way of sharing that view, sharing it by identifying with it, by living in it. Merely believing propositions as such is therefore not faith; it is believing them in a certain way, namely, by loving and trusting the proposer as the one in whom one finds one's fullest delight and final good.[34]

---

34. Eleonore Stump suggests similarly that looking at faith this way, one must recognize that faith's chief importance is in the moral life of the believer. "[T]his approach to faith has the advantage of explaining why an omniscient, omnipotent, perfectly good God would let the epistemic relation of human beings to himself rest on faith, rather than knowledge, and why a person's having faith should be thought to be meritorious in any way, because it holds faith to be the beginning of a moral reform of the will, of a kind that simple knowledge of the propositions of faith by itself could not bring about" ("Faith and Goodness," p. 190).

Without the moral commitment to the teacher, what the teacher has to teach, namely, a vision and certain kind of life, is nothing more than empty propositions. When Aquinas then argues that believing the mystery of Christ is necessary for salvation (ST II-II q.2.a7), it is important to recognize that his context for saying so is that of the inner act of faith. It is the will's commitment to the teacher that matters, although, he adds, one does so according to one's proper time and place. (He, like the tradition, takes key figures in the Old Testament to have had faith, although the incarnate Christ had not yet been revealed.) What is believed is never believed from a spectator's point of view; from beginning to end it is a personal commitment and a realization of one's own self.[35] For this reason, the student-teacher example needs some final revision: the student's commitment to the teacher is not just because the teacher has the answer *qua* answer, but because commitment to the teacher is part of gaining the knowledge. This is no longer a classroom in mathematics or even philosophy, of course. The prime example of this sort of thinking is prayer and meditation in which the deepening understanding of the divine *scientia* is not "intellectual bootstrapping but intellectual apprenticeship."[36]

With this established, Aquinas's borrowing of Augustine's threefold distinction of the act of faith as "believing God" *(credere Deo)*, "believing about God" *(credere Deum),* and "believing for the sake of God" *(credere in Deum)* unfolds as a way of comprising the various aspects of the single act of faith (ST II-II.q2.a2). Taken from the point of view of the understanding, formally one believes God, and materially one believes certain things about God. As it is moved by the will, however, faith, which has committed itself to God, believes in or for the sake of God. Thus the act of faith as a whole is the act by which, from the love one has for God, one believes God as God through what God has specifically revealed. Without any of these aspects, Aquinas thinks, faith is missing. Even to believe God and believe all matters pertaining to God's revelation, as the demons do, is not faith unless the will is moved to believe for the sake of God. Faith is then never mere belief in propositions, but believing them because one believes in

---

35. Aquinas's position would also seem to entail that formally Christian faith is unique, because the will has one proper end and cannot rest in anything else. Assent of the sort he is discussing can only be certain when the will rests in its final end. But again, he recognizes that the material object of faith may vary according to time and place.

36. Jenkins, *Knowledge and Faith in Thomas Aquinas,* p. 218.

THE ACT OF FAITH

God, that is, from a deep and abiding love for God. It is like a mother reading a letter from her son from whom she has been separated. What she reads will not make her love him any more or less; but because she loves him she reads his words, which are his but yet not quite him, over and over again, until she gets some understanding of what his life is like so that she may consciously share in it to the full extent of the love she already bears him.

Having then described the inner act of faith, and having argued that confession is the necessary outer act of faith as the outward speech of what is conceived inwardly in the heart (Q.3), Aquinas turns to describe the act of faith as a specific theological virtue.

2.3.3. Faith as a Virtue

That Aquinas takes faith to be a virtue is crucial to understanding his ultimate point in defining the inner act of faith as "thinking with assent." For as a virtue, thinking with assent is not a single action, or even a series of actions, but a continuing, habitual quality of mind by which the mind is related to its object in a characteristic way, and by which it carries out its defining acts. It defines its subject and the quality of her life internally, and defines it in relation to its object externally. As Aquinas defines it, borrowing from Augustine through Peter Lombard, "Virtue is a good quality of the mind, by which we live righteously, of which no one can make bad use, which God works in us without us" (ST Ia-IIae q.55.a.4).

The defining habitual act of faith is inwardly, thinking with assent, and outwardly, confessing. Its proper object is, of course, God, as both the perfect good in which the will rests, and as the first truth, although as unseen, and in which the understanding tends toward rest. (Thus faith as a virtue disappears in the beatific vision.) The relation to the object, God, however, is not an extrinsic one, but intrinsic as the relation is realized precisely *in* the act. One does not will to have faith; faith is a characteristic way of willing. Aquinas argues in *De Veritate* that the will can only be directed to its end in God if there already

> pre-exists in it a certain proportion to the end, and it is from this that the desire of the end arises in it.... For this reason also, for man to be ordained to the good which is eternal life, there must be some initial participation of it in him to whom it is promised.... We have it through

faith, which by reason of an infused light holds those things which are beyond our natural knowledge. (De Ver. 14.2)

So the virtue of faith *is* participation in the life of God, by God's grace, through the commitment of the will toward God and consisting in the acts of thinking and confessing, without manifest vision, God's own truth. Thus faith is an intrinsic excellence of the human soul, for in faith the human soul already partakes in the end that God has destined for it.

Aquinas can now take the formula of Hebrews 11:1 — "faith is the substance of things hoped for, the argument *(elenchus)* of things unseen" — to define the virtue of faith (Q.4). Truth, because it is not *seen* by faith, is a thing hoped for, but is also faith's substance for "the first beginning in us of things to be hoped for comes with the assent of faith, which virtually contains all things to be hoped for" (ST II-II q.4.a1). It is the argument for things unseen, if one takes "argument" to mean "the effect of argument," i.e., conviction, for "by divine authority the understanding of the believer is convinced to assent to what it does not see" (II-II q.4.a1). Aquinas ventures to put all this in proper definitional form: "faith is a habit of mind, by which eternal life begins in us, making the understanding assent to what does not appear" (II-II q.4.a1). Drawing on pseudo-Dionysius, he further adds that faith can be described as "the persisting foundation of believers, placing them in truth and truth in them," for this is the same thing as to say "the substance of things to be hoped for" (II-II q.4.a1). The virtue of faith is a life lived in truth, by living in the one who is the True and the Good. Faith, then, as a virtue, is far less a matter of finding oneself directed toward believing certain things — although one does believe and confess them — and far more a characteristic way of willing, thinking, and understanding, given that one takes those things revealed by God to be true. They are part of one's imaginative and conceptual apparatus, as it were. However, to put it that way also needs to be qualified to the degree that as a virtue, faith is not in us actually, aptitudinally, or inchoately, by nature, but is thoroughly from the outside.[37] Without the presence of God, without participation in God, it would not exist. It arises not from our nature coming to find the object that will fulfill it, but from the object coming to our nature, reforming it and filling it. It is as such an infused virtue.

These points can be further sharpened by Aquinas's further discus-

---

37. Ia-IIae.63.1.

sion of the *form* of faith, which, following St. Paul in Galatians 5:6, he takes to be charity. There is a problem that Aquinas has to face when he agrees with Paul that the form of faith is, indeed, charity: namely that faith is an intellectual virtue, whereas charity, since it is directed to the good, properly belongs to the will.[38] He resolves it by suggesting that as the form of faith, it is not the essence of faith.[39] Rather, charity is the form of faith because it is through the will's love that the understanding is formed.[40] This seems to be a technical solution; however, religiously there also seem to be strong hints of Augustine's view of faith as that which, directed to the life of the outer man, leads one back to the restoration of the inner man. Faith is a form of life that has its shape and character in its care and concern for others. The manifest characteristic of faith is precisely its love.

Faith's form as love distinguishes "formed faith" from "unformed faith." Unformed faith, that is, faith without love, is a belief in and obedience to God that arises out of servile fear and self-interest.[41] And as Aquinas notes in no uncertain terms, this sort of faith is *not* a virtue, and does not participate in God's life. It is a *privation* of faith proper.[42] It is faith only insofar as, in his way of classifying things, the opposite of faith is unbelief. Since unformed faith isn't exactly unbelief, it has to be described like faith. Formed faith, on the other hand, believes God because it loves God, and loving God, loves others. The key biblical text here is James 2: "faith without works is dead," to which Aquinas adds the gloss that it is revived by works of charity, which is to say it functions and is operative by its acts of love. So the shape of the life of faith is its love for God and others,

38. ST II-II q.3. obj. 2.
39. De Ver. 14.5. answer 1.
40. De Ver. 14.5; ST II-II q4.a3. rep. obj. 1.
41. De Ver. 14.7.
42. IIa-IIae 6.2. In this Aquinas agrees with Calvin, who was confronted with the very real phenomenon of believers who believe out of fear, or who are backsliders, people who have had the virtue of faith but have committed mortal sins and acts of lovelessness, or who believe but never act on their faith. Even Calvin is willing to suggest that such faith is a gift of God, albeit "the lower working of the Spirit in the reprobate" (Instit. III.2.11). For neither Calvin nor Aquinas is such belief sufficient for salvation or to participate in God's righteousness. There is a historical example of some significance that underlines the difference between formed and unformed faith and why the latter is not Christian faith. That example is Augustine, who before his "conversion" in the garden at Milan claims to have believed. Yet he did not have faith until he gave his will unreservedly.

and it is precisely through this activity that the understanding itself is reformed and comes, by grace which has been present in it from the beginning, to participate in the full vision of God and God's life. Loving others is an act of the conscious mind; by the habitual activity of the mind directed by the will that takes God at his word, the mind itself is reformed and transfigured.

Faith for Aquinas is a form of life and characteristic way of thinking that partakes in God's life; it is set out and established by God in Jesus Christ, and involves a personal interaction with God and a way of interacting with others in a historical community materially defined by its doctrinal tradition. This position is sharply distinguished from the sorts of assumptions that guided Catholic thinking on faith at the turn of the twentieth century, for faith is clearly not simply an extension of the natural life and faculties. It certainly is not simply a development of one's intellectual faculties without a concomitant reformation of the will. Nor is it ever mere belief, or even belief based on the foundations of natural theology. It is a fulfilling of the mind that comes from opening oneself up to pay enough attention to be taught.

3. CALVIN AND "REFORMED EPISTEMOLOGY"

Protestant critics of Aquinas such as Alvin Plantinga would not, I suspect, be deeply disappointed to find that Aquinas was not a naturalistic evidentialist or Cartesian foundationalist. If Thomistic faith requires non-natural principles, then Plantinga's much more important point about the nature of modern evidentialism and foundationalism is underscored, namely, that it is artificially anti-theological by an *a priori* exclusion of any sort of belief in God as basic knowledge, as belonging to the primitive cognitive principles from which we derive other discursive knowledge. If faith is based on natural principles, not only does one begin to think about God from a misguided and artificial neutrality, one can easily reduce thought about God to human constructions out of natural experience. What Plantinga wants to argue on the contrary is that belief and trust in what God has revealed is not based on and certified by "natural" knowledge; rather, it depends upon its own proper basic principles. Thus Plantinga might well find an ally in Aquinas, as he seeks one in Calvin, for his important critique of modern evidentialism and foundationalism and in his at-

THE ACT OF FAITH

tempts to establish belief in God as "properly basic," as "among the foundations of my noetic structure."[43]

Yet, Plantinga may get all the right answers for any number of wrong reasons.[44] Rather than fully undermining the props of modern foundationalism, Plantinga seems to expand them by numbering belief in God among them. Rather than redescribing the logical and moral space of the deepest assumptions of naturalism, he seems to try to find room within that space for belief in God. The problem is that such an effort, while defending the epistemological propriety of belief in God, also tends to obscure in an unfortunate and unhelpful way both the nature of faith itself and the personal dimension of knowledge that is its all-important context. It obscures the very sort of knowledge about which Calvin was concerned, for if faith is in any sense basic, it is basic in a very different sort of way than modern epistemology normally allows.

3.1. Basic Beliefs and the *Sensus Divinitatis*

Early in the *Institutes*, Calvin makes the broad and bold claim that the knowledge of God is naturally implanted in all human minds. This is a knowledge, a sense of the divinity, that is not taught, but that comes to us from our mothers' wombs. It is witnessed to by the universality of religion. He writes:

> There is within the human mind, and indeed by natural instinct, an awareness of the divinity. This we take to be beyond controversy. To prevent anyone from taking refuge in the pretense of ignorance, God himself has implanted in all men a certain understanding of his divine majesty.... Therefore, since from the beginning of the world there has been no religion, no city, in short no household, that could do without religion, there lies in this a tacit confession of a sense of deity inscribed in the hearts of all.... From this we conclude that it is not a doctrine that must be first learned in school, but one of which each of us is master from his mother's womb and which nature itself permits no one to forget, although many strive with every nerve to this end. (Instit. I.3.1, 3)

43. Plantinga, "Reason and Belief in God," p. 59.
44. As James Ross also suggests in arguing that Plantinga omits the positive role of the will in belief. Cf. Ross, "Cognitive Finality."

This is the key passage that Plantinga uses to develop what he calls a "Reformed Epistemology." The belief that God exists is not a belief derived from other foundations, but is itself as basic as any other sort of belief, he claims. We do not need other arguments to prove that God exists in order to say that God is creator; the belief in God is not to be reduced to an extension of our other beliefs.

There are, of course, large and numerous issues that can and have been raised about this sort of claim, including warranting it, and distinguishing it from bizarre beliefs that somebody might also want to claim are properly basic. Plantinga has spent a career carefully sorting these issues and defending his claim. What is most useful, though, is to note how Plantinga thinks this *sensus divinitatis* of Calvin operates epistemologically and what sort of question it actually answers. Plantinga shows early and later strains. In earlier arguments he tended to take the *sensus divinitatis* as a sort of internal foundation for knowledge, especially for claims that involve reference to God. If it can be shown that it is such a foundation, Plantinga has then succeeded in showing that classic foundationalism is wrong because it excludes important properly basic beliefs. He has also provided reason to think that there can be a theistic foundationalism, with beliefs about God forming part of the foundations of one's noetic structure. In later discussions, Plantinga has been less concerned with such beliefs as foundations themselves and more with showing that the *sensus* is a sort of "mechanism for providing true beliefs when it functions properly in an appropriate environment."[45] In either case, however, while Plantinga has used the *sensus* to provide an alternative to naturalistic foundationalism, as an alternative he has made it answer the same sorts of questions that foundationalism has critiqued. It is a matter of defending the rationality of religious belief and of generating true statements, indeed even a Christian worldview, based on the belief that God exists.

This is a perfectly justifiable and admirable thing to do. And, indeed, if our mode of knowledge is propositional we need to take it seriously. What

---

45. Cf. Paul Helm's discussion in *Faith and Understanding* (Grand Rapids: Eerdmans, 1997), ch. 8, "John Calvin's *Sensus Divinitatis*." Another discussion of Plantinga's position, especially vis-à-vis Calvin, is Dewey Hoitenga, *Faith and Reason from Plato to Plantinga: An Introduction to Reformed Epistemology* (Albany: State University of New York Press, 1991). Vos, in *Aquinas, Calvin, and Contemporary Protestant Thought,* also discusses "reformed epistemology" in relation to Calvin and Aquinas, but chiefly concentrates on Nicholas Wolterstorff's version.

THE ACT OF FAITH

we say makes a difference to Christian philosophy and theology, and it makes a difference that we believe that it is true. Plantinga's project in this way is then not entirely unlike Aquinas's attempt to integrate, logically and theologically, all of human knowledge. Calvin himself made no such attempt, although he too thought that "the book of nature" and the "book of Scripture" did not conflict and could provide an ultimately unified witness to God. But where Plantinga's project is unlike Calvin's is that Calvin is not very interested in the issue of the rationality of religious belief.[46]

What Calvin is interested in is the *way* that Christian beliefs are taken. The issue of "unformed faith" is a case in point. For neither Calvin nor Aquinas is such a thing faith; it is a distant spectator's belief. So while the beliefs we have and their truth certainly matter, faith is something more than having beliefs, including all the correct ones. It also matters that we love their truth. The way one holds the beliefs of the Christian faith is something more than simply assenting to them; the very understanding we have of them, especially their *pro nobis* character, also depends upon the state of our wills.[47] A spectator's beliefs may be *other* than Christian beliefs unless they are personally engaged.

This can be seen in Calvin's use of the *sensus divinitatis*, although the

---

46. Paul Helm suggests: "[W]hat we find in Calvin... is little or no interest in the rationality of religious belief. (Rationality in this sense is perhaps as much a child of the Enlightenment as strong foundationalism; certainly one struggles to find any interest in such an issue in Calvin.) Rather, what Calvin emphasizes is not rationality but responsibility. His interest in the *sensus* is not due to an interest in the rational grounds for theistic belief, but to a concern to establish that since all men and women in fact have some knowledge of God, they are culpable when they do not form their lives in a way that is appropriate to such knowledge" (*Faith and Understanding*, p. 198).

47. James Ross argues that Reformed Epistemology produces simply a "thin theism" that often ignores the believing community, and the authority and warrant of tradition. "[T]hose sources are evidently normative for belief. The very notion of norms for belief makes no sense unless the will has a role in our cognitive design. It is the individual will to believe that has to conform to the proclaimed faith. If an ecumenical council declares 'The Son is of one substance with the Father,' you do not come to *see* that is so but must willingly believe that it is so. Thus for faith to be rational the will has to have a suitable cognitive function. By failing to undertake inquiries into these elements, the Reformed Epistemologists look too much like their opponents, too much like a 'repaired evidentialism,' with foundationalist leanings still attached to much narrower conceptions of human knowledge than are required now. They seem still stooped over by the evidentialist burdens they have thrown down" ("Cognitive Finality," p. 229).

sensus is not the same thing as faith, a point ignored in Reformed Epistemology. Calvin, echoing Augustine, makes it eminently clear in the opening chapters of the *Institutes* that "nearly all the wisdom we possess, that is to say, true and sound wisdom, consists of two parts: the knowledge of God and knowledge of ourselves" (Instit. I.1.1). Wisdom joins these two types of knowledge. On the one hand, when we think of ourselves truly, we are immediately driven to think of God. For not only are we obliged to understand that all our endowments come from God and not ourselves, our miseries also cause us to look to God: "From the feeling of our own ignorance, vanity, poverty, infirmity, and — what is more — depravity and corruption, we recognize that the true light of wisdom, sound virtue, full abundance of every good, and purity of righteousness rest in the Lord alone" (Instit. I.1.1). On the other hand, unless we know God, we will not know ourselves, especially our need and lowly state. This knowledge is not the result of a distanced judgment. To know God in this way is also to know what befits God and what our advantage is in knowing him. It is a knowledge gotten and exercised in worship; "indeed, we shall not say that, properly speaking, God is known where there is no religion or piety" (Instit. I.2.1). "For how can the thought of God penetrate your mind without your realizing immediately that, since you are his handiwork, you have been made over and bound to his command by right of creation that you owe your life to him? — that whatever you undertake, whatever you do, ought to be ascribed to him?" (Instit. I.2.2).

The awareness of God is, indeed, naturally implanted in the human mind. The evidences of God are also displayed in the creation, and both the natural sciences and liberal arts penetrate into the secrets of the divine wisdom.[48] This awareness for Calvin, however, is an inclination to worship God, and not an urge to generate rationally acceptable statements. But here is also the rub. While the universality of religion testifies to the *sensus divinitatis*, it also testifies to the misuse of it. Calvin states flatly that it is scarcely one in a hundred who fosters it, and none in whom it ripens; indeed, "all degenerate from the true knowledge of him" (Instit. I.4.1). Due to pride and vanity, God does not measure human life, but is measured by it. The knowledge of God, due to the fall, degenerates into false worship. So despite the fact that God manifests himself clearly enough to the human mind, these testimonies "flow away without profit" (Instit. I.5.1).

48. Instit. I.5.1, 2.

THE ACT OF FAITH

The interest in providing rational foundations for religious beliefs arose only in a very intense way for Calvinists in the century after Calvin's death. But even if Calvin were interested in these foundations, the *sensus divinitatis* is not the place to look for them. His own examples of religions and philosophies based strictly on the *sensus* are universally a catalogue of error, superstition, pride, and vanity.[49] Even in an age of universal belief, Calvin was no more impressed by theologies and beliefs based on the *sensus* than Plantinga is by the theology of Gordon Kaufman. In this, Calvin has been followed by Reformed theologians such as Barth, whose objections to natural theology are directed more vehemently against any development of a natural religious sense than they are against the effort to establish the existence and nature of God by natural, rational means; or, the former is the problem with the latter.

There is something positive, however, that can be gleaned from what Calvin says about the *sensus divinitatis* with respect to the nature of the knowledge of God. The *sensus* largely functions in Calvin, as it does for Paul in Romans 1 from whence Calvin got the notion, as making humans responsible for false worship. It functions as conscience.[50] It is not entirely effaced by the fall, and because it is not, humans are not in utter ignorance about what they are doing, even if they inevitably do it. But this responsibility highlights a key feature of the knowledge of God throughout Calvin: it is something that creates a moral obligation, although this is often manifested before grace, as guilt. Not only does it create such an obligation, the full knowledge of God is linked to the moral response of the human believer and is correlated with self-knowledge. The knowledge of God, insofar as it also includes knowledge of the self, is a reflexive knowledge that locates the believer in a conscious moral relation to God that is had in worship.

Calvin does not base Christian faith on the *sensus divinitatis*. But because he does think that the knowledge of God is both possible and desirable, he does need to find another way to have that knowledge. That way is by the instruction of Scripture. Scripture, however, does not simply tell

---

49. John Beversluis gives a trenchant critique of Plantinga's use of the *sensus* along similar lines in "Reforming the 'Reformed' Objection to Natural Theology," in *Faith and Philosophy* 12, no. 2 (1995): 189-206. Also, Derek Jeffreys, "How Reformed Is Reformed Epistemology? Alvin Plantinga and Calvin's 'Sensus Divinitatis'" in *Religious Studies* 33, no. 4 (1997): 419-32.

50. Cf. Dowey, *The Knowledge of God in Calvin's Theology*, Appendix II, pp. 263-64.

one what is the case; it also generates and requires a personal response. That response is faith, which is not simply a development of the *sensus*, but a new pattern of believing and acting. It gives what the effaced *sensus* in its best moments can only long for. It points to the gift of God, the peace of faith, for which the gift of conscience was given.

3.2. Faith as Personal Knowledge

The *sensus divinitatis* for Calvin makes fallen humanity responsible for its guilt. It does not provide clear knowledge that allows one to distinguish true God from false gods, nor does it allow whatever sense of God that we do retain to flourish properly in worship. Scripture alone provides this knowledge of God that nature does not.[51] It does this in two ways: first, by teaching us that it is God who founded and governs the universe; second, by teaching us about the Redeemer.[52] Through the path it sets out, we can then aspire to the contemplation of God.[53] It is the school of God's children, whose authority comes from God — as living words of God. But because it is a matter of living words, faith is needed to appropriate it. The knowledge that Scripture gives is not impersonal; it gives us knowledge of God's promise to us, the living Christ. It witnesses to the person who is the promise, and to know Scripture is to know Christ.

Calvin makes no bones about declaring faith to be knowledge. It is a "firm and certain knowledge of God's benevolence towards us." What is not immediately obvious, however, is what exactly Calvin means by knowledge. The knowledge of faith is not the sort of knowledge and comprehension of things that fall under human sense perception.[54] The knowledge of faith grasps things that are beyond the natural cognitive capacity of the human mind. For this reason, the knowledge of faith consists "in assurance rather than in comprehension" (Instit. III.2.14) and is often interchangeable with "confidence." But how is this knowledge? Calvin, like most thinkers trained in Humanism, does not have a thoroughly articulated theory of knowledge, one that spells out what it means to "compre-

51. Instit. I.6.1, 4.
52. Instit. I.6.2.
53. Instit. I.6.3.
54. Instit. III.2.14.

THE ACT OF FAITH

hend."[55] He seems to be using "know" here in a common, intuitive sense that designates the fact that one knows what is going on with respect to an art or science. What is clear, though, is that the knowledge of faith is not the same sort of knowledge that one has or can have with respect to the arts and sciences. Something more is required.

Furthermore, the sort of knowledge Calvin has in mind is not distant, third person knowledge. "In understanding faith it is not merely a question of knowing that God exists, but also — and this especially — of knowing what is his will toward us. For it is not so much our concern to know who he is in himself, as what he wills to be toward us" (Instit. III.2.6). Unless it makes us rely on God's goodness, even knowledge of God's goodness is not very important.[56] The knowledge of God is something that is necessarily attached to sanctification. Calvin even wants to go so far as to suggest that without such a corresponding transformation of the person the knowledge of God simply is not there, despite all outward appearances. For example, outwardly, the reprobate may confess nothing any different than the elect. Yet, Calvin firmly denies that they "proceed so far as to penetrate into that secret revelation which Scripture vouchsafes only to the elect" (Instit. III.2.12). Even Scripture, unless it is inwardly appropriated, is not a foundation on which to build other knowledge.

Philosophically there is something maddening about these sorts of qualifications. Faith's knowledge does not seem criticizable on the basis of anything else one knows; even agreement in confession would seem not actually to constitute real agreement. But they do make sense in a context of personal communication. Like Augustine or St. John, Calvin sees Scripture as personal communication, the communication of the person of Christ to human persons. The ambiguity that arises throughout Calvin's writings from calling Scripture the Word of God and also calling the Son of God the Word of God is rhetorically deliberate. Scripture's words communicate the Word itself to us. Calvin puts it succinctly: "This then is the true knowledge of Christ, if we receive him as he is offered by the Father: namely, clothed with his gospel" (Instit. III.2.6). Faith for Calvin is always *ex auditu*. As with all other spoken words that we use to understand and know the speaker, we need to be predisposed to listen sympathetically to the speaker. Understanding and taking another's words to heart depend on

---

55. Cf. Vos, *Aquinas, Calvin, and Contemporary Protestant Thought,* ch. 1.
56. Instit. III.2.7.

more than simply a speaker speaking and an ear to hear. It is the role of faith to listen and receive those words sympathetically, to discern and to understand their *pro nobis* character. "There is a permanent relationship between faith and the Word" (Instit. III.2.6). Faith does not float freely; it is bound in its genesis, maintenance, and completion to the activity of the Word. Calvin, like Luther, is particularly concerned to make sure that his readers do not take the ability to listen to and receive the Word to be any sort of innate human capacity. Indeed, he insists that faith, the very capacity to receive the Word, is created by the Word itself. Its possibility depends upon the offer of the promise; the ability to take it to heart and to embody likewise depends upon the indwelling of the Word through the Spirit. Faith for Calvin has a phenomenological structure that is rooted in the activity of the Word.

This structure can be unfolded by describing the act of faith as a succession of its various aspects. Initially, the very possibility of faith and knowledge of God and ourselves is given, *ex auditu,* in the promise who is Christ. This involves Calvin's first two uses of the law: to convict the sinner of sin, and to cause us to seek grace.[57] If there is any role in faith for the *sensus divinitatis* it is that in being confronted by the Word of God, it knows its own guilt and looks toward the true source of its aspiration and its hope for forgiveness. But the *sensus* does not create faith. It is God's promise of Christ that creates the space in which faith operates. What the promise includes is at least forgiveness of the past, a restoration of righteousness or justification, and ultimately, union with God in Christ. Since the very possibility of these things depends upon God's freely given promise, the knowledge of faith exceeds human capacity.

If the promise given creates the possibility of faith there still remains a gap between the recipient and the promiser, the object of knowledge. Calvin thinks that the mere declaration of the promise should have been sufficient to engender faith if the *sensus* were healthy; however, "our blindness and perversity prevent it" (Instit. III.2.33). The promise is a promise of transformation; by itself, strictly speaking, it does not effect that transformation. The knowledge of the promise, the knowledge of God in Christ, is not like a natural fact that can be asserted to be true regardless of whether there is anybody who knows it or not. Because it is *pro nobis,* there is, for Calvin, no genuine knowledge of the promise that is not transforming.

57. Instit. II.7.3-9.

THE ACT OF FAITH

Faith as the transforming knowledge of the promise is what overcomes the gap. But the response of faith, because it depends upon actually embodying the promise, does not arise from human capacity, nor can it be something that can be entertained *in abstracto*. The gap between recipient and promiser is crossed only by the activity of the Holy Spirit, which illumines the mind to receive the Word and which strengthens and supports the heart steadfastly by its power.[58] Faith is a gift of God.

Calvin conjoins aspects of the theological virtues that Aquinas tends to keep theoretically separate. The Spirit not only illumines the mind and gives power to the heart to receive the promise, the Word; its gift of illumination *is* the transformation of the believer and her engrafting into the Word itself. Faith as a gift of the Spirit is one's full and willing *participation* in Christ, and the enjoyment of Christ's own presence.

> Therefore, as we cannot come to Christ unless we be drawn by the Spirit of God, so when we are drawn we are lifted up in mind and heart above our understanding. For the soul, illumined by him, takes on a new keenness, as it were, to contemplate the heavenly mysteries, whose splendor had previously blinded it. And man's understanding, thus beamed by the light of the Holy Spirit, then at last truly begins to taste those things which belong to the Kingdom of God, having been formerly quite foolish and dull in tasting them. (Instit. III.2.34)

The religious import of this can be seen in Calvin's way of describing the doctrine of justification by faith. Justification, or righteousness, is not a reward for believing, nor is it an external infusion of the quality of righteousness into the believer, but arises from being bound to the one who is righteous life. Righteousness is always Christ's, but because we participate in him it becomes ours by our being his. Christ, his promise and his righteousness, is not for the faithful simply *extra nos,* but *in et intra nos*. Strictly speaking, faith — the act of belief as such — itself does not justify, as Trent accused the Protestants of thinking; but *by* faith, given by the Spirit, Christ's righteousness dwells in us. This also means that faith as a gift of the Spirit is righteousness. Because the gift and the giver are the same, Christ is our righteousness.[59]

58. Instit. III.2.33.
59. Cf. Victor Shepherd, *The Nature and Function of Faith in the Theology of John Calvin* (Macon, Ga.: Mercer University Press, 1983), ch. 2, "Justification and Faith."

This puts a somewhat more mystical cast on Calvin than he is usually credited with, although the import of his language is not unrecognized.[60] But leaving aside the question of mysticism, what now becomes clearer is in what sense faith is knowledge for Calvin. At its root it is a deeply personal form of knowledge, for it is a communication of God's very self to the human self in which human self-knowledge is transformed. The person of faith is one who has been transformed from a manipulatively proud and self-centered and self-seeking being to one who understands, and is conscious of, himself as God's creature, redeemed by and dependent on God's own life, and enjoying life in God. It is knowledge of God that is also a self-knowledge that depends upon a hitherto unimagined space opening for it in which it is not the center, and it is a matter of forging for itself a new identity fixed in relation to God. It fulfills what conscience, the *sensus divinitatis,* was a vestigial intuition of.

To put Calvin's understanding of faith in this very Augustinian way leaves, however, one last problem. Calvin, like Luther, in the face of what he saw to be the Pelagianism of the late middle ages, was deeply concerned to avoid any suggestion that the human self contributed to its salvation, or even had any capacity to do so. This, of course, fueled the interminable debates between Protestants and Catholics over the freedom of the will. The problem in the reading here suggested, though, may not be whether or not the human will contributes anything to the act of faith as an act of believing but that, if this knowledge is personal, it is somewhat difficult to see *how* it is interpersonal. Interpersonal knowledge requires some sort of push and pull, give and take, some sort of interaction. What worries one about Calvin is that while the knowledge of faith is personal, that is, its content and form is the person of Christ, how is there left any room for self-knowledge? Where are the phenomenal qualities that allow us to say

---

60. Cf. e.g., Dowey, *The Knowledge of God in Calvin's Theology,* pp. 197-204; Dupré, *Passage to Modernity,* p. 210; R. S. Wallace, *Calvin's Doctrine of the Christian Life* (Edinburgh: Oliver and Boyd, 1959), esp. ch. 3; and Dennis E. Tamburello, *Union with Christ: John Calvin and the Mysticism of St. Bernard* (Louisville: Westminster/John Knox Press, 1994). Barbara Pitkin (*What Pure Eyes Could See: Calvin's Doctrine of Faith in Its Exegetical Context* [New York: Oxford University Press, 1999]) notes that this mysticism comes to the fore especially in the *Institutes* of 1559, although it is not sudden. Previously Calvin did tend to emphasize a stronger Lutheran-like position. (But on Luther cf. below, section 4.) I note that the present exposition of Calvin is of his position in the 1559 work, as his latest and most considered position.

THE ACT OF FAITH

that there is a change in self-knowledge, and not simply a replacement of one self by another? If there is a problem with "mysticism" it is here in the question of how faith is played out in the concrete life of the believer.

Calvin, like Augustine or Aquinas, does not see faith or even union with Christ as obliterating the creator-creature distinction. How is this more than a verbal parry? The key is that Calvin does not see faith as an all-or-nothing, or all-at-once, proposition. For what is accomplished in eternity is achieved in time by faith for the believer. If faith is God's sure action in us, it is still acted out within temporal dimensions, and that gives it its qualities. For Calvin, faith's participation in Christ is played out very concretely as, in Calvin's eyes, a constant struggle between the "old man" and the "new man," a process of becoming fully engrafted into Christ. Calvin's account of the *life* of faith abounds in paradoxical formulations — for example, faith is combined with unbelief,[61] participation in Christ's righteousness is combined with lingering sinfulness.[62] These are paradoxes of the Christian life that assume faith, and are what might be called teleological paradoxes — they arise and make sense because in faith life has a direction and a goal. For Calvin, faith as lived is a continual shaping of the self. Faith is our openness to and reception of the promise, and in that some sort of transformation of imagination and intention already occurs. Yet one's participation in Christ, one's faith, is the continual reforming action of the promise in us, an action whose conclusion is fixed and sure. Faith as the reception of Christ is lived out as the continual shaping of one's life, and having a form already characterized by a willingness to be shaped by another. The life of faith is Christ conforming us to him. This is the third use of the Law, to shape us in Christ's image. "He is the shape which existence-in-faith assumes in obedience to him. Jesus Christ is not only that to which obedience is oriented, but also the reality which is effected in believers through their obedience. Existence-in-faith is formed as Jesus Christ 'forms himself' in it."[63]

Faith results in a certain kind of life, which can be characterized by certain actions, and by a certain orientation and intentionality.[64] With re-

---

61. III.2.4
62. Instit. III.3.10-15.
63. Shepherd, *The Nature and Function of Faith*, p. 166.
64. For a full examination of the Christian life in Calvin, cf. Wallace, *Calvin's Doctrine of the Christian Life*.

spect to actions, the Christian life of faith is first a moral life with respect to both giving God proper due and living charitably with others. But it is also a communal, interpersonal life. For Christ gathers all the faithful into his body, and then through the preaching of the Word and the Sacraments feeds them by his own self, which Calvin calls the "ordinary means" by which God teaches and shapes the believer.[65] Faith is formed not out of subjective experience for Calvin, but within the give and take of certain institutions and interhuman contexts. Experience comes within these; it does not precede them. To know God and to have faith is to struggle within those human contexts. It is, for example, to base faith on neither experience nor reason, but on the personal authority of an institution, even though Calvin recognized that this institution could at times fail its Source and Founder.

Faith's orientation is less a matter of comprehending the truth than a deep willingness to be taught. What truth and certainty it has is because it has found and fixed its attention on a teacher. Throughout the *Institutes* Calvin repeatedly uses the metaphor of Christ as "schoolmaster" and "teacher." He also stresses the church's value as that of a teacher. Faith, although it is certain for Calvin, is always a matter of the heart, a willingness to trust God. And that willingness, that confidence *(fiducia)* in God, is the willingness *(assensus)* to set one's own certainties and projects aside and to be ready to be taught, slowly and in uncertain situations, by another, and to learn another so well that in time we would be conformed to him and to share his life.

3.3. Between Two Worlds

There is a considerable congruence to the shape of faith in Aquinas and Calvin. Neither is a foundationalist in anything like the modern sense; both ultimately see faith and the knowledge of God begun in faith as a deeply personal and moral act involving participation in Christ by Christ's own gracious action. For both, faith is a personal shift of the self from the center that involves the humility and deep desire to listen and to be taught, to wait, and to engage others in a way that is charitable to them and that can change us. They, along with Augustine and the key writers on faith in

---

65. Instit. IV.1.5.

THE ACT OF FAITH

the New Testament, understand the act of faith and the self as constituted by its moral response to the offer of the Other in a very different light than it has frequently been understood since the Enlightenment, not only in philosophy but in much of modern theology. For both, faith is an apprenticeship in God.

Some further context for taking all this in is still needed, though. That context is Calvin's. The sort of Calvin who writes on faith can look to be a very different sort of Calvin than is often given to our view, either historically or theologically. There is another side to him and to his thinking — its style and its conclusions — that also needs to be brought to attention. This is a side that William Bouwsma has shown so carefully, but that he has also kept together with a kinder, gentler Calvin. Bouwsma points out that there is something to Calvin of the intellectualist and rationalist, traits that he carried throughout his writings: "Fundamental to this kind of Christianity in Calvin was a conviction that all truth, having its source in God, is objectively *given,* that it is the same for all people in all times and places, and that it is self-consistent and intelligible."[66]

This gives a certain daring logical quality to Calvin's writings that can lend them a bold clarity and order that is missing in Luther. But Calvin also shows little reticence in taking a doctrine all the way to its logical conclusion. Even when he stands on much the same ground as his predecessors he often says too much, too sharply, and sometimes with unhappy results, as in his discussion of predestination. Often in these cases in Calvin's theological writings Scripture does function as a body of propositions, and what it means to interpret it involves drawing out its syllogistic conclusions. Religious truth is often treated as if there were no ambiguity, wanting only appropriate application.[67]

Now in this, Bouwsma suggests, Calvin, ironically, shows something of the medieval schoolman he so detested. But he also links it to a deep anxiety Calvin, as well as his age, felt in a time of moral, political, and intellectual uncertainty. His very confidence in the certainty of reason is a way of fending off that anxiety, and his worry about error and the need to root it out witness to that anxiety and need for certainty. Surely some of this anxi-

---

66. William J. Bouwsma, *John Calvin: A Sixteenth Century Portrait* (New York: Oxford University Press, 1988), p. 98. For this side of Calvin cf. especially chapter 6, "Rational Religion."

67. "Reformed epistemology" in this way does have genuine Calvinist credentials.

ety underlies his pressing concern to call faith certain, even when he does not have any particular criteria for certain knowledge.

None of this ought to be denied. Its features are plain enough in reading Calvin. For those who do not share his presuppositions or methodology they can make that reading an irritating and unattractive experience. But this is combined with another side of Calvin in which, "when momentarily forgetting the philosophers, he recognized that the heart, as the spiritual center of the personality, belonged to a different cultural universe in which what is best is not located at the top but at the center."[68] There is a side to Calvin in which he stands in awe of the heart and its integrating possibilities for the human personality, just as Augustine had. In this, the more humanistic Calvin, there is a recognition of the ambiguity of human life, a certain gentle Montaigne-like skepticism, in which words were a matter of communication for shaping human and divine relations, and less a vehicle for timeless, universal truths.

What is interesting about Calvin's treatment of faith, which in many ways is not innovative but conservative, is that he stands on the edge of a new age full of anxieties and in which, for so many, distanced reason will provide certainty. Yet in the end, at least in his understanding of faith, he stands firm on a personal sense of faith; he develops faith as a matter of personal knowing that depends upon a moral space that engages and demands a response of the will, of love and charity, in the believer. What is interesting is that he had a choice, and in this central doctrine he was willing to live with all the anxieties that personal interaction and trust create. Calvin was not a foundationalist. What he did rest on was a sense of trust and attention and a willingness to wait. He did not remain distant, in full possession of his autonomy, as neither one's reason nor one's own experience finally provide certainty; it is the grace of God's own gift.[69] In this, despite occasional unattractive aspects of his writings, Calvin remains a par-

---

68. Bouwsma, *John Calvin*, p. 132.

69. Cf. Dupré, *Passage to Modernity*. Dupré suggests that Calvin's stress on the certainty of experience links him to earlier mystical traditions, but it also reflects a certain modern feature of his teaching. Nevertheless: "that subjective experience . . . is not a substitute for the divine foundation of faith, for according to Calvinist doctrine, the experience of salvation reaches the elect from a trans-subjective source. . . . Faith, then, surpasses a merely subjective certainty insofar as it attaches that certainty to a transcendent source. On this crucial point Calvin abandons the modern concept of the wholly autonomous creative subject" (pp. 212-13).

ticularly important exemplar in his treatment of the act of faith, especially in an age that approaches knowledge and the relation between persons in a way that oscillates continually between instrumental rationality and unshakable confidence in autonomy and one's own creative subjective experience. In the end Calvin did not have more to say about faith than Augustine had. He probably did not care to do so. But in a world that was just as anxious as ours and that entertained dreams of autonomous grandeur and rational certainty, he may be an example of how to read and reach a tradition of knowing by personal trust and dealings.

4. SUMMARY

The life-world of Christianity through the Reformation was conceived within a horizon that gave life a teleological orientation in which it was understood that one is fulfilled by knowing God and enjoying him forever. It was a world in which union with God — *theiosis* — is the human end. God's acts — including nature — were understood within that horizon. Creation was God's gracious act; God is present to humanity through it. But humanity had also lost its way and damaged its nature; Christ came to heal it, and to guide it to an end that it did not understand. He did so by teaching, yet this teaching had its meaning in his union with his lost race. By his union with the faithful, given through the words of Scripture, through his body the church, and through the sacraments, their alienation from God and from neighbor was overcome, although that work is not finished this side of death. Christian life then for Paul, John, Augustine, Aquinas, and Calvin was in some sense a matter of participation in God's own life, and God's indwelling of the human soul by Christ and the Spirit.

Even Luther is no exception.[70] Despite his insistent use of a forensic metaphor meant to smash pride and self-reliance, i.e., righteousness is *im-*

---

70. If the recent "Finnish interpretation" of Luther is at all accurate. Cf. the essays in *Union with Christ: The New Finnish Interpretation of Luther*, ed. C. E. Braaten and R. W. Jenson (Grand Rapids: Eerdmans, 1998). E.g., Tuomo Mannermaa, "Why Is Luther So Fascinating?": "According to Luther, Christ (in both his person and work) is present in faith and is through this presence identical with the righteousness in faith. Thus, the notion that Christ is present in the Christian occupies a much more central place in the theology of Luther than in the Lutheranism subsequent to him. The idea of a divine life in Christ who is really present in faith lies at the very center of the theology of the Reformer" (p. 2).

puted to the faithful, and never their possession, he is also bold to say that "Christ is the object of faith, or rather not the object but, so to speak, in the faith itself Christ is present." And: "Therefore the Christ who is grasped by faith and who lives in the Christian heart is righteousness, on account of which God counts us righteous and gives us eternal life as gift."[71] Not only is he not an exception, his jarring juxtaposition of the transcendent, external God who imputes righteousness and the internal, indwelling Christ actually underlines the distinctive Christian idea of the God who is beyond, but who is also closer to us than we are to ourselves. God is neither the Kantian lawgiver and guarantor of human autonomy and morality, nor the Stoic indwelling *logos*. Nicholas of Cusa put it aptly: God is the other that is not-other *(aliud non-aliud)*.

Within this life-world, Christian faith certainly believes what cannot be seen or proven. It believes doctrine. But just as important is that it is a way, indeed, the Way. The act of faith is first and foremost a certain radical openness and willingness to be entered into by the Spirit — but not simply privately, rather through an openness to the community of faith, present and historical, and its means of grace. Historically, Christian faith thus reveals a self in which the Good is not chosen, but in which one's very being is bound up with that Good, in which one finds oneself claimed. This is a reflective self, for it is conscious of being claimed; it is also conscious of its standing before God and conscious of God's presence. But it is not one that is radically reflexive, standing outside its own character. This is a self that chooses, but the choices that are made are made from and for this openness; they are to increase it in order to be like the God one thinks. The thought of life's Good is self-involving. So there are choices, but choice flows from an inner character that has already been claimed; choice consents to let the "new man" to whom God is present become the real self. Thus faith is also an apprenticeship in which the art of the teacher enters into the body and soul of the learner. Faith is indeed intensely personal, and even held in solitude — prayer is its sustenance — but it is not private in anything like the liberal sense of privately chosen personal goods, for its inner springs are fed through its community with God in God's own chosen community. Herein lies its difference, and its challenge in the modern world.

---

71. *Lectures on Galatians*. Quoted in Braaten and Jenson, p. 37.

CHAPTER VI

Attention and the Embodied Self

Kierkegaard in his imaginative pseudonymous works presents us with numerous pictures of what it is like to hold or not to hold certain beliefs about an ultimate good in life. His portrayals are effective because he understood that these sorts of beliefs are forms of life, and not just beliefs about the contents of the world. They lie at the heart of our very sense of ourselves; we cannot make proper sense of them when they are divorced from our lives as a whole. Indeed, they have no such sense. To see the nature of faith, the context has to be broad. Faith in God — at least Christian faith in God — is all encompassing, played out not only in private life, but in the very way we connect our inner lives to our outer lives. The broader narratives of our lives are at once both the most difficult obstacles to faith, and the only way to conceive it at all. They are also important because what we say we believe needs to have some empirical bite to be taken seriously. What we believe has to make a difference, and it has to make a difference across a very broad range of human life. So we now return to the issue of faith and the moral self in the modern world where the self is largely individualist, psychically distanced, and often lacking any substantial inner side, and which is played out in politics and social relations as much as it is in philosophy of religion.

When the late Iris Murdoch published her seminal essay, "The Idea of Perfection," in 1964[1] she offered a sharp and early criticism of the picture

---

1. Reprinted in Iris Murdoch, *The Sovereignty of Good* (New York: Schocken Books, 1971).

of the moral self presented by contemporary moral philosophy as "behaviourist, existentialist, and utilitarian."[2] She explained: "It is behaviourist in its connection of the meaning and being of action with the publicly observable, it is existentialist in its elimination of the substantial self and its emphasis on the solitary omnipotent will, and it is utilitarian in its assumption that morality is and can only be concerned with public acts."[3] In short, what "I" am objectively is given in publicly acceptable reasons and publicly discernible behavior; what I am subjectively is what I choose. Thus "personality dwindles to the point of pure will."[4] And there is continually the problem of "the big fat ego." Murdoch argued that the self needs to be seen as something weightier and more profound, something that actually involves an inner life. What she had in mind was something different than celebration of our own inner depths; romantic, expressivist alternatives were not what she intended. What she meant by an inner life she gave by means of an example: A woman of impeccable manners dislikes her son's wife, a girl she finds bumptious and unrefined. However, after the younger woman moves away or dies (it only matters that the mother-in-law have no chance to act publicly) the mother-in-law rethinks her relative. She pays just and kind *attention* to the girl. As a result she changes her opinion of the girl, even though she has no chance of showing or expressing it. Murdoch wanted to claim that attention to others, an inner activity, *is* a real, significant activity, and the mother-in-law should be seen as being engaged in a real and significant moral activity. This is an activity that belongs to the inner self; we should be loath to say that nothing morally important was going on here in her thinking about the girl.

If an inner self is revealed by this sort of attentive activity, then it would appear that it functions in one's "perception of particulars"; this is what it does. Our consent to the world, and the self-involving descriptions under which we consent, matter to us not only because we act on them, but also because they produce the very quality of our evaluations. But the quality of our evaluations is what we see or don't see in the world. Loving what is, and being open to it, being attentive, is not a theory from which we practice, but our going out to another, a letting into our lives of another that occurs because we have seen the other. The truly perceptive descrip-

2. Murdoch, *The Sovereignty of Good*, p. 8.
3. Murdoch, *The Sovereignty of Good*, p. 9.
4. Murdoch, *The Sovereignty of Good*, p. 16.

tion of another is a just description that reveals the inner justice of the perceiver, his or her openness to another.

An inner self like this is vital to making sense of Christian faith, especially as "participation" and "indwelling," and as the focus of faith's apprenticeship. It distinguishes the self of faith from the obviously distanced, autonomous self, as well as from contemporary offerings that have tried to find a deeper, more genuinely human space within the structures of rational autonomy. Or so I shall argue, and need to argue, since such offerings often look as if they were compatible with and attractive to faith. To this end we shall examine the work of Martha Nussbaum. In her efforts to link literature and politics, and in drawing on ancient philosophy, Nussbaum has gone to some lengths to argue for a richer conception of personal life that can take place within rational liberal social structures, and even reorient and reform them. So her context is sufficiently broad. Her proposals also rely on the ability to perceive particulars. First known for her work on Aristotle's ethical theory, especially the concept of *phronesis*, which goes beyond a general ethical rationalism and involves a perception of particulars, she has found in it a way to read literature as moral philosophy.[5] The narration of novels relies on an ethical ability that she calls "perception" — ". . . the ability to discern, acutely and responsively, the salient features of one's particular situation."[6] Here she thinks there also can be a link to politics. Literature extends our moral experience and increases the material we have available for moral reflection: "The importance of this for both morals and politics cannot be underestimated. . . . [Novels can depict] the imagination of the novel-reader as a type that is very valuable in the political (as well as the private) life, sympathetic to a wide range of concerns, averse to certain denials of humanities. It cultivates these sympathies in its readers."[7] In short, a politics rooted in the moral ability to see people as they are would be more humane, and more conducive to human flourishing. It would help make our associations a matter of respect for persons. It would make them more just by putting a personal heart in the otherwise ironically alienating structures of the modern self. It would genuinely protect our concern for individuals and shield us from intrusive, oppressive

---

5. Cf. Martha Nussbaum, *Love's Knowledge: Essays on Philosophy and Literature* (New York: Oxford University Press, 1990).
6. Nussbaum, *Love's Knowledge*, p. 37.
7. Nussbaum, *Love's Knowledge*, p. 47.

THE ACT OF FAITH

structures and authoritarianism. Yet, what Nussbaum gives us is little more than an enriched liberalism, failing precisely to pay the real sort of attention to the human person that faith demands. Rather, it is Simone Weil, from whom Murdoch first got the notion of "attention," who gives a consistently deep enough sense of the sort of openness of the self that supports a conception of participation. It is in the contrast that we also find a socially embodied moral self and a specific way of imagining the act of faith within a broader life-world.

1. NUSSBAUM'S ENRICHED LIBERALISM

1.1. Defining the Political

First, we must begin by coming to grips with just what sort of problem or problems we are dealing with in trying to relate the perception of particulars to politics, in trying to relate the personal to the larger social context. The problem is that personal desires, actions, and perceptions within a *polis* need to be configured within general rules. This problem can take a number of different forms, and it is well to be aware of some of the most important of them.

Most generally, it is a problem of having to think the general, collective notions that politics necessarily involves through visions, ends, and needs of individuals that are, by definition, singular. For justice in the *polis*, common ends and needs and solutions are needed. However, there are two different, although not incompatible, ways of approaching this general problem.

The first has to do with the degree to which general political solutions must be a matter of "rule-guided toughness." We simply *have* to legislate by rules; some philosophers think they need to be unbendingly rational to guarantee universality. Put that way, justice seems best exemplified by the sort of ultra-rationalistic utilitarianism exemplified by Mr. Gradgrind in Charles Dickens's *Hard Times*. (Nussbaum is explicitly reacting to this sense of justice in much of her work.) Other philosophers think that some sort of flexibility is required for justice. This question of degree is largely a question that is internal to a system of justice.

The second way of taking the problem of the general and the particular has more to do with the sort of concepts we use in thinking about justice at all. It is concerned with trying to say something about where those concepts are rooted and about the very nature of political and moral space. Are the political and social structures of justice first and foremost rooted in a personal concern for individuals and derived from sensibilities that come from interacting with them, from loving them? Or are they rooted in something else, say simply preservation of life, liberty, or property? In either case, there will always be *some* tension between the general and particular. At a social level politics and justice are matters of finding channels for power to run in, and justice in the first instance within a society is a matter of cutting those general, wide channels that will contain the flood of particular powers, needs, and desires. Here political justice, whether unbendingly rationalist or personalist, cannot be particular, for better or for worse. By its very nature justice at this level is rough. As Adam puts it succinctly after Hetty is sentenced in George Eliot's *Adam Bede,* "there's no law so wise but that it's a pity for somebody or other." Even so, when justice is rooted in the perception of individuals, it is there in personal interaction that we look for the standard that measures whether it is a pity or not. When the rationality of justice is strictly procedural, when it shields the individual and is not meant in itself to increase interaction or to call forth the obligation to care, however, another sort of standard will be applied.

1.2. Nussbaum's Liberal Vision of Persons

1.2.1. Perception and Revolution

We now turn to Nussbaum's account of the political import of the perception of particulars, beginning with "Perception and Revolution," an examination of the political value of Henry James's novel *The Princess Casamassima*.[8] That value, Nussbaum suggests, consists in three elements that James presents as vital to social life: "socialism as the guiding principle in the economy; liberalism as the guiding principle in politics; conserva-

---

8. We will examine Nussbaum's meditations on the political import of the "perception of particulars" in three works: the essay "Perception and Revolution: The Princess Casamassima and the Political Imagination," in *Love's Knowledge*; "Patriotism and Cosmopolitanism," which appears with several responses in *For Love of Country: Debating the Limits of Patriotism* (Boston: Beacon Press, 1996); and *Poetic Justice: The Literary Imagination and the Public Life* (Boston: Beacon Press, 1995).

THE ACT OF FAITH

tism as the guiding principle in culture."[9] How does this come out of the perception of particulars?

Socialism is recommended to us via the ability of the hero, Hyacinth Robinson, to recognize and sympathize with the poor, and his consequent recognition "that thinking, imagining, and even desiring are very much affected by the material circumstances of life. . . ."[10] Liberalism is recommended in a "conception of the human being according to which our essential dignity resides in a free and responsive activity of thought and the free creative use of language."[11] It is linked to a certain demand in the novel for the artist's freedom of expression. Hyacinth's sensibilities are also liberal in that they are anti-revolutionary, showing a preference for patient, slow change. Conservatism in culture is not mere traditionalism, but a recommendation of the finest in culture, precisely to give us access to vital and enriching fellow feeling.

Here certainly seems to be a political program, involving both a conception of the human and a sense of what it takes for the human to flourish; as such, it involves justice. What is not entirely clear, however, is how this comes from any perception of particulars in the novels. The novel may simply be illustrating already established general philosophical principles. Hyacinth's perceptions may be no more than *instances* of rule-guided behavior. So what is distinctive here? Where is the perception of particulars and how is *it* political?

Nussbaum argues that much of what Hyacinth sees is, in fact, the result of his ethical values and "his active love of human beings." Without this active love, he simply would not see what he, in fact, does see; he would not act in the caring way that he does act. It is thus the ability to see the lives of others, clearly combined with a general desire for goodness and justice "that makes Hyacinth a fine and ethical and political agent."[12] How he is such a political agent is made clear by a contrast in the novel with other political agents who are rule-driven, and who act without emotion. In contrast with them, Hyacinth is incapable of certain cruelties and violences; he is capable of a compassion that rules cannot give. Thus "the

---

9. Nussbaum, "Perception and Revolution," in *Love's Knowledge,* p. 196. NB: This essay was originally written for a *Festschrift* for Hilary Putnam and the formula for a healthy politics is originally his.
10. Nussbaum, "Perception and Revolution," p. 201.
11. Nussbaum, "Perception and Revolution," p. 205.
12. Nussbaum, "Perception and Revolution," p. 207.

commitment to the person *is* political."[13] It is political insofar as it is a critique of the actual justice rendered by mere principle; it is political insofar as "any real solution to the problems of hunger and misery must take place in the context of an ongoing sense of life's richness and value and full humanity."[14] Politics without art can only give a truncated sense of justice. So if there is a revolution called for it is a "revolution in the heart that consists in learning to see and to love."[15]

There is no doubt that what Nussbaum is describing is indeed more just, with a view of persons superior to "a general rule-guided toughness." There is no doubt that the utilitarianism of Mr. Gradgrind is not nearly so just. But so far, this is only one form of the problem about rules; it chiefly answers to the question of the degree to which behavior ought to be guided by rules. What Nussbaum is describing, however, does not generate a theory of justice because it doesn't yet suggest a reason why we should respond in this way to humans, why this sort of sensibility ought to be the measure of justice. Nor does it describe what channels ought to be cut for power; it only improves a theory already existing.

This need not be pressed yet. There is a point here, though, about the relation between justice and the ability to see particulars that needs to be considered before going on. It can be put in Aristotelian terms. If the perception of particulars plays any role in the moral life, surely it is the one Aristotle describes as *phronesis*. But if *phronesis* has a role in political life, in the administration of justice, it is that of equity, the moral recognition that a strict application of the rules of justice does not always produce the most just situation. Equity is the ability to see the particulars of a given situation and to adjust the situation and make it more just, given those particulars. That, of course, is precisely the political value Nussbaum is claiming for Hyacinth Robinson's finely tuned moral sense. But this can be looked at in two different ways. Equity may be the grace in a system of rough but rational justice, the gravy on the roast, something that adds flavor to what is basic. Or, it may be regarded as perfect justice itself, the *telos* of justice, on which our rougher justice depends for its legitimacy and chief distinctions. Which does Nussbaum see it as?

In Nussbaum's other writings, it becomes clear that the perception of

---

13. Nussbaum, "Perception and Revolution," p. 209.
14. Nussbaum, "Perception and Revolution," p. 211.
15. Nussbaum, "Perception and Revolution," p. 216.

particulars is the gravy on the roast of liberal theory. In the later *Poetic Justice,* the real contribution novels seem to make to political culture is to give a richer view of the human being than one gets simply by reading and writing abstract economic and political treatises. They expand what we know. Nussbaum recognizes full well that governments cannot run by seeking out each individual's story. She does think, though, that they can be aware — as too often they are not, and as too often rational choice theorists and utilitarians are not — that people do have stories and are not mere instances of rules. Government has to run by rules; it might be better, however, if people in government read a book of moral consequence once in a while. With this said, it should then be noted that novels, however, do not exclude political thinking by rules; in fact, she suggests, they "can go wrong and need theoretical corroboration."[16]

All this is politically and morally significant. Because of the view of the human being it presents, it not only critiques, it actually excludes certain theories of justice, such as Bentham's. If it is significant that human beings have rich and varied lives, if it is important that we consider what those lives are, and that we need to listen to their stories, that their telling their stories is vital to human flourishing, then there is a rather substantial view of the human being here that is important to a theory of justice and hence of politics. Nussbaum personally thinks it leads "in the direction of a liberal theory of the Kantian or Aristotelian sort, in which separateness, freedom and a complex account of human flourishing will all play a role." But how *far* does that go?

1.2.2. The Thinness of Cosmopolitanism

In the last of her writings to be considered, there is an answer to that question. In an article titled "Patriotism and Cosmopolitanism,"[17] written in response to a piece by Richard Rorty that extolled the virtues of patriotism, Nussbaum argued, *au contraire,* for a Stoic model of education, that is, a cosmopolitan approach to education in which we learn to see ourselves *first* and foremost as citizens of the world. Among the many values

---

16. Nussbaum, *Poetic Justice,* p. 45.

17. This article was originally published in *The Boston Review* with twenty-nine replies. It was later published in book form, along with sixteen of those replies, as *For Love of Country: Debating the Limits of Patriotism* (Boston: Beacon Press, 1996).

she sees in this model is that it might rid us of a sort of irrational education that teaches us to see our own national characteristics as natural, "lending to what is an accident of history a false air of moral weight and glory."[18] This is, of course, an updated liberal approach to Stoicism and Kantianism, for Stoic organicism and Kantian rational essentialism are not meant to be taken too far, viz., where they might be taken "to deny the fundamental importance of the separateness of people and of fundamental personal liberties."[19] There is little *amor fati* here.

Many of her critics were quick to point out that this was a somewhat surprising position for anyone to take who emphasizes *phronesis*. If *phronesis* comes from anywhere, Aristotle thought, it is from well-legislated local communities teaching their citizens. But it is also clear here that for Nussbaum, the rules (where else would universal "fundamental personal liberties" come from than rules? — surely they are not the result of perceiving individuals as individuals) comprise justice in the first instance, and not *phronesis*. It is the rules that define what ought to be seen — and limit it. Ironically, for somebody who has worried about how thinking in universals affects our ability to see the particular, she has seemed quick to give up particulars. And that she recognizes that there is a problem is evident at the end of the article when she tells the bizarre story of Crates and Hipparchia, two Cynic philosophers, who were so taken with each other, and so immediately taken, that they copulated in public. Ap-

---

18. Nussbaum, *For Love of Country*, p. 11.

19. Nussbaum, *For Love of Country*, p. 10. For Nussbaum's consideration of Stoicism see chapters 9-12 of her *The Therapy of Desire: Theory and Practice in Hellenistic Ethics* (Princeton: Princeton University Press, 1994). Her appreciation of Stoicism clearly lies in its appeal to autonomy and control of one's life. Speaking of her imaginary gypsy scholar Nikidion who traverses the Hellenistic schools, she says after Nikidion leaves the Skeptics: "Moving now to the Stoa, Nikidion feels that to give up the aim of taking charge of her own life, by her own thinking [as Skepticism requires], is to give up something too deep and essential. . . . She wants to become more, not less, of a distinct self, healthier, stronger, thinking only her own thoughts, and thinking them actively, rather than being a passive vessel for the dogmas of another" (p. 321). She will find this in Stoicism, Nussbaum thinks. Summarizing Seneca, she claims "[t]he result of philosophical instruction is that the mind itself can bring itself before its own bar, autonomous, secret, free" (p. 341). And, Epictetus: "Philosophy builds an impregnable wall around the self, fortifying it against all possible assaults of fortune." There is nothing here in this examination, however, of Stoic pantheism, and the self that is the self only by giving itself up to the immanent cosmic *Logos*.

parently this is to show that holding positions of philosophical universalism is not incompatible with love of an individual. Yet if bizarre, it may be exactly all that she means in making the political personal as she continually returns elsewhere to the most private of acts to find the personal, as if it were nowhere else.[20]

One may be excused for doubting that this act of Crates and Hipparchia was the moral high point in Greece's public space. Indeed, Nussbaum's position has not convinced many. The poet Robert Pinsky suggested that Nussbaum's utopianism is "bloodless" and a sort of "moral esperanto."[21] Hilary Putnam thought she had confused a universal ethics with a universal way of life, and arguing "that any Sittlichkeit that is not part of a universal ethic construed as a universal way of life is simply absurd."[22] Far from teaching us how to see embodied individuals lovingly, in all their limitations, it appears that Nussbaum has simply suggested that the standards and lifestyles of the academic tribe, which are always more international, replace those of the *rudes*. Rather than establishing what she called a "perfectionist standard," her recommendation of literature is less a love of particulars than the tastes of a certain educated class. Artists are simply its priests, not its real conscience (a problem James had, too). She herself seems less what Murdoch had in mind, and more a Rawls who reads novels.

The basic idea of universal caring in Nussbaum's cosmopolitanism is not wrong. But one does come away believing that the sort of justice to which she is committed is procedural liberalism, simply improved (and probably vastly improved) by the richness of having to face the variety of human lives. In that she shows a marked taste for expressivism contained within rational, liberal, political forms. But, in the end the view of the per-

---

20. Fergus Kerr notes that Nussbaum concluded her Gifford Lectures with a discussion of Molly and Bloom "in which she argued that Molly and Bloom in bed together at the end of the day, imperfect unromantic creatures, sweaty and smelly, somewhat unfaithful to one another, no doubt self-deceiving, and so on, nevertheless offer a paradigm of love that turns the ascent downwards, so to speak, into the everyday world, the only place where our humanity would not be eliminated" (*Immortal Longings: Versions of Transcending Humanity* [Notre Dame: University of Notre Dame Press, 1997], p. 2). Apparently the paradigm of love, while personal, cannot be realized outside the private. The social still cannot receive it except as bizarre.

21. Nussbaum, *For Love of Country*, p. 89.
22. Nussbaum, *For Love of Country*, p. 95.

son at stake has not changed too much, nor does it really involve the "perception of particulars." It does not get us too far out of our own skins. She is simply trying to expand what the universal rules actually cover. That is important enough; it, however, is very limited in it what it says about compassion and love. It is also limited in the attention it is willing to pay to the particular communal commitments of individuals, which are often the most important things to *them*.

The problem is that, despite a promising beginning, in the end there is a curious lack of *engagement,* for the rules are all *a priori*. There is a *representation,* indeed, often a very full one, of the other; there is still not a relation or a meeting of the other, except perhaps in the private — but that was the problem from the beginning. And what especially of people who do not have rich, interesting stories, or whose lives are eccentric beyond easy harmony with those of their neighbors, or whose lives are fragmented, or even repulsive, sometimes even by their own fault? A revolution in love needs to go further than simply respecting separateness.

To reiterate: cosmopolitanism is not *wrong,* nor are Stoicism or Kantianism wrong — so far as they go. The problem is that they are just terribly thin, even when beefed up by the insights of art. They get to their universal respect for humans too quickly, forgetting, as Plato said, "all the intermediaries." For the love of all humanity needs to be gotten to by actually loving individuals, individuals whose values are embedded in and inseparable from the way the institutions of their lives and the history of their particular communities have gone. To love humanity without first taking these seriously is so ethereal it threatens to blow away at the first wind — and does. In rejecting human transcendence Nussbaum has barely moved us out of ourselves.

2. SIMONE WEIL AND THE FORMATION OF ATTENTION

2.1. Attention

When Murdoch first started talking about paying attention to other human beings as an important, even primary matter of being a moral agent, she admitted from the outset that she had borrowed the idea from Simone Weil. "Attention" is, indeed, a key contribution Weil has made to understanding the nature of moral thinking. Used regularly throughout her notebooks, she develops it at greatest length in the essay, "The Right Use of School Studies with a View to the Love of God." As she describes it there, paying attention to something is a matter of refusing to fit it into any pre-established categories, epistemological or practical.

> Attention consists of suspending our thought, leaving it detached, empty, and ready to be penetrated by the object; it means holding in our minds, within reach of this thought, but on a lower level and not in contact with it, the diverse knowledge we have acquired which we are forced to make use of. Our thought should be in relation to all particular and already formulated thoughts, as a man on a mountain who, as he looks forward, sees also below him, without actually looking at them, a great many forests and plains. Above all our thought should be empty, waiting, not seeking anything, but ready to receive in its naked truth the object that is to penetrate it. (SW 96)

Attention is not a matter of willpower; it is intellectual and moral humility.

The moral importance of attention is that it is through attention to others that we see *them,* and not simply what we imagine of them. This includes seeing people we might otherwise ignore.

> The love of neighbor in all its fullness simply means being able to say to him: "What are you going through?" It is a recognition that the sufferer exists, not only as a unit in a collection, or a specimen from the social category labeled "unfortunate," but as a man, exactly like us, who was one day stamped with a special mark by affliction. For this reason it is enough, but it is indispensable, to know how to look at him in a certain way.
>
> This way of looking is first of all attentive. The soul empties itself of all its own contents in order to receive into itself the being it is looking at, just as he is, in all his truth.
>
> Only he who is capable of attention can do this. (SW 99)

The religious significance of attention for Weil is central; prayer and the love of God, she says, have attention as their substance. As such, it is the key to understanding faith as living from something other than one's own resources. But it also has crucial social and political significance for her as well, which responds to a concern for universal human justice. This comes in two ways. First, it can be seen in the essay, "Human Personality." This essay, written at the beginning of Weil's work with the Free French in London, explores the root moral notions of social life generally. Specifically, it served Weil as the foundation of the work she was to do in the remaining months of her life in describing what the nature and shape of a legitimate French government after the war might look like. In it Weil begins to look for a sense of justice more profound than the procedural justice of modern liberalism.[23] Earlier, when she was resituated in Marseilles because of the Nazi occupation of the north, she spent much time observing court cases. She discovered that even when they were procedurally fair, there was something missing. Somehow through the flow of the words of justice, the deepest concerns of the defendants were not heard. That is unjust, and so in "Human Personality" she insists on recognizing the absolutely vital importance of listening for the unexpressed word behind the spoken words of procedural justice in order to ensure that justice is not merely rough. She is driven to look deeper than the notions of rights provided to her by Kantianism and Stoicism, not because Kant and the Stoics were wrong (she admired both), but because they missed and could not accommodate cases of humanity at the margins. The problem was that they could not deal with people who could no longer be respected as rational agents, or who had been cut off from the organic body of humanity that Stoicism presented. Weil did not look to do away with Kantianism and Stoicism, but to make their rough justice of rights an imperfect derivation of a more perfect sort of justice, one where those who do not count are nevertheless paid attention to and made to count. Attention alone is truly inclusive and universal.

The second area of importance that the notion of attention played in Weil's social and political thinking is that it caused her to shift thinking about root moral and political problems from a "third person perspective" to a "first person perspective." This was for her a shift in thinking about problems of justice in terms of rights to terms of obligations,[24] a shift that allowed her to move beyond "the separateness of people" to a

---

23. For a detailed explanation of this reading of the essay, see E. Springsted, "Rootedness, Culture and Value," in R. Bell, ed., *The Divine Humanity: Simone Weil's Philosophy of Culture* (Cambridge: Cambridge University Press, 1992), reprinted as chapter 10 of D. Allen and E. Springsted, *Spirit, Nature and Community: Issues in the Thought of Simone Weil* (Albany: State University of New York Press, 1994).

24. This distinction forms the opening pages of *The Need for Roots,* trans. A. Wills (London: Routledge & Kegan Paul, 1952).

fundamental engagement with them. What this shift means is spelled out in her essay, "Are We Struggling for Justice?" also written in this same period in London.

2.2. Are We Struggling for Justice?
Justice and Mutual Consent

In the beginning of "Are We Struggling for Justice?" Weil defines justice simply as mutual consent. It is a definition that allows her to discuss both general, imperfect justice and particular, perfect justice. Justice defined this way has a certain *prima facie* obviousness to it, even bearing certain relations to Kantian autonomy and Stoic assent to fate. She explains: Human action in a material world does not proceed automatically from desire and design to accomplishment. Instead, it must negotiate certain obstacles. With respect to the world of matter, it must therefore find a way to bring about the desired goal, or, by use of other obstacles, to circumvent them; the dove does not fly except by using the resistance of the air. Within the human world, the same necessity applies. In the case of the human world, however, since other agents have projects and are capable of action, we have to seek their consent. We have to ask them. Respect and justice consist in seeking this consent, and are constituted by treating humans as humans and not as passive things. It is a basic recognition of the human world. To the degree that one's consent is sought, one has freedom and insofar as justice is asking permission, it is always a matter of dealing with individual particulars.

But, of course, Weil notes, when our "will finds expression outside ourselves in actions performed by others, we do not waste our time and our power of attention in examining whether they have consented to this" (SW 122). If we went around asking each individual if he consented to participate in our projects, things would never get done. There is a sort of presumption in all of our daily dealings that does not bother us. When that presumption becomes overweening, civil justice is there to outline and enforce our rights. Through the administration of public justice, one can put her foot down and refuse consent, and make sure that she is taken seriously. While there is a certain vital efficiency in justice of this sort, it is nevertheless imperfect. Weil suggests: "Because of this action is tainted by sacrilege. For human consent is a sacred thing" (SW 122).

This efficient sort of action is the realm of the rough sort of justice. It is to be contrasted with — and hopefully rooted in — the sort of justice in which consent is always sought, and never presumed, especially in those cases where it is not necessary to obtain it, or where we would not in the course of business normally think of asking. Such cases are those of the afflicted and weak, those who present no effective obstacle to the achievement of our desire. The perfectly just person is the one who, although in a position of strength, still asks consent. This Weil calls a sort of madness, for "it would be absurd and mad for anyone at all to impose upon himself the necessity of seeking consent where there is no power of refusal" (SW 123). But, she adds, it is the madness of love, the same sort of madness of a God who seeks a human's love and service in creating and providing for the universe. Perfect justice *is* love according to Weil. And, as she points out, it is this madness, this deep-seated love for others, that alone is capable of transforming human action from efficient, half justice to a morally respectable concern for human beings.

When Weil introduces God into the discussion at this point, it is to set the ultimate defining context of what she has in mind when she talks about "consent." For God as creator and provider of the universe has put humans in a world that they experience as necessity — an obstacle to their desires — but which also makes them the beings that they are. We cannot help but obey Necessity; "obedience is the imprescribable law of life" (SW 126). Yet, God still seeks human consent and love for the universe. So with respect to both the universe and the realm of the social, freedom is never a matter of "negative liberty," a lack of restraint; it is a matter of consent sought to what is, an invitation to full-bodied participation. Thus freedom and dignity in the universe are not a matter of our advice being sought on its forms and ends, or an ability to withdraw from it. It is a concern on the part of the one who loves us that we love in return.

In the *Genealogy of Morals* Nietzsche introduced the concept of *ressentiment*, a root reaction to the world of the strong by the weak willed, a reaction that generated an entire morality Nietzsche believed was fundamentally life denying. Weil's "consent" *(consentement)* is its polar opposite, for it is an embracing of the world as a whole, an embracing from which life and character flows. As such it has wide-ranging import in moral philosophy,[25] particularly in seeing the relation of "consent" to political "le-

---

25. Of course, Nietzsche is also looking to move beyond *ressentiment* to consent. While Weil and Nietzsche are clearly polar opposites in what they regard as life enhancing

gitimacy." Legitimacy is not a question of the "best" political system; it is not a request for designing the political ambience. It is a question of whether a people, collectively and individually, actually believe in, love, and support their life together. It is a matter of whether they flourish morally or not in that common life.

To put it this way may be helpful in coming to grips with exactly how consent is justice, and in also dispelling what may be an unfortunate way of understanding "the perception of particulars." When one uses vision words such as perception, there is often a sense of simply being a spectator to what is seen. This is particularly true in modern formulations of rationality and aesthetics. A phrase such as "the perception of particulars" can be taken to imply a recognition of individual qualities that are not obvious except to artists and people who are willing to pay careful attention to other people. What then is seen is a matter of information. This actually seems to describe Nussbaum's "perception of particulars." To know particular lives through art, she says, is to enrich our sense of justice, to flesh it out. But Weil is at pains to go much farther. What makes attention a matter of justice is not simply that we have taken time to see something that is there. Weil never bases her case on *qualities* that need to be in humans to make them worthy of respect, and that we are to perceive. What makes perception a matter of justice is that in seeking the consent of others and in consenting to their existence, we actually have to make an adjustment of our imaginations to let them have their own play therein, and then adjust our lives and plans to accommodate their reality. Dealing with them as particulars means a full-bodied accommodation to them, pure and simple. Weil at one point calls perception "a kind of dance." If, for her, the phrase "perception of particulars" is at all helpful, it is chiefly in the fact that it describes a willingness to dance with a partner, to be engaged, and not simply to be a spectator. This is underlined in her very definition of attention as "detached, empty and ready to be penetrated." Where the standard English translation uses "detached," it renders the French *disponible* only halfway. For to be *disponible* one is detached in that he is not engaged somewhere else; he is *available* and free for use.

Throughout her later writings on justice Weil regularly employs the

---

(Weil found that reading Nietzsche made her nauseous), this does not mean that in the absence of *consentement*, *ressentiment* does not adequately describe the shape of moral life in the West.

metaphor of a balance to describe justice. It is a particularly helpful way of describing exactly what she is after. Real justice as a matter of mutual consent is a matter of taking another's will and projects seriously. But taking them seriously is not simply recognizing that they exist; it is bringing our own being, thought, and projects into balance with them, of adjusting our weight in the world to theirs so that neither is overwhelmed, and so that each contributes to the overall effect, which is to the good of each — which includes the sense that one has contributed to the well-being of others. Justice is not simply recognizing autonomy and separateness; justice comes into play when difference is engaged, and when we do not always insist on our separateness. It is responding to the call of others, and it is perfected when there is no necessity other than concern for others to do so.

2.3. Consent and Communities

Justice for Weil then is found in balance, which is somewhat more than a respect for the separateness of individuals or a recognition that the human good is relatively complex.[26] Perhaps the best way to come to grips with what Weil is suggesting is to recognize that she is trying to effect a change in moral thinking, and hence in the political thinking connected with it, from a "third person perspective" to a "first person perspective," a change from thinking about what ought to be done generally to what I ought to do and what I ought to be. This surely is the switch in moral thinking she is arguing for when, in *The Need for Roots,* she replaces the concept of rights

---

26. What does the balanced society mean for Weil? It is *not* a question of the best-designed political system. Even wide-open democracies that invite the participation of all can violate the most important sort of consent, especially when mixed with certain economic motivations. Weil points out the important political difference between a society rooted in consent and one in which *ressentiment* rules: "Democratic thought contains a serious error — it confuses consent with a certain form of consent, which is not the only one and which can easily, like any form, be mere form. Our parliamentary democracy was hollow, for we despised the leaders we chose, we bore a grudge against those we did not choose, and we obeyed all of them unwillingly. Consent cannot be bought or sold. Consequently, whatever the political institution, in a society where monetary transactions dominate most of social life, where almost all obedience is bought and sold, there can be no freedom. Just as oppression is analogous to rape, so the dominance of money over work, pushed to the point where money becomes the prime motive for work, is analogous to prostitution" (SW 126-27). (The democracy in question is France in the 1930s.)

with that of obligations as the prime moral category. It is only from the perspective of the first person that we can seek the consent of others. *We have to do it.* Similarly, balance is a matter of singular human wills balanced against each other. Such balance cannot be described from behind a "veil of ignorance." It can only come from one person seeking the consent of another, without any prior guarantee of his or her answer; it can only be achieved within their interaction.

This would seem to make any general rules for political association or moral behavior utterly capricious. Yet general rules and laws will always be written or formulated. Indeed, the commitment of people within a community to rational, general laws should be seen as a form of commitment to other individuals. The two perspectives — general and particular — are not on the same plane, and success on one is no guarantee of success on the other. But there is a hierarchy. The first person perspective does not replace rationality or law; it does, however, shape it and complete it. For example, if justice is seeking the consent of another and fully recognizing that there is another to ask, it is to that end that, on the level of generalized law, we cut the channels for power to run in. The channels are neither an end in themselves, nor is our dealing with human beings over and done when they are cut.

This does mean, though, that human collectivities themselves are not just or unjust in themselves. They *are* essential media, some better, some worse, for the *virtue* of justice. They *are*, at their best, also a nested form of the actual consent generations of a people have made to each other and to the world in which they live. For each present individual they should invite her participation, and shape her in such a way that she will seek the consent of others. They are living and ongoing histories that cannot be violated or even managed with a distanced, rational efficiency without damaging the souls who hope through them. This is why Weil insists that there is a need of the soul to be rooted. "A human being has roots by virtue of his real, active and natural participation in the life of a community which preserves in living shape certain particular treasures of the past and certain particular expectations for the future."[27] This is the importance of tradition, which is not otherwise important in itself. Tradition is important for the ongoing shaping of our moral space and of the individual souls who live within that space. But that is to put it in a way that is perhaps too in-

---

27. Weil, *The Need for Roots*, p. 41.

strumental itself and too external to the people who live within a tradition. Traditions are not the external deadweight of the past; they are the concrete forms and practices of consent. They are the ongoing consent of the souls who form them, consent not only to the natural world that constrains and opens possibilities for them, but also to other living beings of past and present. They are in practice the balances we have between ourselves and others, past and present, and the natural world. They are not simply the rules of non-interference; at varying levels, and in varying ways — speaking, singing, dancing, reading, teaching — they are how we become available to others and they to us, including God. Living from a center that is not simply one's own *cannot* be an isolated act; it is also a communal one, for which a past is crucial.

Weil illustrates why a past is crucial in an essay in which she discusses the problems of French colonialism. In that system Algerian and Vietnamese children could be regarded as French as long as they became part of the French educational system and recited phrases such as "Our ancestors, the Gauls, had fair hair." That uprooted them. But why should that make a difference? It would not, Weil thinks, if we are self-sufficient and could produce justice and human flourishing out of our own resources and reason. But if we are not self-sufficient, if we need help outside ourselves, then maintaining a past that preserves our spiritual treasures is crucial to human life. "It is only the radiance from the spiritual treasures of the past which is the necessary condition for receiving grace."[28] "Culture is the formation of attention" (SW 119).

3. CONCLUSION

Because of her own classical sensibilities Nussbaum is well situated to raise the question of how any sort of personalist view of human flourishing and interaction might be compatible with modern social structures. She is somebody who has a foot within each of the contrasting moral frameworks of the West, at least as much as anybody might be able to have a foot in each at the same time. She highlights the tension between the two, and her solution is attractive, as are most attempts to split the difference when

---

28. Simone Weil, *Selected Essays: 1934-43* (Oxford: Oxford University Press, 1962), p. 207.

a genuine dilemma arises in how we are to regard ourselves. After all, splitting the difference promises everything and sacrifices little. But what does splitting the difference come to? It may well be as Murdoch once observed of much modern moral philosophy: the command to be perfect as your Father in heaven is perfect has become "Be ye therefore slightly improved."

Contrasting Nussbaum's approach to the dilemma with Weil's is a way to contrast moral spaces and selves. From *within* the modern moral framework, Nussbaum's approach looks both attractive and sane. However, its sanity avoids — and of course this is its appeal — the "madness" that Weil thinks is at the root of loving attention. Consider the contrast. While Nussbaum is not an advocate of Christianity, she would seem to give one a way to talk about faith, at least insofar as faith is personal and makes sense within interpersonal dealings. Her recovery of the personal in morals and politics does show how the personal can be encompassed and considered within the spheres of modern life. As what enriches human life and makes it human, friendships and particular loves and their inherent joys and struggles *have* to be taken into account. A similar case might be made for faith insofar as it is personal and enriches human life. Even if Nussbaum herself is not interested in Christianity *per se,* some analogy for the place of faith as a personal act might be derived from her meditations. She has found religious symbols attractive, although shown little sense of how they are generated out of religious life and held within it. But, if so, it is well to be aware that in this solution the personal clearly is encompassed within the limits of procedural justice and individual separateness. Yet perhaps this is not quite the right way to put matters. More deeply, Nussbaum is very suspicious of self-transcendence.[29] That is to say, her position is perhaps not so much a compromise between the personal and a rational politics, but a view of the personal that demands rational constraint. The problem with both the ultra-rationalism of Mr. Gradgrind and the madness of faith is that *both* are attempts at self-transcendence. Both modern rationalism and Christian faith are dreams of a humanity that go beyond the personal and moving gropings of Molly and Bloom, although they do so in very different directions. So if Nussbaum emphasizes the personal but puts it within the constraints of a rational, universal, but non-transcendent order, perhaps she has done so

---

29. On this issue see Fergus Kerr's "Transcending Humanity: Nussbaum's Version" in Kerr, *Immortal Longings.*

because such rational constraints are demanded by her view of the personal. The individual still remains at the center, and this limits both what is required of him in loving his neighbor and what his community might give to him as a personal heritage. Of course, on this view, one can love a lot even through a lot of human stink, but still there are limits.

This is also an ultimately tragic view and a pagan one. Nussbaum has reintroduced tragedy to moral philosophy; it is the result of moral demands that conflict without any satisfactory solution. Clear-sightedness demands that its place in moral life be recognized. But hers is also a pagan view because it is *ultimately* tragic. The sources of personal good do conflict within individualism, and not just within the limits of moral imagination. Good is polytheistically plural. So there are limits to the good we would do; the hubris of transcending them can only break us. Like the ancient Greek tragedians, the lesson of suffering is to learn the goodness of human life within limits.

By way of contrast Weil is no less a serious participant in the modern world's concern for the ordinary; what she offers is hardly a naïve "premodernism," a frequent refuge for those who have found the modern wanting. Indeed, she is far less willing to accept limits to justice and love than most people. But for Weil the limits of justice and love are not those of the natural self; rights are encompassed by duties to another. This is to invoke a very different sense of self, one that is called out of itself to become something greater; but this is done by recognizing that there is something greater than the self. This is a key to attention. Attention's home is in moral transcendence and transformation. To pay attention to another *is* to take another into one's life and to change one's life. To want to do so, to even assent to the possibility and to keep one's eyes focused on it, Weil thinks, is already to have taken God into one's life and to have transformed the deepest desires that make us what we are, to have transformed our sense of the ultimate good that shapes our self-identity and gives coherence to our projects. That is to participate in God's life at the most basic level. This is not to escape the human situation, an inhuman striving for perfection that is damaging to the self. It is to discover ourselves and our true freedom — and to discover them as a gift.

If faith operates within a distinctive moral space, it does so as a response to the very particular, personal proclamation that opens that space; it is personal from its inception. It is not a dream of human possibilities or a moral strategy, which really would be a dangerous act of hubris, but a

THE ACT OF FAITH

space that is opened by the words and Word that are addressed to human souls. This, of course, was what was meant in the traditional assertion that faith was based on authority, i.e., on the personal authority of the proposer, the credibility of the one who told you about the Good News. Augustine observed that if it were not for the church, he would not believe. He believed on its authority because in its life and words it conveyed an essential personal authority. So when he, as any number of others after him including Calvin, described the church as Mother, they meant it had *that* kind of authority. Faith lives within an ongoing community, a tradition of nested consent where consent to the community's words is living by its words, by being taught by them. It is by patient attention, by actually being taught by others and by teaching others, that one even comes to understand the God that encompasses the self and in whom we live and move and have our being.

CHAPTER VII

Conscience, Faith, and the Knowledge of God

1. SOULS AND LIFE IN THE GOOD

If God dwells in us, and if faith is a radical *disponibilité* to let God and others enter our lives, and if those phrases are not simply hyperbole for the shared ideals of otherwise separate minds and wills, then we would seem to be souls, filled with responsibilities and fulfilled in virtues, natural and theological. We are not *just* selves. But what does it mean to be a soul anymore? Is a soul an object, a monad that generates and guarantees our individuality? Or might having a soul actually mean experiencing the world in a certain way, say, in the light of a good? And what is its relation to that good: is it inescapably heteronomous? Is talk about soul a matter of seeing something about persons, or is it a way of being a person?

What, then, is it to be a soul? Newman in one of his earliest sermons, "The Immortality of the Soul," raises the question in a way that even now seems strikingly clear and contemporary. From our birth, he notes, we are apparently dependent on the things around us. Our lives are built up by acquiring relations to things. That, of course, in the end makes us largely the sum of those relations. As Augustine had put it, we come to think of ourselves according to the image of the "outer man." "We look off from the self to the things around us, and forget ourselves in them" (PP I.2). But, Newman claims, "to understand that we have souls, is to feel our separation from things visible, our independence of them, our distinct existence in ourselves, our individuality, our power of acting for ourselves in this

215

THE ACT OF FAITH

way or that way, our *accountableness* for what we do" (PP I.2; emphasis added). In time we begin to recognize that we are not just the sum of our relations. We come to recognize their "unprofitableness and feebleness"; they do not fully satisfy us and even disappoint us. "We still crave for something, we do not well know what; but we are sure it is something which the world has not given us." We have some sense of a far greater good. Should we take this to heart, he claims, we eventually begin "to perceive that there are but two beings in the whole universe, our own soul, and the God who made it" (PP I.2). To be a soul is to have first a sense of our own existence, "next of the presence of the great God in us, and over us, as our Governor and Judge, who dwells in us by our conscience, which is His representative" (PP I.2).

Newman's argument bears directly on modern senses of the self. Either we become the mere sum of our relations, or the sole image of any deeper, hidden self to which we can point is one that is constituted by the sum of its phenomenal properties, all of which are accidental, which for the most part comes down to the same thing as the first option.[1] The narcissism of having to check ourselves in mirrors and photos to make sure we have selves and to see what they are is a necessity, if not an obsession. To have a soul, on the other hand, is to have an essential relation to God. We are not, as selves or souls, accidentally related to God, an external object; God is what makes us what we are. So our selves are in God; to recognize that we have a soul, that we are souls, is to recognize that "our lives are hid with Christ in God" (Col. 3:3).

To leave matters at this, however, might be simply to revisit worn out metaphysical platitudes about "inner selves." That is not Newman's point; his own constant insistence on "reality" in religion is as suspicious of that kind of metaphysics as Locke and Hume were. Rather, what makes us souls, what gives us a sense of being essentially related to God as Governor and Judge, is that we are accountable, that we have consciences. So, for Newman, to be in God is to act as one who is responsible; it is to have obligations *before* we have relations. God's impress on the soul is a sense of

---

1. This, of course, is the Lockean self, which is identified with its phenomenal properties, and which leads into the interminable, truly weird discussions in contemporary philosophy of mind of mad scientists transplanting brains, or even half brains, into other bodies. Who then would be the resulting person? The Parfitean conclusion that there is no soul, that we are only phenomenal properties, is then not a difficult one to reach.

moral obligation. Having a soul for Newman is to experience life as a moral self. To "participate" in God is to see and to act as a moral person; to act on conscience is to live out that essential relation in time. What, however, does it mean to talk about the soul in terms of a "moral self," whose identity is constituted by its obligations to others, fulfilled in attention and *consentement*?

It is in the first place to suggest that while reciprocity in personal meeting (as, e.g., in Buber) may well be the glory of personal life, that such reciprocity comes about *because* of one's care for another. One goes out to the other, and is established, not first in spiritual friendship but often before there is any reciprocity at all. The soul finds its home in its consciousness of the other and its concern for the other's good. It is because of that care that the distance between persons is overcome. The overcoming of the distance is not first and foremost a matter of reciprocity; it is, as Levinas suggested, often a problem of *height,* of caring, for example, for the hungry and naked as hungry and naked when one is not so circumstanced himself.[2] The soul exists in its obligations *before* reciprocity. Weil put it: "A man left alone in the universe would have no rights whatever, but he would have obligations."[3]

There are two points I want to argue to clarify this priority of obligations as lying at the heart of what it means to be a soul: (1) that the moral relation of the self to the other is not in the first place reciprocal but a prior stance to the other; (2) that, nevertheless, an other plays an indispensable role in this stance. I shall do so by looking at the parable of the Good Samaritan.

---

2. Cf. his "Martin Buber and the Theory of Knowledge," in *The Levinas Reader,* ed. S. Hand (Oxford: Blackwell, 1989), pp. 59-74. For fuller argument on Levinas and Buber see my "Loving Neighbor: Having a Soul and Being a Moral Self" *Arob@se: Journal des lettres et sciences humaines* 4, nos. 1 & 2 (2000).

3. Simone Weil, *The Need for Roots,* trans. A. Wills (London: Routledge & Kegan Paul, 1952), p. 3. More fully Weil argues: "The notion of obligations comes before that of rights which is subordinate and relative to the former. A right is not effectual by itself, but only in relation to the obligation to which it corresponds, the effective exercise of a right springing not from the individual who possesses it, but from other men who consider themselves as being under a certain obligation towards him. Recognition of an obligation makes it effectual. An obligation which goes unrecognized by anybody loses none of the full force of its existence. A right which goes unrecognized by anybody is not worth very much."

This parable is told by Jesus in response to a lawyer who, wishing to "justify himself," wants to split hairs over the sum of the law — to love God with all of your heart, mind, and soul, and to love your neighbor as yourself. The lawyer wants to debate the point about just who exactly his neighbor is, just to whom he owes moral obligation. The story Jesus tells in response to his question is startling and paradoxical: a wounded man (a Jew) lying by the side of the road is helped by the moral heroism of a stranger, and not by those who are ethnically and religiously closest to him. But not only is the moral hero a stranger, he is a Samaritan, one of the traditionally hated *enemies* of the man. So it is startling and paradoxical. But it is also obvious. It is obvious who the real neighbor of the wounded man is, and the smart-aleck lawyer knows it full well. So the neighbor is not defined by kinship of blood or creed — neither the priest nor the Levite would help — but by the Samaritan's willingness to take the responsibility of caring for him. He doesn't have to care for the wounded man; expectations are that he would not. So Jesus is pointing out, and the lawyer cannot really argue with him on this, that it is the man's care that makes him a neighbor. It is also that which commands our immediate respect and recognition.

There is no question of reciprocity here. We hear nothing of the wounded man's reaction; it plays no role in the Samaritan's action. He does not seek it and he does not stay around long enough to enter into a reciprocal relation. He purely and simply cares, and we admire him and find him the exemplar of loving neighbor precisely for this reason. More difficult to recognize is that the Samaritan does not act, or at least does not initiate his action, in *response* to a recognition of value that is apparent in the wounded man. The wounded man's worth does not cause his caring.

Weil's exegesis of the story helps make clearer just what this last point is. She suggests that the worth of the wounded Jew is not at all apparent to the Samaritan. Nor is the wounded man's worth simply hidden under a veil by his affliction. It isn't there at all, she observes. Because he is afflicted, he has ceased to count. It is small wonder that the priest and the Levite pass him by. He commands no more attention than any other lump of matter by the road. What then makes the Samaritan just, the best sort of example of a neighbor, is therefore not his responding to the inherent worth of the wounded man; he is not responding to the man's *rights*. It is his readiness to give worth where it had disappeared, and to elevate the wounded man. The Samaritan pays *attention* to him, Weil suggests, and such attention is creative. This is in a double sense: by giving of himself, by opening up a place in human life for the man once again, he creates or re-creates the worth of the other who has disappeared from lived human space, for he is powerless to command respect any longer by himself. Nothing causes him to respond; by his openness, by his consent to the existence of the wounded man, he then lets the wounded man affect him. But second, he then "creates" himself as a soul, a moral self. He is no longer simply the sum of his relations. He is the creator of the form of such relations as he has in this world. He is not moved except by his compassion, although his movement, his compassion, is a matter of consenting to be moved, of taking the wounded man to his heart.

Being a moral self, a soul with obligations, is the willingness to recognize another as human, sometimes despite the objective evidence. It is also a matter of being vulnerable in its openness to others. To give genuine love to another is frequently to put oneself in the very vulnerable position of receiving their gratitude, to let oneself in turn be the object of compassion, and to then be created by them. It is *then* that reciprocity is born, not in a world outside the concrete interplay of human language and tradition, but in it. But in this case reciprocity is the *desiradatum* of love, not its originating condition. Love brings about whatever reciprocity there is.

This, of course, does not mean that all obligations are of the higher to the lower, nor that love is indifferent to worth. Indeed, in explicit religious faith the obligation is from the lower to the higher, for we are the wounded man; for us it is a matter of giving way to be taught and led, and a matter of gratitude. Obligations within the human realm also are frequently from lower to higher as one gives gratitude and compassion to those who have given up something for one's sake, and they are also from equal to equal, as in the case of friendship. But whether from lower to higher, or vice versa, or between equals, the ensuing relation is the result of one's care for the other, the fruition of the desire for the existence of the other's good, even if it is other.

Yet, despite all this talk about vulnerability, one may well be suspicious that the specter of Kantian conscience is lurking in the background. If one is not responding to some sort of inherent worth by which the other commands our attention, there would well seem to be a temptation here to locate care in a set of self-generated formal imperatives. A genuine other would seem to disappear, and hence genuine contact and community.

There is a second reading of the story of the Good Samaritan, however,

THE ACT OF FAITH

that dispels this concern and that adds a different texture to the story as a whole. For if the story about the Samaritan underlines his self-generated care, the story about Jesus telling the story of the Samaritan to the lawyer yields another layer of interpretation. On the one hand, of course, *this* story stresses the lawyer's own responsibility. It is a story about the pricking of his conscience (and the conscience of the reader as well), both with respect to his self-serving attempt at self-justification, and with respect to his predatory behavior toward the Galilean without the law degree. On the other hand, insofar as it is a story about the pricking of conscience, a call to the lawyer to recognize his responsibility, the lawyer — and the reader — is the object of compassion. To become, then, a moral self, to generate compassion and care, one has to be willing to be the object of compassion; one has to be an other to the good to which one is called. To be a moral self and to exercise care, one has to see this good as incumbent upon oneself, and has to take it to heart as one's own.

This then brings us closer to the heart of Newman's point that we begin "to perceive that there are but two things in the whole universe, our own soul, and the God who made it," and that the sense of the presence of the God in us and over us is "as our Governor and Judge, who dwells in us by our conscience, which is His representative." To have a sense of the self as a soul is, for Newman, to have a sense of our accountableness. But it is not to have a sense of aloneness, or of oppressive heteronomy. For it is precisely in the accountableness that exists in the movement of conscience that we feel a sense of an other, who while "over us" is also within us, and who calls us to be a soul, to care and to have compassion. Thus at its very heart, a soul's care and compassion are a matter of openness and vulnerability — a willingness to open itself, to desire the good that it does not possess, and to be taken into the life of an other and to take another into its life.

Newman says that, at the bottom of it all, we are accountable to a Governor and Judge who makes us what we are. Yet any lively sense of the person of *that* Other is not where we begin. It is rather in small acts of conscience exercised in the social world, in beholding the faces of our neighbors, that conscience and moral selfhood are developed. It is only through acts of accountability, and not through mere theory, that we ever come to that deep personal openness to the most intimate of all our relations. It is through being vulnerable that our deepest vulnerability is ever exposed. And for this to happen we often need to be reminded and taught by others around us, as Jesus teaches the lawyer. The lawyer is the real wounded man needing care. Our care and accountableness, even if they are inescapably ours, need a human community of care and concern in which to arise, and the call of conscience first arises there.

To talk this way about the soul and "the moral self" is to move in the sphere of religion, for the self's very being stands under a perfect good that is not its own possession. But that good does not weigh us down, for the soul is linked to that good, not by an external but by an internal relation. For the good that obligates us is not a good that we know independently, imposed on us from the outside; it is a good that makes itself felt in the obligation itself as we seek to understand others and the world around us. One is not related or obligated to God as one is to other beings. God, the good, is the good we participate in and which lies at the heart of whatever intentions we have toward the world. Our obligations and our acts are the response we make as persons to being addressed personally, the living out of ourselves in the light of the good we understand. This is a personal and concrete good that obligates us, not an abstract one, nor an urge to metaphysics.

We come alive in that relation. Nevertheless, we also feel a distance from that which makes us alive. Wittgenstein remarked: "People are religious to the extent that they believe themselves to be not so much *imperfect*, as *ill*. Any man who is halfway decent will think himself extremely imperfect, but a religious man thinks himself *wretched*."[4] To see oneself as imperfect is to see one's acts as flawed, perhaps in execution or design, or both, or perhaps to regret a missed opportunity. It is to *possess*, nevertheless, the standard of judgment and health; one has just made a *mistake* in applying it. To see oneself as ill, however, is to see oneself as crooked, to feel out of joint with what one knows one ought to be, to not will the good that one knows is right, and to wonder — and to care deeply — about that. To see oneself as *ill* is not moral breast-beating; moral breast-beating implies that one is intact. Rather, it is to feel the lack of symmetry of one's acts — or orientation to the world — with a good that can be dismissed only at the peril of losing all sense of integrity and coherence. It is thus precisely because one believes that there is such a good and because one is committed it, indeed loves it and identifies with it, that one feels so deeply that lack of symmetry. Or, better put, this is what it even means to believe that there is such a good.

---

4. Ludwig Wittgenstein, *Culture and Value*, trans. and ed. Peter Winch (Chicago: University of Chicago Press, 1980), p. 45e.

THE ACT OF FAITH

We come close now to the very nature of religion. Once one begins to talk in such ways about human beings that one uses phrases such as "enduring obligations" of the human subject, or of humans to whom we have obligations phrases such as "inviolable," or that "humans are always to be treated as ends and never as means," or that they have "infinite worth," some sort of appeal to religion seems nearly inevitable. But why? Not because of a metaphysical urge to hypostatize the sense of value we feel belongs to human beings and to put the self in an inviolable distant realm, or to give permanence and immortality to our otherwise tragically ephemeral human projects. Religion is not a matter of taking the wood of our very ordinary concepts which we use in very ordinary ways and then taking the remainder, carving an idol out of it to represent the unseen, and worshiping it. It is not a matter of representing, for example, the worth of human beings in such a way that it logically creates and demands obligations. That is an attempt to derive the first person perspective from the third, the participant's view from the spectator's. It is a sense that in the face of another the obligation to her is unconditional, that it is mine, that I am claimed by it, that I ought to pay attention to her. Here Kant appears to have had a genuine insight into the relation between religion and morality.

If, however, Kant did have such an insight, he also tended to reverse the relation between the moral self and religion. God is not the guarantor of the self's moral autonomy; God's relation to the soul — God's breathing of life into mortal clay — is experienced as a moral relation that makes itself felt, and that is lived out in the obligations we have to the world around us. The "cosmological relation" is not, *simpliciter,* between us and an external cause; we exist only in the relation. We are human only insofar and to the degree that our agency is the life of that absolutely prior relation, to the degree that God's goodness is impressed upon us as agents. The issue is that, and I hearken back to Newman's rather traditional point, our relations, our meetings, always come out of the primary relation to God. And for us as souls, as human beings, that is manifest in our concern for others, and acted out through the history and media of that relation with God. We are not necessarily conscious of that relation; Newman thought that only a fully formed conscience could find the face of that good, although we often get anxious and invent one. But conscious or not, the relation exists in our activity and is discovered through it. It is not something we step outside of our own skins to examine and affirm.

2. THINKING WITH ASSENT: THE "INNER" ACT OF FAITH

2.1. Conscience

2.1.1. The Fixed Will

How then does the idea of a "moral self" that is a soul affect how we understand faith? Initially, it gives a way of understanding what the participant's standpoint is. Faith is not chosen, willed, and judged from a critical spectator's standpoint; it is, rather, thinking and willing and doing from a participant's standpoint. The idea of a soul yields a way to see oneself as responsible and obliged, to see obligations as inextricably linked to even being a self. It also gives a sense to faith as participation in the life of God; to act on a good that is at the heart of our identity, that is not our own creation, is to act within God's own life and to have God act in our own. To judge good and evil absolutely is reflexive. It is not simply to make a judgment *about* the nature of the good; it is to make a good judgment, to be of good judgment. Reflection on and consciousness of that judgment is, of course, possible. But that is posterior. Faith is life lived within a perspective and standard of judgment to which we assent. What I believe about the good *is* my moral perspective; it is where I stand.

Newman argues that to have a soul is to have a sense of our own existence and of the presence of God in us and over us as a Governor and Judge, who "dwells in us by our conscience." Although an underused concept, "conscience" is particularly helpful for explicating just what it might mean to think about faith as participation, and can move us to more traditional definitions of faith such as "thinking with assent."

Iris Murdoch's story of the refined woman who pays attention to her daughter-in-law, and changes her opinion about her, is an apt illustration of how conscience works. The mother-in-law finds that the girl is good-hearted, but certainly "lacking in dignity and refinement as well as being inclined to being pert and familiar, insufficiently ceremonious, brusque, sometimes positively rude, always tiresomely juvenile."[5] She is inclined to picture her with resentment, imprisoned by the cliché "my poor son has married a silly vulgar girl." Yet, the mother-in-law is an intelligent and well-intentioned person, capable of self-criticism, and so pays just atten-

---

5. Iris Murdoch, *The Sovereignty of Good* (New York: Schocken Books, 1971), p. 17.

THE ACT OF FAITH

tion to her, until her vision alters; in the end she finds her "not vulgar but refreshingly simple, not undignified but spontaneous, not noisy but gay, not tiresomely juvenile but delightfully youthful, and so on."[6] Murdoch points out that the mother-in-law might be moved by any number of motives: a sense of justice, love for her son, attempted love for the girl. She may even be moved by a fear of thinking of her son as unfortunate, which is perhaps less worthy. But of the positive motives we might imagine all bear a common feature: each involves a personal commitment and value. Thus she reasons about the girl from within those personal "value" commitments. And the degree to which her reconsideration is correct, to which she sees the girl better than she had before, is the degree to which those personal commitments led her to that judgment. Her sense of obligation leads to her vision. That is conscience: a thinking within the moral participant's view.

There is a similar example from Trollope's *Framley Parsonage* that may focus this even more clearly. The young Lord Lufton wishes to marry Lucy Robarts, the parson's sister, but finds himself opposed by his mother, Lady Lufton. Lady Lufton is not at all unaware of Lucy's many apparent virtues; indeed, she herself knows that it is possible for her to love Lucy. Yet in considering her as a wife for her son who will be a man of significance, she finds Lucy unsuited to become the next Lady Lufton because she is "insignificant." But after a row with her son over this issue, she returns to her room to think.

> We may say that as Lady Lufton sat that morning in her own room for two hours without employment, the star of Lucy Robarts was gradually rising in the firmament. After all, love was the food chiefly necessary for the nourishment of Lady Lufton — the only food absolutely necessary. She was not aware of this herself, nor probably would those who knew her best have so spoken of her. They would have declared that family pride was her daily pabulum, and she herself would have said so, too, calling it, however, by some less offensive name. Her son's honour, and the honour of her house! — of those she would have spoken as the things dearest to her in this world. And this was partly true, for had her son been dishonoured, she would have sunk with sorrow to the grave.

---

6. Iris Murdoch, *The Sovereignty of Good*, p. 17.

But the one thing necessary to her daily life was the power of loving those who were near to her.[7]

In time, Lady Lufton's love for her son overcomes her resistance, and Lucy's star indeed rises to its full height. How has this come about? Lady Lufton's will, her love, is fixed on a good, her son and his happiness — not the honor of her house or her own narrow happiness — and with it so fixed she then thinks. She thinks *from* this fixed point, not to it. That is, in the first instance, the nature of conscience. It is not an infallible inner voice; it is a sense of a good that we care about that guides and focuses our thinking. It does so at least by restraining our other impulses. But it also causes us to regard others and the world in a certain light, a light that lets us see others differently. It does not make up the evidence, but because of its commitment to the good it can open up things.

2.1.2. Newman on Conscience

Newman's meditations on the nature of conscience are particularly instructive at this point. Not only does Newman give explicit discussion to the role of conscience in the formation and life of faith, highlighting in important ways matters that are often crucial, but implicit, in earlier writers; he also, as we have already noted, does so in consciously attempting to give a "grammar of assent" that rejects the view of distanced, critical rationality. "Conscience" is a vital and central concept in Newman's philosophy of religion and crucial to his apologetic. It provides the material for the illative sense, and as such is the basis of the real (i.e., personal) assent that makes Christian faith intellectually defensible and attractive. How the illative sense works on the conscience need not directly concern us here. What is pertinent to our purposes is to give some sense of how conscience itself actually operates, for in Newman it is the prime example of how religious and moral thinking is a matter of a personal participation.

Initially we may be struck by the very Victorian nature of Newman's view of conscience. It is a "personal guide," and is "carried about by every individual in his own breast, and requiring nothing besides itself, it is thus adapted for the communication to each separately of that knowledge

---

7. Anthony Trollope, *Framley Parsonage* (New York: Harcourt Brace & World, 1962), pp. 420-21.

THE ACT OF FAITH

which is most momentous to him individually . . ." (GA, 389, 390). Thus it appears as a sort of infallible inner voice that constantly gives us direction. As such, it would also appear to be easily explained away, particularly because of its varying cultural differences, as something like Freud's "superego," the cultural moral strictures of the empirical self.[8] Newman's view is not so easily dismissed. He does not view conscience as innate or naturalistic, an infallible inner voice implanted in all rational beings, and a *private* guide. Although a part of "natural religion," conscience clearly arises for Newman out of revelation, a being spoken to.[9] It is the consciousness of a personal demand. But it is not an external voice, like Socrates' daimon; it is operative in one's very judging. The *voice* of conscience is our voice; the absolute obligation it lays on us is a Word behind the words. But we know that Word only through the words. So if conscience is a personal guide, it is personal in that it is inextricable from the act of moral judgment itself: "I use it because I must use myself; I am as little able to think by any mind but my own as to breathe with another man's lungs. Conscience is nearer to me than any other means of knowledge" (GA, 389).

Conscience, in the first instance, for Newman is not personal because of its object. Rather, "conscience implies a relation between the soul and a something exterior, and that, moreover, superior to itself; a relation to an excellence which it does not possess, and to a tribunal over which it has no power" (US II.7). It may well begin a quest for a person as that "something exterior," which Newman thinks Christianity gives and paganism invents. However, at this point its personal quality lies largely in the sense that it implies a moral obligation of the person of conscience. It is a personal obligation, a matter of will, to follow conscience. The power and distinctness of conscience in giving direction is initially quite formless; it only gains content and actual discernment in being obeyed: "the more our moral nature is improved, the greater the inward power of improvement it seems to possess, a view is laid open to us both of the capabilities and prospects of man, and the awful importance of that work which the law of his being lays on him" (US II.8). As such, *when improved*, it can give a system of morals. But, Newman cautions, it is not a system of morals; it is a religious

---

8. Cf., e.g., Anthony Kenny, "Newman as a Philosopher of Religion," in *Newman: A Man for Our Time*, ed. David Brown (Harrisburg, Pa.: Morehouse Publishing, 1990), pp. 119-20.

9. US II.4-6.

phenomenon "which is implied in the remorse and vague apprehension of evil which the transgression of Conscience occasions" (US II.8). It is a sense of perfection that haunts and claims us.

Conscience works from certitude. One should not, however, confuse certitude with analytic certainty.[10] Newman, thinking that certitude is a quality of mind, and not of propositions, rejects an analytic model of certitude, i.e., that only analytic propositions are certain and can generate certitude, compelling it, as it were. Rather, for him, informal reasoning, especially in the illative sense, can also give it. However, it is not through the nature of the reasoning *per se* that certitude is gained. It also depends upon assent, an act of the will. But how can this be, since Newman clearly claims that the will cannot force or create certainty? The way out of this apparent dilemma is to recognize that in Newman there are two senses of willing, which can be explained by a moral analogy. There is a distinction between "seeing X as what I ought to do" and "choosing to do it." While the latter is clearly an act of the will, Newman thinks that *accepting* the ought, of experiencing it as an ought, is also an act of the will. There is then a subsequent willing to do it. While the will does not create the force of the moral argument, to experience it as forceful — which simply comes in the judgment of the conclusion, especially when it is not analytic — is an act of assent. Similarly, in the case of intellectual judgment, "choice does not come in to bring about an acceptance (i.e., experience) after the judgement; the judgement *is* the intellectual acceptance which can be followed by practical affirmation or negation of that acceptance."[11]

We talk about the will in two ways. One is that it is the agent of choosing, a usage that since Hume has tended to overshadow all others. But it is also the agent of desiring, the active reaching out of the mind for what it thinks. It is in this sense that one does not *choose* the judgment; one can, however, desire it and see it as incumbent on oneself. So the will does not create the certainty of a line of reasoning; but certitude as an act of staking oneself on the conclusion is dependent on the will. This is especially the case in moral judgments. The moral judgments of conscience then are personal in that they are in themselves *moral judgments*, not just judgments *about* moral matters. To make them is to be committed to them, to make

---

10. Cf. M. Jamie Ferreira, *Doubt and Religious Commitment: The Role of the Will in Newman's Thought* (Oxford: Oxford University Press, 1980).
11. Ferreira, *Doubt and Religious Commitment*, p. 57.

THE ACT OF FAITH

them incumbent on oneself. To fail to act subsequently is a personal failure, and ultimately, a betrayal of that superior good by which one feels called.

Conscience, while rooted in an idea of perfection that imposes permanent and enduring obligations on us, however, operates and exists in particular judgments. It has, as Newman asserts, both "a critical and a judicial office" (GA, 106). Judicially, it is a testimony that there is a right and wrong, and its "sanction to that testimony [is] conveyed in the feelings which attend on right and wrong conduct" (GA, 106).[12] The judicial office lies at the heart of being a moral self. The critical office is conscience' actual judgments in matters of right and wrong. It is here that conscience as a sort of moral vision does give us access to others.

In a discussion of Coleridge's *Rime of the Ancient Mariner* J. R. Jones gives an example of how these two offices of conscience might be construed. The poem is the story of a sailor who one day kills an albatross for the mere fun of it. And it was mere fun, since one can neither eat albatross nor use it for any other purpose. That bird merely decorates the sky and sea. As a result of that wanton act, the ship on which the mariner is sailing is becalmed and the other sailors justly blame him for the misfortune. For a punishment they force him to wear the dead albatross around his neck. But at first this is no lesson at all. The mariner had the sort of conscience that can be guilty; he knew the difference between right and wrong, and perhaps was guilty over what was surely a malicious act. That is the role of the judicial office. In killing the albatross he has failed to act in accord with the judicial office of conscience; he has failed to make the actual judgment that the judicial office prompts him to, and his conscience is uneasy. But in the course of the poem the sailor looks over the side of the ship. He sees

> . . . the slimy things which infested the water round the ship and he began to be *aware* of them. . . . Something then welled up within him to which he could only give the name of "love" and he *suddenly felt grateful*

---

12. Cf. PP I.17: "As . . . progress in sin continues, our disobedience becomes its own punishment. In proportion as we lean to our own understanding, we are driven to do so for want of a better guide. Our first true guide, the light of innocence, is gradually withdrawn from us; and nothing is left for us but to 'grope and stumble in the desolate places,' by the dim, uncertain light of reason. Thus we are taken in by our own craftiness. This is what is sometimes called *judicial blindness;* such as Pharaoh's, who, from resisting God's will, at length did not know the difference between light and darkness."

228

for them. Not because they were of any use to him, because they were not; and not necessarily because he *liked* them: he found them strangely beautiful but possibly not attractive. The experience was something quite different from this — it was gratitude for their existence.[13]

Jones points out that the sailor's awareness is a recognition both of the particularity of these creatures, their independence from him, and of their vulnerability. This awareness is *going out* to their existence. "To go out to a thing in this way when it is a living thing, and particularly when it is a living person, is fundamentally to have pity for it.... For the insight into its existence is at the same time an insight into its offering, its defencelessness, its profound vulnerability."[14] (Newman claims that faith, as a judgment about facts in matters of conduct, is "formed, not so much from the impression legitimately made upon the mind by those facts, as from the reaching forward of the mind itself towards them..." [US XII.5].) This concern for the particularity and vulnerability of others, Jones claims, is at the heart of the moral vision. Conscience is an ability to see what cannot be seen apart from love and concern, or apart from an awareness of the good. It cannot be put in abstract categories, for "the moral position is such that distinctions between good and evil, suffering and happiness... do not affect the requirement that [things that are independent of us] are to be loved."[15] To put this in Newman's terms, the mariner's critical judgment of the worth of these creatures is a fitting and full response to the absolute requirement of the "judicial office" of conscience.

This illustrates how the conscience operates. The epiphanic nature of the illustration ought not to mislead us, however, into thinking that conscience is not also and even largely a developed capacity, and a mark of character, as *phronesis* is in Aristotle. It is developed — or destroyed — by practice and habit as the certitude of one moral judgment becomes the antecedent consideration of future judgments. It is by acting on specific certitudes that one's experience is expanded and can lead to further moral certitudes. The ability to make particular good moral judgments then depends upon having made them before. The ability to care for others in this sense is a function of one's character, and to see them as needing care often

13. Quoted in Diogenes Allen, *Finding Our Father* (Atlanta: John Knox Press, 1974), p. 40.
14. Allen, *Finding Our Father,* p. 41.
15. Allen, *Finding Our Father,* p. 40.

depends upon what we have made of ourselves. In moral matters, then, knowledge of the good is a matter of being good. According to Augustine: "The one who knows righteousness perfectly and loves it perfectly is the righteous man."

While conscience exists as a judgment of the moral self, and is often directed to others, it is not an isolated act, or one without human context. It is not a judgment whose certitude depends upon its own sheer luminosity. It is not something that is just going on in our heads. Nor is it first and foremost a matter of the individual choosing himself; it is only in entering into actual relations that conscience is formed. Diogenes Allen gives a sort of negative example of this. Drawing upon Iris Murdoch's novel, *The Unicorn*, he cites the example of Effingham Cooper, a colossal egotist, who in the face of death has an experience of what he calls "perfect love," the sort of experience that the ancient mariner had. He begins in the light of this experience to *see* people for the first time. But, Allen observes, he is unable to put his newfound point of view into practice, and in rather short order returns to his egotistical ways.[16] Because his body and passions cannot follow, his heart fails in the end. Weil suggests: "Human nature is so arranged that a desire of the soul has no reality within the soul until it has passed through the body by means of actions, movements and attitudes. Until then it is like a ghost. It has no effect on the soul" (SW, 56). The development of conscience is our apprenticeship to the Good that stands over and within us, so that God's art might fully enter our bodies and souls.

Conscience is developed and practiced within an intersubjective context, within specific human communities; it has its meaning within them. This is certainly the case insofar as the judgments of conscience are particular themselves, and insofar as whatever moral certitudes that one reaches and that serve as the antecedent considerations of future judgments are similarly concrete. These judgments are reached in the push and pull of specific human interactions, which is why morals can, in Newman's eyes, never be a strictly abstract science, or a matter of mere information. Nor, for Newman, are they reached, confirmed, or rejected as acts of an isolated thinker, moral or otherwise. Often they are accepted because we trust and accept people who offer their judgments for us to use as a guide in particular and general situations. Many of our antecedent principles therefore are

---

16. Allen, *Finding Our Father*, ch. 2.

ones that we accept on testimony, that is, from other agents of conscience, say, our parents, or our teachers and other moral and spiritual guides, or our church, or the Bible itself. The very founding of our initial moral judgments comes in moral interaction. (And thus conscience, and faith as well, ought always to have the air of a gift.) It is then by actually reasoning with these principles that they become the basis of further judgments. While Newman is no pragmatist, it is because we can reason with such principles, and can come to understand ourselves and others morally with them, that they have their truth. They have their illuminating power, not because we establish them independently by reason, but because we do reason with them and render true judgments with them. Their very use is within that human context and needs to be understood within it. For example, Newman notes, "texts have their illuminating power, from the atmosphere of habit, opinion, usage, tradition, through which we see them" (US X.36). The truth of religious texts and doctrines needs to be assessed and used within their proper human context. But, conversely, insofar as they do play a vital role within moral judgments, conscience and its judgments need to be situated squarely within the context of the community. And, of course, human communities then need to be seen not as neutral spaces, but as fundamentally and inescapably moral ones. They are not simply the recipients of good deeds; they culture and form the souls within them as those souls act and judge within them.

2.2. Thinking with Assent: Faith as a Spiritual Concept

Augustine defines faith as "thinking with assent" (De Praed. II.5). In describing faith this way he argues that faith is not of ourselves; we do not create the religious truths to which we adhere in Christianity, but assent to them. Even our assent, he contends, "our sufficiency, by which we begin to believe, is of God" (De Praed. II.5). The grammar of conscience gives sense to what it means "to think with assent." Faith is not thinking in order to assent, or, more precisely, thinking and then assenting, but thinking in the light of a good we hold dear to ourselves, indeed at the very heart of our souls, as conscience is seeing, acting, and judging from a moral position that we hold. For Newman, the similarity is more than striking; conscience is the key to understanding the "grammar of assent"; any dictate of conscience, and judgment made thereon, is implicitly, if not explicitly, reli-

THE ACT OF FAITH

gious. "Faith is the *reasoning* of a religious mind, or of what Scripture calls a right and renewed heart . . . " (US XI.1).

This sheds light on how religious doctrines and concepts are held as "personal," and what makes them religious, and spiritual, and not simply propositions of neutral fact. They are held and *used* within religious communities and gain their sense in that intersubjective context, both immediate and historical. They are held as true. But as Wittgenstein suggests, they are not believed in the same way that historical claims are believed by historians; believing them means making a quite different place in one's life for them. They are not simply assertions; they are used. Assenting to them is to think with them, and in their light to see the promised light. To think with assent, of course, is not simply to pursue a way of life, it is to believe in God; nevertheless, faith and its assertions are embodied in a way of life, and inextricable from it. The point of view is understood in what is seen and how it is seen.[17]

Religious concepts, even ones such as "God," are not *explanations* as Hume took them. Their force and their use is not, say, to explain where the world came from, nor do they arise from wondering about that question, nor is their primary sense in the context of such questioning. They are not things we balance in our lives as if we were the fulcrum, that which is outside the system of weights. Rather they function as active principles of thought by which the mind goes out to grasp and participate in the world it thinks. They function to put the *thinker* in the balance where God's good is the fulcrum. While I shall want to say something below about how

---

17. In a striking set of epigrams, Weil puts the point forcefully: "The soul's attitude towards God is not a thing that can be verified, even by the soul itself, because God is elsewhere, in heaven, in secret. If one thinks to have verified it, there is really some earthly thing masquerading under the label of God. One can only verify whether the behavior of the soul bears the mark of the experience of God. In the same way, a bride's friends do not go into the nuptial chamber; but when she is seen to be pregnant they know that she has lost her virginity. There is no fire in a cooked dish, but one knows that it has been on the fire. . . . In the same way, the proof that a child can do division is not that he can recite the rule, but that he can divide. If he recites the rule, I don't know if he understands it. If I give him some difficult sums in division and he gets the answers right, I have no need to make him explain the rule. . . . A painter does not draw the spot where he is standing. But in looking at his picture I can deduce his position by relation to things drawn. . . . The value of a religious or, more generally, a spiritual way of life is appreciated by the amount of illumination thrown upon the things of this world. Earthly things are the criterion of spiritual things" (SW 108-9).

Christian faith is faith in *God, extra nos,* what needs to occupy our attention at this point is what taking religious concepts as assented to, and as through which we think, says about the inner *act* of faith itself.

When Augustine describes faith as "thinking with assent" he does so in the course of arguing against the Pelagians, who believe that faith is of human origin and that grace is given according to the merits we earn for ourselves. By thinking and doing the right things, the Pelagians thought, God will give strength to the will as a reward and to assist them in thinking and doing those things. Augustine wants to maintain, on the contrary, that even the act of faith itself is a matter of grace, not only in assent, or in something added to the deed, but in the thinking of faith. He bases his argument on 2 Corinthians 3:5 — "Not that we are sufficient to think anything of ourselves, but our sufficiency is of God" in his version. But in doing so his argument does not rest on the fact that the object of what is thought is divinely given because revealed, or that thinking in faith is therefore a matter of grace because of its object (although he does believe this, too). Nor does he appeal to an argument that would suggest that in thinking and assenting we have to have help in order to assent; he does not appeal to external forces as being responsible for and as explaining what we do. Rather, he simply says: ". . . everybody who believes, thinks — both thinks in believing, and believes in thinking" (De Praed. II.5). Augustine regards faith as a holistic act, unlike the Pelagians who assume that there are gaps between thinking and assenting, and between doing and reward. The Pelagians are talking about a will to believe, Augustine about faith's willing. But if it is a holistic act, as Augustine argues it is, and if it is divine (the Pelagians would guardedly admit this in that God gives *some* help), then it is divine throughout — which the Pelagians deny. For Augustine faith itself is religious, and does not need anything additional to become so. It does not *become* divine. If faith is divine, it is so not because it can appeal to an external divine sanction, but because the act of faith itself, because thinking with assent, is itself spiritual. It lives and dwells within the divine, and is a way of thinking within it. It therefore needs to be understood within those terms, and within the spiritual practices appropriate to it.

Christian faith thus lives and moves within a space that is given by the Incarnation and Resurrection. It lives within this space, and cannot create it or enter it without God's activity — either in the giving of that space or in God's own concurrence in the soul's assent. That is to state the "objective" situation. Without God's gift there is no Christian faith. Nevertheless, viewed subjectively, even if that is a backward glance, faith is not entirely a leap to understanding from utter non-understanding, but something more like a movement from a limited moral understanding to a full one under the pressure of the "judicial office" of conscience, the pressure to judge good perfectly. It is a judgment made upon the basis of a prior "faith" or a positive judgment made in response to whatever new is offered. This was Newman's considered view on the arising of Christianity itself. The Faith may be something new in the world, although the world was created for it and it is true from the beginning. But it still did not appear unheralded in the world; its appeal lay in that, for those who believed, it was the moral and spiritual conclusion to what had been announced before in Judaism; Christ came to fulfill the law and prophets and not abolish them. Its appeal was that it was spiritually fulfilling — a way of life, a way of looking at things and people; it was as spiritual that it was believed. There may be only a single example of unheralded faith in the Bible itself: Abraham's initial decision to respond to God's call (Genesis 12); even his great faith displayed in his willingness to sacrifice Isaac has a history of faithful judgments behind it. This, of course, does not mean that specific Christian faith is an obvious step; Newman did not think it was. The virtue of faith, its excellence, lies in the very courage and willingness to act and believe on conscience and a few certitudes, just as the excellence of a just person lies in seeing the full extent of justice, even when there is not fulsome evidence for it.[18] It has reasons that are internal, and the reasons for assenting to the good that the gospel offers are the spiritual ones that the gospel fulfills. The hope of faith and the certitude of truth that comes from practice are what lead the mind toward fulfillment.[19] But, of course, this is also God's own gracious activity within the soul.

---

18. This is to leave aside the question of sudden conversions. But even in their case there is no need to appeal to an outside force to justify them. They can possibly be described as changes of religion or sudden recognition of the demands of conscience, inchoate as they may have been in one's life before, or even ignored. Even in such experiences as Allen describes above — the case of the ancient mariner and Effingham Cooper in *The Unicorn* — what makes them conversion to faith is that the experience doesn't just happen to them; it rests in the judgment. Their judgment about the worth of other things, as Allen says, is the moral point of view.

19. Such would seem to lead to any number of possible judgments, including superstitious ones. That may well be the case. Newman, however, in a fascinating sermon titled

Newman's view about the arising of Christianity particularly underlines the need of faith to grasp the truth and the form of the whole in a particular historical instance. Thematized, it provides an important contrast with the view of religious faith given by Hume. In the *Dialogues Concerning Natural Religion,* Philo systematically takes apart the reasonable basis of Cleanthes' deism. The evidence that Cleanthes thinks is so solid is ambiguous at best. Philo also offers a devastating critique of Demea's orthodoxy by suggesting that it is conceptually empty. But in the conclusion, he makes a surprising concession to Cleanthes after Demea has slinked out. He says that everybody ought to be struck by the design of the universe; only careless and thoughtless people are not. Nevertheless, he adds, this motivation to think of God acts on us only by fits and starts; it is not habitual to the mind. To try to make it so encourages a habit of dissimulation and falsehood, and over time, hypocrisy. Therefore, he suggests, we ought to take the experience simply for what it is, and return to more quotidian reasonings over which we have more control, and which, he thinks, are more honest and less dangerous. (This is the religious version of safe sex.) Why Philo/Hume wants to entertain the wonder of the design of the world need not concern us here. What is of interest is his assumption that it is the basis of religious motivation, that it nearly alone carries us along in religion, and that religion is the simply systematic development of this sense of wonder, an attempt to capture and rationalize it. But if this is so, then Christian faith would not only be a system of beliefs to explain this wonder, its habits, so dependent on moral and personal motivations, would seem to be incommensurate and discontinuous with its originating motivations.

Neither Judaism nor Christianity began in positing God as the explanation for the order of the world. Rather, the ancient Hebrews worshiped the Lord because yesterday they were in Egypt; today they are free. Both Judaism and Christianity live and breathe, and find their beginning and end, in God's promises and in dealing with God in a particular history. Faith is not a metaphysical compliment to that history, imported from somewhere

---

"Love the Safeguard Against Superstition" (US XII) suggests that since faith is an intellectual act, although on little evidence, but "done in a certain moral disposition," e.g., reasoning upon holy presumptions, that it does not easily admit worshiping evil, idolatry, and superstition. But it resists superstition out of its moral character, not the fullness of external evidence.

THE ACT OF FAITH

else with a different sort of sensibility. Its sensibility and motivation are throughout enmeshed with that history: they are matters of gratitude and obedience, matters of conscience reaching out to grasp the fullness of the good that lies before it. Faith's movement from premises to conclusions, as Newman suggests, should therefore be seen within the personal realm of that sort of history as well, that is, as a matter of grasping and waiting upon God's purpose. The soul's movement to faith is from faith. To say then that faith is a spiritual act throughout is to say that the nature of faith, its characteristic modes of willing, feeling, and thinking, are not incommensurate with its first subjective movements. But to say this is not to suggest that faith is built up from these movements as from a ground. Explicit faith is rather a final cause that shapes and determines the nature of movements toward it. Insofar as the end of faith is personal, moral, and spiritual, it draws and fulfills the movements of conscience. It shows us what conscience really is. Faith is not built up from conscience; conscience is suspended from faith.

Newman particularly stresses grasping the form in the historical particular. This is right, although we can now see how that thought can be thematized as a movement of conscience. The reaching out of the conscience, its movement from assent to assent, can further be thematized to highlight the holistic, spiritual nature of faith without leaving Christianity's historical specificity. I offer two other versions of this idea, one from the British theologian and philosopher, Austin Farrer, and the other taken from Weil.

2.3.1. Farrer's "Initial Faith"

Farrer is a particularly helpful case because, by virtue of a shift in his own thinking, he provides an angle of vision that illumines just what is at stake in calling the concept of faith "holistic" and "spiritual throughout." In the early 1940s Farrer had already produced a massive, impressive, and profound work, *Finite and Infinite*, that sought to explicate the evidence for a first, spiritual cause of the universe. While no positivist on matters of evidence, Farrer in that work, nevertheless, tried in the broadest sense to show that reason itself demands that we see such a cause. Yet, twenty years later, while still holding to the view that there was such evidence, Farrer claimed that simply presenting it as a demand of reason misrepresented both the sort of evidence it was, as well as the form and content of faith. Rather, he suggested at that later point, the reason in faith, as in any other form of reasoning, had to be looked at more "empirically"; it had to be understood squarely within its life's context of dealings in the world and within interaction.

In his later works, Farrer recognized from the outset that it is fairly clear that serious continued thought about God does not come about because we have wondered about the universe, then proposed "God" as a possible hypothesis among others to account for phenomena, and finally found inescapable evidence that makes us admit the hypothesis, like it or not. Rather, he argued, the story is more plausibly something like this: we hear about God, or perhaps apprehend the idea of God independently, and then entertain it. It is only after entertaining it in a sort of experimental way that we seek the evidence for it. Simply put, the intelligence, as is its role in a thoughtful life, first imagines what it would be like for there to be a God, a God that is presented to it. This imagining is already a kind of faith — "initial faith" he calls it.[20] But as the mind imagines what it would be like for there to be a God, it also comes to think of what sort of evidence would incline us to commit ourselves to the thought. But why should we continue to entertain it, much less commit ourselves wholeheartedly to it? Farrer argues here that at this point evidence is not irrelevant, but also points out that because of this "initial faith" we are in a subjective condition favorable to the reception of the evidence insofar as the evidence is revealed by our sympathy to receiving it.[21] This sympathy, though, does not replace evidence, it only inclines us to consider it. We thus continue the experiment, he thinks, because of the evidence, although it is now evidence that we have a particular interest in pursuing.

But what is the evidence? Consider what the idea of God is that it is supposed to support. God, if he is God as theists present him, is at least creator, sustainer, and perfectly good, the alpha and omega of our lives. This is important, for in experimenting with the idea of God we are not experimenting with the possible existence of an item in the world, but with an entire picture of the world. And, Farrer adds, this picture carries with it a number of built-in attitudes, just as a supposed orphan who wonders about whether he has a living mother does not wonder disinterestedly, but with the expectation that if it should turn out that he does, his entire view

---

20. Austin Farrer, *Saving Belief* (New York: Morehouse-Barlow, 1964), ch. 1.
21. Farrer, *Saving Belief,* p. 22.

of his life would change. To experiment in thinking God, then, is to experiment in thinking oneself God's creature and finding in God the very meaning and purpose of our existence and the existence of all that is. Already we see here that the thinking that goes on in faith is not, as Farrer later pointed out, really in the range of the sciences, which view the world with a necessarily limited methodological perspective or from a disinterested distance; rather, it is a surveying of the whole in its relation to the creator. It is very interested, and rightly so, for to imagine a God is to imagine being a creature. But in that case only certain sorts of evidence are even appropriate for convincing us of God's existence. One sort is that which Farrer sought to explicate in *Finite and Infinite*, namely, that the world is capable of being read as the effect of a first cause, and that it even demands such a reading.

Yet as Farrer went on to explain in his last major work, *Faith and Speculation*, that is not the only evidence; in fact, it is actually only correlative to the evidence by which believers are actually convinced. *That* evidence is far more personal and the sort that comes from living the life of faith; or, in other words, it is experimental evidence. It is the evidence of having sought for God's goodness and having found it in one's life. Farrer succinctly put it: "The Gospel offers God to me as good, not simply as fact. In embracing the good I am convinced of the fact."[22] Simply put, I am motivated by a good that I desire, which is promised to come from the life of faith; as I pursue that good I find that it is, indeed, forthcoming. The desire is spiritual; the promise is directed to the desire.

Now there are two good reasons for Farrer's embracing this position. The first is related to his notion of "initial faith." The believer in experimenting with the idea of God is dealing with a question of whether or not she should submit her will to a creator. What will motivate her to do so is less the evidence, which may be ambiguous or not easily forthcoming, than the importance of religious interest. What she then looks for to confirm that she has actually gotten a hold of anything real in faith is also going to be religious. Thus the position of *Faith and Speculation* far more closely represents how God is actually thought by theists. The second reason has to do with what Farrer by this time had clearly understood about the metaphysical defense contained in *Finite and Infinite:* it relied on a

---

22. Austin Farrer, *Faith and Speculation* (New York: New York University Press, 1964), p. 10.

metaphor of vision that allowed us to think that an idea's sheer luminosity gives us knowledge.[23] But this he later thought was a mistake. Instead, he now argued, knowledge arises only from interaction with the object of thought. There is "no thought about reality about which we can do nothing but think."[24]

Farrer's concern about interaction extends beyond the "inner" act of faith to the content of faith, insofar as he rightly understands *what* faith believes and confesses to be thoroughly interlinked with its practices. We shall need to discuss this below. At this point, however, what needs to be observed about his position is that by linking the knowledge and evidence to the actual holding of faith, again, there is no gap between knowing and assenting in the act of faith. The good that faith desires and wills is the good that it thinks.

2.3.2. Weil's "Proof by Perfection"

Within Weil's writings there are a number of references to what she calls a "proof by perfection" or an "experimental ontological proof."[25] Sketchy as her discussions of this "proof" are, they are valuable in helping to draw together the roles of the idea of perfection that both Newman and Murdoch engage in developing the idea of conscience, and in showing how that idea is thought in religious life. It can also provide a transition to the outer act of faith.

The "proof by perfection" is, Weil says, the only valid proof there is of God. Briefly stated, it runs like this: It is only by desiring something perfect that I am made any better. If what I desire is unreal, it clearly has no power to effect anything. If it is imaginary, it is effective only psychologically; it is no better than its source, the imaginer. If, however, in the course of desiring I am made better, then this something that draws me is real. Although Weil in places where she speaks of this proof does not say what counts as real effect, elsewhere she makes it very clear. Even as Aquinas took Paul's phrase, "faith working through love" as defining the form of faith, so in her own

---

23. Cf. Jeffrey Eaton, *The Logic of Theism* (Lanham, Md.: University Press of America, 1980), p. 35.

24. Farrer, *Saving Belief*, p. 22.

25. Cf. Simone Weil, *Pensées sans ordre concernant l'amour de Dieu* (Paris: Gallimard, 1962), p. 136; *Notebooks* (London: Routledge & Kegan Paul, 1956), p. 434; *First and Last Notebooks* (London: Oxford University Press, 1962), p. 342.

THE ACT OF FAITH

way does Weil. Really engaging perfection, for her, is the ability to sacrifice our personal perspective and egos for the life of others. Engaging perfection *is* paying attention. Since for her the will is a part of that ego, any such real sacrifice would not be in the will's possibilities of self-realization. If the sacrifice is made anyhow it must be made out of a source of action that is beyond our wills.

What is the point of this "proof"? If it is to suggest that there must be an outside cause to account for certain of my actions, say, altruistic ones, it would be a miserable failure. That I did them at all would surely argue that they are not non-natural and impossible except by an external agency. The point of Weil's proof is far more subtle than that, though. It is to say that the concept of perfection, of a perfect God who bears on the conscience, is not empty. To have it, to think it, is to will *ab initio,* if not always *in consequentio,* certain things and not others. It is to regard people and to act toward them in certain ways that one would not if one didn't have it. We know somebody has it if he does certain things. Again there is no gap between thinking and assenting.

This much has already been discussed and is not new ground. Where one can go deeper is in recognizing that thinking and assenting are one, not only in thinking and doing, but also in the relation one has to perfection. For to hold the thought of perfection is to hold it with a certain reverence and respect, and with a certain desire for its good. And, for Weil, to hold it with that desire is already to engage it. She provocatively puts it: "Whereas the desire for gold is not the same thing as gold, the desire for good is itself good."[26] Like possessing mathematical concepts, having a moral or spiritual concept is shown in the ability to use the concept. If one wants to discover if a child understands long division, one has him divide. In doing so, there is no need to determine whether this proves that the laws of long division exist or not; that is not the problem. Similarly if one understands what it means to care for people, one simply cares for them. But unlike mathematical concepts, moral and spiritual concepts are also held in a certain way that is essential to possessing them at all. For example, doing good to others by ceasing to occupy the center of moral gravity, especially when we do not have to cede that center, goes hand in hand with a deep respect for the idea of perfection. We do not simply employ the concept; nor do we judge it. We submit to it. The dictates of conscience in this

---

26. Weil, *First and Last Notebooks,* p. 316.

sort of instance are not advice; we feel them to be binding on us as persons. We not only seek to do the best for others, we judge our efforts and ourselves in the light of the perfection that led us on in the first place.

We *wait* upon the perfect good. Weil thought that "patient waiting" — waiting *en hypomenē* — is the New Testament definition of faith. This waiting, however, is not passivity, but in her words "non-active action," an activity of the middle voice. To have any sense of such a good then is initially less to have a specific sense of its content, or grasp on it, and more to have a sense that we do not construct it and that we cannot anticipate it, or run ahead of it, or that it is within the domain of our own wills. It is to have a sense that we are responsible to it, and that the integrity of our thinking and willing depends on it. To wait then upon that good, to desire it for itself and not for what one can make of it is an important good itself, a good that is at the heart of spirituality. But we still act on it, or through it. Thus the "desire for good is itself a good."[27] It is to this good that the good speaks.

It is this waiting that therefore ultimately provides the holistic, spiritual dimension of thinking with assent and that closes the gap between thinking and assent, for all particular acts of thought or will become acts within that primary stance to the good. How can be seen in the way Weil discusses faith. Weil, as she makes clear in numerous places, does not consider faith as an *intellectual* adherence;[28] rather, she calls it a "submission of those parts [of the soul] which have no contact with God to the one which has" (SW 114). What she means is that faith is not an isolated act. It is a consent of the whole person to God's action. Not all of what we think, feel, and do, of course, is directed toward perfection; some of it is simply directed to getting across the street. Where faith enters is when all of our life is ordered to our deep desire for the good. This is not a procedure or a method; it is narrative and dramatic. Practically, on the one hand this means that we do nothing to oppose the fulfillment of desire, either morally, or intellectually, such as by

---

27. Newman in commenting on Hebrews 11:1 — "faith is the evidence of things hoped for . . ." says: "It is the reckoning that to be, which it hopes or wishes to be; not the realizing of things proved by evidence. Its desire is its main evidence . . ." (US X.34).

28. E.g., "Last Text," in *Gateway to God*, ed. D. Raper (New York: Crossroad, 1982): "When I say 'I believe' I do not mean that I take over for myself what the Church says on these matters, affirming them as one might affirm empirical facts or geometrical theorems, but that through love, I hold on to the perfect, unseizable truth which these mysteries contain, and that I try to open my soul to it so that its light may penetrate me" (p. 62).

THE ACT OF FAITH

constructing ideologies that no longer represent but attempt to wholly embody the good. On the other hand, it means that our entire being is engaged by the object of desire and open to its call. When Weil then criticized the church for undue authoritarianism in imposing dogmas on the intellect, she did not think that faith was below the intellect. It is above it. The church had debased the function of doctrine, not elevated it.

Weil's usage of the term "faith," of course, is a form of faith as trust. But she develops the idea further by pointing out the spiritual nature of *why* we trust and how that involves our very being, namely, in order that the good in which we trust might be expanded. Or more accurately, that trust is precisely what refuses to be anything but what God makes of it; it is a life given over to God's good. She notes that the relevant article of faith is "concerned with fecundity, with the self-multiplying faculty of every desire for good" (SW 115). Faith is not only a consent of the whole person to God's action, it is a consent motivated by the desire that God's goodness might be shed abroad — in and through us and even despite us. So it is in its nature to reach from good to greater good when it is given the power to see it.

Yet, Weil adds, this is nevertheless faith because we do not know, prior to our commitment, that the Good is actually fecund and will be effective; it is only by our experience of having been made better by having chosen to live this way that we are convinced of its efficacy. There is no direct observation of God's action, for, if it is seen, it is only seen in the end result. Ironically, though, once we actually desire it, it is embodied and shed abroad not only because we as embodied agents desire it but because as embodied agents we act on it. It is only a seeming paradox then when Weil says that "faith creates the truth to which it adheres" (SW 114). To desire and wait on the good is to know something of the truth of that good, for faith *is* a good, made by the Good. It is participation in the life of God and God's participation in our lives from the very core of our souls.

3. FAITH IN GOD

3.1. The Inner Act of Faith and Its Object

There is an obvious point at which the description of the personal nature of faith when undertaken chiefly as a description of the inner nature of faith begins to strain and crack. There are limits to what can be said about faith simply by reference to our moral and personal commitments, histories, and ways of seeing things. What is lacking is the most obvious sense of "personal" in Christian faith, i.e., that faith is in *God*, who is in some sense personal. How is faith not only personal in terms of our living in faith, but interpersonal, as dealing with God as person?

Before dealing with this question head-on, however, the ground that has been cleared needs surveying. The limits of what can be said about faith by reference to our personal and moral commitments are *not* a matter of failing to provide anything like a proof for God, or to make an appeal to "God" as an external reference in order to ground the moral sense. Proofs of God within Christian theology, rather than being attempts to convince the neutral intellect of the need for faith, are best directed at articulating just what is thought and assented to, and to bring the mind responsively into congruence with what the will is fixed upon. Anselm's ontological argument in the *Proslogion* is preceded by prayer; Anselm's joy in discovering the proof is not assurance that his faith actually had an object. His joy is in recognizing, in understanding more clearly, the undeniable perfection of the God in whom he believed. Similarly, Augustine's "ideological" proof is primarily a matter of understanding his own relation to God.

Nor are the limits the obfuscation of what might be called the plain, personal model of interaction, a fancy but devious way of avoiding having to talk about God speaking and the human person responding. The model, formally and rhetorically underwritten by the drama of salvation in Scripture and as Scripture, *is* religiously and morally to the point. But that is precisely why the inner act of faith needs to be stressed. God is not just "out there," an object like others in the universe, a conversational partner like any other. God acts and speaks in our very act of existing as humans. If faith is the response to a call, as Christianity sees it to be, that response therefore needs to be seen as an act of the soul moving in the room that God has opened for it. The response is a way of life and a way of seeing ourselves and others in a certain way. Faith in God is not an explanation for this; nor is God an explanation for it. Faith in God is the response to what lies closer to us than we are to ourselves.

Where the limits *do* lie are along lines prescribed by Newman when he distinguishes *fides acquisita et humana* from *fides divina*.[29] Christian faith

---

29. Cf. Newman, *The Theological Papers of John Henry Newman on Faith and Certainty* (Oxford: Oxford University Press, 1976), p. 38.

is confessional; it believes that there is a God, *extra nos,* and it believes in response to God's having revealed himself. Where the division lies is here: It is not only possible to describe the inner act of faith, insofar as it is *fides acquisita et humana,* without this outer confession — it may not recognize what its good really is; it is also possible, insofar as faith waits, to live with the tension that comes from not recognizing the face of the one for whom faith waits. But *fides divina* on the other hand, not only confesses that there is a God, known through his revelation in Jesus Christ, in confessing and assenting to that revelation it confesses and assents to the revealer. In doing so it is explicitly dealing with the revealer, even if faith does this through the mediation of the thing revealed *(res revelata)* and its witnesses. That is a clear division. Still, there is important descriptive overlap. Indeed, the unity of the inner act of faith generally underlines the fact that faith is an inner, unified, and spiritual act *particularly* in the case of *fides divina.* Here there can no longer be any question for the conscious believer about what she thinks and wills and who her divine source is. Faith's confession recollects conscience and its source, unifying the soul, and unifying the soul with God.[30]

To recognize this unity is then to recognize that the question of faith in God stays put within the context of *faith* and not outside it. As Newman put it in describing his project in *The Grammar of Assent:* "I am not to draw *out a proof* of the being of God, but the mode in which practically an individual believes it" (GA, 139). Faith is the mode of believing in God. Anything else is at best dealing with the god of the philosophers. The ques-

---

30. Newman notes that Scripture is indiscriminate in its uses of "faith" and "obedience." It doesn't move from faith or self-understanding to obedience; they are coextensive. "To believe is of the heart, and to obey is of the heart; to believe is not a solitary act, but a consistent habit of trust; and to obey is not a solitary act, but a consistent habit of doing our duty in all things" (PP III.6). Consistent habits of trust and doing one's duty are habits of *character,* matters of identity. But as Christian faith they also have a distinctive quality. Noting that in Paul faith is stressed over and above the other parts of a religious character, Newman explains why this is so: "[T]he Gospel being pre-eminently a covenant of grace, faith is so far of more excellence than other virtues, because it confesses this beyond all others. Works of obedience witness to God's just claims upon us, not to His mercy: but faith comes empty-handed, hides even its own worth, and does but point at that precious scheme of redemption which God's love has devised for sinners. Hence it is the frame of mind suitable to us, and is said, in a special way, to justify us, because it glorifies God, witnessing that He accepts those and those only, who confess they are not worthy to be accepted" (PP III.6).

tion of having faith in God is not therefore a question about the doctrine of God — about the articulated grammatical rules — but one about how *faith* interacts with God. It is to make faith a spiritual matter, not one of explanation. To talk about interaction with God is not to talk about how faith is possible, or to uncover the "causal joint" where God acts or where we act in faith. To talk about interaction with God is to talk about *faith* in the first instance. God is *extra nos;* the relation to God, and what we know of God, except in a strictly notional sense (and this may well be possible), is not *extra fidem.* Confession of God the revealer is within the internal relation we bear to God. To know God, to think God with assent, is not first to know *about* God and then to assent to it, as Locke suggested. In the case of a revealed, and hence personal religion, it is to take God at his word and to live within the covenanted conventions God has revealed.[31] The knowledge of God and dealing with God are precisely then in those practices that constitute taking God at his word.

"God" and "knowing God" are not epiphenomena of Christian practices, nor is God separable from them. Nor is God an external guarantee or grounding that provides the real certitude of faith. To take God at his word is to live a new life in a certain kind of community and fellowship and to treat even strangers and enemies with the care we normally reserve for our friends. It is also to participate in listening for God's word preached, and to participate in the sacraments, as well as to pray and to meditate on Scripture. To think God with assent is to will and think through those practices. Christian faith *in* God is to participate in those practices because it is taking God at his word that this is a revealed way of life; it is to come to know God in those practices, and to participate in God's life.

---

31. Weil talks about sacraments as a *convention.* The French term includes both a sense of "convention," i.e., what is not inscribed in nature, and "covenant," a promise made by somebody. Thus sacraments are conventions deliberately set out by God by which God promises his presence for the partaker. Cf. "Theory of the Sacraments" (SW 101): "By a covenant *(convention)* established by God between God and human beings, a piece of bread signifies the person of Christ. Since by virtue of the fact that a covenant ratified by God is infinitely more real than nature, its reality as bread, while remaining, becomes simple appearance relative to the infinitely more real reality that constitutes its significance."

3.2. The Life of Faith

Faith is divine when it consciously accepts its way of life as a gift offered, when conscience not only bears the impress of the divine good, but also focuses on the revealed, and sees this way of life, these words, and these sacraments as fulfilling, even in surprising and unanticipated ways. But faith is also divine in a second way. The gift of a revealed way of life is received and assented to not as utterly fulfilled, but as the very way of fulfilling. The practice of Christian faith is not an end in itself, a replacing of orthodoxy with orthopraxy or orthopathy. It is rather that in hungering and waiting for the good within the forms of Christian life one is fed. It is the active moral sense that reaches out to see and live life and that finds its full activity — reaches out best — in the place God has given it. There the conscience sees people best, and feels best the presence of God the giver in this life. In receiving the gift, one receives the power to receive and recognize the giver.

Conscience is the gift of God; its peace in Christ is a gift of God for which the gift of conscience is given. That is what it means to talk about faith as a matter of participation. For to act on the impress of the good in conscience is to be led to conscious awareness of one's own being in God, to recognize as Newman thought, even if he was being hyperbolic, that there are but two beings in the universe, the soul and the God in whom we live, move, and have our being.

Is this mysticism? Unfortunately mysticism, even when not used as a way of contemptuously dismissing a line of argument as being beyond the pale of the discussible, is misleading. For mysticism's place in Christian faith is as a particularly distilled version of faith, something that gains its sense within the more common practical space of Christian faith, and not its alternative. To know God is a part of quotidian Christian faith, even if, *qua* faith, that is to see in a mirror darkly, just as to know others is a part of moral life. The knowledge of God, that which makes faith divine, is not an epiphenomenon that supervenes on practice; it is the knowledge gained in practice. Prayer, reading and hearing and meditating on Scripture, partaking of the Eucharist are ways of interacting with God. They are, as such, the way by which faith gains its content and direction, not as external directing principles, but as the internal ways by which God becomes known, just as conversation, eating, and shared projects are ways by which we come to engage others.

Consider the parallel between a child coming to know his parents well and how God is known through prayer. A child requests, pleads, and simply lives with a parent. A parent in turn gives advice, provides an example, and compromises as well as grants and denies requests. The interaction is not, however, episodic, or static, beginning with a blank slate each time the child and his parent come into each other's presence. Rather in time, by heeding advice, and by learning what requests are granted and how, a child changes his requests and ways of looking at things, not as a matter of efficiency, but because he is in important ways forming a character through this process. He is learning to see through a sort of apprenticeship. He is also *learning the parent* as another person who is to be respected, and who is to be seen. Although we are often entranced by the unconditional and innocent love between infants and parents, the fulfillment of love comes in its adult form, which involves a certain moral equality and respect between parent and child. Without those things, it is clear that somebody's moral development has gone awry. In a parallel way, in prayer, we do not *just* ask God for things and thank him for other things, laying out our requests before him. In prayer's asking, thanking, complaining, and moaning we also lay ourselves out. And we do so in light of what we know of God in Scripture and the sacraments and participation in ecclesial life. But that knowledge, because it is moral knowledge, changes as we continue to pray and attentively apply ourselves to life's tasks. The knowledge of God as God comes also from the patient attention one pays in practices. It comes as we come to learn how to know an Other, and that arises from attentive interaction.

The dialogical element of this parallel ought not to obscure, however, the deeper aspects of prayer that are not so conversational. Prayer is also found in meditation. It may be in the reading known as *lectio divina,* where the imagination by dwelling on a biblical word, image, or phrase lets itself be penetrated and reshaped. Or it may be in contemplative forms of prayer, such as recommended by *The Cloud of Unknowing,* where, by paying attention to a single name of God, one sweeps away all discursive thought, and even all consoling images for a moment in order to be spoken to in the silent recesses of the soul. "The element of dialogue does not abolish the justified element of monologue; it is impossible simply to reduce thought to 'dialogue' for the very good reason that God is not a finite partner but the ontological basis *(interior intimo meo)* of the personal act of thinking,"[32] observes von Balthasar. Here we find an epitome of thinking with assent.

---

32. Hans Urs von Balthasar, *The Glory of the Lord: II: Studies in Theological Style: Clerical Styles* (San Francisco: Ignatius Press, 1984), p. 110.

How we know God is further epitomized in sacramental life. The real presence of God in the Eucharist is rarely an epiphany; it dwells within faith's life. To desire God, and to approach the sacrament with the belief that God has established by covenant and promise his presence in it is, in accepting the promise by coming to partake, to have the soul accept and wait on God's presence. Just as the thought of gold is not gold, but the thought of good is good, so the waiting upon and humble participation in God's promise is reception of God's life through accepting the promise. Weil suggests: "If you believe that contact with the piece of bread is contact with God, in that case in the contact with bread the desire for contact with God, which was only an impulse, passes the test of reality" (SW 101). Partaking of the sacrament not only gives reality to the good of the desire; it becomes its focus, the place to which desire returns time and again, intensified and transfiguring.

All this is to place the confessional knowledge of God squarely within the context of moral and intersubjective certitudes (and vice versa). After recounting what was perhaps the most significant religious experience of her life, "when Christ himself came down and took possession of me," Weil claimed of that contact that "I only felt in the midst of my suffering the presence of a love, *like that which one can read in the smile on a beloved face.*"[33] Her previous questions about God which, as intellectual questions *simpliciter*, she had thought insoluble, were grounded and transfigured by the certitude that can only belong to persons. This is the mark of the knowledge of God. That knowledge, deep in the innermost reaches of the soul, lives, like being able to read the smile upon a beloved face as the certainty of love and care, in a wider intersubjective context. Its history, metaphors, analogies, and allegories are not code for some underlying reality that are better described in more "objective" terms; it is the way personal and spiritual thinking in fact goes on. Outside this context, the very ability to understand becomes terribly thin, even incomprehensible.

Conversely, the health of the community depends upon that knowledge. The point, for example, of the prophet Ezekiel's vision of the valley of dry bones was that the community only lived and breathed when the Spirit of the Lord in the prophetic word was breathed into it. "'I will put my spirit within you, and you shall live. . . . Then you shall know that I, the

---

33. Simone Weil, *Waiting for God* (New York: Harper & Row, 1973), p. 69. Emphasis added.

Lord, have spoken and will act,' says the Lord" (Ezek. 37:14). But that health depends upon communal practice actually living this way. It is only in the intersubjective care for each other in the community that the author can be known.

3.3. The Nature of Theology

If this is the way it is with the knowledge of God, what does it mean to call theology knowledge? It would mean that if what Augustine, Newman, and Weil are pointing to is at all right, then the ultimate task of theology is the transformation of the thinker, of fitting him or her to the inner life of God. Theology is an intellectual discipline; but it is a spiritual one as well. Its goal is not simply description of God as referent; it is to make the thinker as much like its object as possible. It is to become what one thinks. For much of modernity, theology, once queen of the sciences, has had to establish itself as a science at all. No longer that which defines "knowledge," its intellectual worth has been measured by scientific methodology. Even in the presently more generous time of post-positivism, a time when theology has been conceded some kind of distinctive subject matter, it has faced attempts to make it in the image of the established natural sciences, even by its friends. Thus, for example, Wolfhart Pannenberg has called for "a general concept of science . . . which would . . . transcend particularity and unite theology and the other sciences."[34] Ian Barbour, in a well-meaning attempt to find some sort of *rapprochement* between science and religion, has made theology "critical reflection on the life and thought of the religious community . . . [whose] context is always the worshiping community."[35] It is in the way it organizes its knowledge and in its rational models that Barbour finds a link to science and sees the possibility of fruitful interaction between theological and scientific knowledge.

There may be something to be harvested from such suggestions. Insofar as theology is a notional and intellectual discipline it includes critical thought. Insofar as it is a function of faith, it does, too, for insofar as it

---

34. Wolfhart Pannenberg, *Theology and the Philosophy of Science* (Philadelphia: Westminster, 1976), p. 19.

35. Ian Barbour, *Religion in an Age of Science* (San Francisco: HarperCollins, 1990), p. 267.

THE ACT OF FAITH

seeks the multiplication of the good to which it is committed, it seeks that good in intellectual life as much as anything. So it includes critical thought because that enables the multiplication of the good through teaching, apologetics, exegesis, and even interreligious dialogue. Faith is not innately unscientific, dogmatic, and credulous. Insofar as it is earnestly attentive to unexpected movements of God's action in multiplying his good, it does invite method, freedom of opinion, and critical judgment so that its object may be universal.

Nevertheless, to leave it at that level is to understand things at what well may be a secondary level. It may well be to leave intact numerous assumed mischaracterizations of both faith and theology, such as taking belief to precede faith, and to take faith as *chiefly* an intellectual position opposed to knowledge, which can be discussed strictly notionally. In each of these cases the sense that faith is also an order of the heart that reason does not know (Pascal) or an inner word, the shape of our minds and knowledge (Augustine), or the ordering of our lives in the light of the Good we desire (Weil) is ignored. It forgets what Evagrius of Pontus observed, that theology is the life of prayer, for that is the prime example of thinking with assent, and theology is thinking with assent.

In this sense, what its real place is in intellectual life may well be ignored. The primary importance of theology is not simply to contribute to the construction of intellectual representations of the world — although it can do that, too; it is to submit them and to submit the representing mind to a higher order. Science is about the world as we think it; theology is about the soul of the thinker.[36] Theology ought to make us recognize that

---

36. In a discussion of how human life can re-rooted in the world of necessity, and by its mediation, in the life of God, Weil suggests that the key to much of modern science is understanding its lack of motivation to think upon any sort of overarching Good, its failure to think about the relation of the Necessary to the Good. Thus when modern science studies truth by studying the web of necessity of which the universe is composed — as it ought — it has left matters at that: blind, brute necessity. It has not put the surveying intellect and the order it discerns within the world within any larger context; it has not sought to think about how its symbolic world signals an overarching order that is the presence of the Good. And Weil thinks it does — or should — signal such an order. She writes: "The order of the world is the same as the beauty of the world.... It is one and the same thing, which with respect to God is eternal Wisdom; with respect to the universe, perfect obedience; with respect to love, beauty; with respect to our intelligence, balance of necessary relations; with respect to our flesh, brutal force" (*The Need for Roots* [London:

there is no knowledge worth having that does not involve self-knowledge or moral and spiritual questions. It ought to cause us to recognize another dimension to thought, which in the modern world has been so monodimensional.

4. CONCLUSION

We have tried in the foregoing to give a sense of the nature of faith if the believing self is what we have called a "moral self," that is, a self for whom moral questions are not questions of chosen policy, but constitutive of one's very identity, where human and personal space is inescapably moral space. Through a use of the concept of conscience, particularly as Newman developed it, I have suggested that we get a distinctive reading of the inner act of faith as thinking with assent. For thinking with assent on this account does not presuppose a gap between thinking and willing. What we think is the good that we will. This goes to the heart of moral self-identity; our selves are linked to the good we will and to which we aspire. This is not to deny that our knowledge of God is intellectual, but it is artificial to separate it from the good to which we assent. In Samuel Johnson's phrase: "We are perpetually moralists, but we are geometricians only by chance." In all our understanding of humans and ourselves, our moral nature is involved.

This says something about Christianity's revelation. Conscience may well demand that we care for others and give them worth and human space, as the Samaritan did to the wounded man by the side of the road. In Christian faith, however, we are not in the first instance the Samaritan but the wounded man. We are on the receiving end of care, for we need to be healed, to be reminded of the good that claims us. Faith accepts and *sees* the space opened to us, and the gift of new life. The assent of faith then means, on the one hand, that we accept the duty to fulfill our obligations to others, and to give others human space. We have been given the room to do so. But it also means from our end to give thanks and return compas-

---

Routledge & Kegan Paul, 1978], p. 281). Newman in a similar vein argues that a grave risk that the modern scientist runs is that he may admire the creation but overlook the wonder of its — and his — being created. Cf. "Letter VII" of *The Tamworth Reading Room*. Also Stanley Jaki's comments in chapter 11 of his *Newman's Challenge* (Grand Rapids: Eerdmans, 2000).

THE ACT OF FAITH

sion to the one who gave that space and to know the one who first knew us. It is to give our attention to the one who paid attention to us. We live humanly in human space as room that is given to us, not as created by us. We cannot live well in that space without having recognized and assented to our being the recipients of such a gift, and the objects of the compassion of a giver. We fully occupy such space only in recognition of the Giver.

I stress this last point, for it underlines a central theme that is present in pre-Enlightenment understandings of faith and lacking in modern versions, where the self becomes the center of value. Both versions actually see God as *pro nobis*. In the modern version, however, as Taylor carefully notes, "the legislative, self-proclaiming God is a great benefactor to mankind" (Sources 241); God is the one who enables ordinary human life. God's revelation is directed chiefly to restoring and enabling human life, and does this by making possible that which constitutes human dignity: self-responsible autonomy, productiveness, just social systems, freedom, expression. Speaking of the time of Locke, Taylor observes, ". . . it is the preservation of [the centrality of ordinary life] which now takes on prime importance. The goodness and providence of God are shown above all in his designing the world for the preservation of its denizens, and particularly so that the various parts of it conduce to reciprocal conservation" (Sources 244). The motion is unidirectional — from God to the world, throughout the world, and the action is in the effects produced. The world is the *telos;* God is its architect and handyman. The ancient version shared by the New Testament writers, Augustine, Aquinas and Calvin, and most of the world, religious and philosophical,[37] to which they appealed, is not so unidirectional and has a different sort of teleology. God's going out to humanity was to give new life, including a new way of life to be lived in human community. But *that* going out was to bring humanity back into communion with God. The fullness of the human community and individual human was not the fullness of expression of its inhabitants; "the chief end of man," is, in the famous Calvinist creedal phrase, "to know God and enjoy him forever."

The difference highlights how the sense of self affects the very nature

---

37. Pierre Hadot in *Philosophy as a Way of Life*, ed. A. Davidson (Oxford: Blackwell, 1995) suggests that the driving force of much of ancient philosophy was wisdom, and that as such philosophy was a way of life and involved routinely spiritual exercises precisely to elevate oneself out of the ordinary.

of what faith is understood to be and the nature of faith's practices. Both may involve a sense of responsibility to others and responsibility for living one's life. In the modern version one may even be grateful to God for having redeemed human life. But the sense of one's communion and knowledge of God, and hence the point and nature of religious practices, changes dramatically when one no longer sees one's assent to God as what constitutes the fullness of human life and the heart of one's own identity. Religious life for the autonomous self may strengthen one in resolve and even purity and good works, but it is not communion. Nor can religious life in the modern version be understood any longer as sanctity, or as anything more than the natural good. But even the natural good becomes truncated when it is no longer defined by the supernatural good. The givenness of human life thus tends to define what the operations of grace must be, rather than vice versa.

It may be left to the conjectures of historians and sociologists what the future of this illusion is and how it may affect the future of Christianity as a living religion. Philosophically, however, the task is somewhat different. In the first place, it is to take care when dealing with questions of faith to have the right concepts and to understand what they are. Theologically, the task is for the church to recover a living partnership with its own heritage, and to participate in it with heart and body, as well as mind. That is to recover a theological community; it is also the only way to have one at all. Doing so cannot happen without recovering within the community of faith itself the words that give way to the Word. It cannot happen without participation. For the theological task is, as it has always been, to recover personally and communally the space that God has set out and in which God dwells with his people.

BIBLIOGRAPHY

Adams, Robert M. *The Virtue of Faith and Other Essays in Philosophical Theology.* New York: Oxford University Press, 1987.

Allen, Diogenes. *Finding Our Father.* Atlanta: John Knox Press, 1974.

———. *The Reasonableness of Faith.* Washington: Corpus Books, 1968.

———. *Three Outsiders: Pascal, Kierkegaard, and Simone Weil.* Cambridge, Mass.: Cowley Publications, 1983.

Allen, Diogenes, and Eric Springsted. *Spirit, Nature, and Community: Issues in the Thought of Simone Weil.* Albany: State University of New York Press, 1994.

Aquinas, St. Thomas. *On Faith. Summa Theologiae 2-2. qq. 1-16 of St. Thomas Aquinas.* Translated and edited by M. D. Jordan. Notre Dame: University of Notre Dame Press, 1990.

———. *Summa Theologica.* 5 vols. Reprinted; Westminster, Md.: Christian Classics, 1981.

———. *Truth.* Three volumes. Translated by R. W. Milligan, S.J. Indianapolis: Hackett Publishing Co., 1994.

Aristotle. *The Nicomachean Ethics.* Translated by T. Irwin Indianapolis: Hackett Publishing Co., 1987.

Augustine, St. *Confessions.* Translated by H. Chadwick. Oxford: Oxford University Press, 1991.

———. *Earlier Writings.* Edited by J. H. S. Burleigh. Philadelphia: Westminster Press, 1953.

———. *The Nicene and Post-Nicene Fathers.* Vols. 1-8. Edited by Phillip Schaff. Reprinted: Grand Rapids: Eerdmans, 1974.

———. *On Free Choice of the Will*. Translated by A. S. Benjamin and L. H. Hackstaff. Indianapolis: Bobbs-Merrill, 1964.

———. *The Trinity*. Translated by E. Hill, O.P. Brooklyn: New City Press, 1991.

Aubert, Roger. *Le Probleme de l'Acte de Foi*. 3rd edition. Louvain: Publications Universitaires de Louvain, 1950.

Ayer, A. J. *Language, Truth, and Logic*. New York: Dover, 1946.

Baillie, D. M. *Faith in God and Its Christian Consummation*. New edition. London: Faber and Faber, 1964.

Baillie, John. *Our Knowledge of God*. New York: Charles Scribner's Sons, 1939.

Balthasar, Hans Urs von. *The Glory of the Lord*. 7 vols. ET: San Francisco: Ignatius Press, 1982-91.

Barbour, Ian. *Religion in an Age of Science*. San Francisco: HarperCollins, 1990.

Barrett, William. *Wittgenstein on Ethics and Religious Belief*. Oxford: Basil Blackwell, 1991.

Barth, Karl. *Church Dogmatics* I.1. Rev. ed., IV.1. Edinburgh: T. & T. Clark, 1956, 1975.

———. *Natural Theology: Comprising "Nature and Grace" by Emil Brunner and the Reply "No!" by Karl Barth*. London: G. Bles: The Centenary Press, 1946.

Becker, Jürgen. *Paul: Apostle to the Gentiles*. Translated by O. C. Dean, Jr. Louisville: Westminster/John Knox Press, 1993.

Beker, J. Christiaan. *Paul the Apostle: The Triumph of God in Life and Thought*. Philadelphia: Fortress Press, 1980.

Bellah, Robert, et al. *Habits of the Heart: Individualism and Commitment in American Life*. New York: Harper and Row, 1986.

Bentham, Jeremy. *An Introduction to the Principles of Morals and Legislation*. Oxford: Clarendon Press, 1876.

Berlin, Isaiah. *The Roots of Romanticism*. Princeton: Princeton University Press, 1999.

Bernstein, Richard J. *Beyond Objectivism and Relativism*. Philadelphia: University of Pennsylvania Press, 1983.

Beversluis, John. "Reforming the 'Reformed' Objection to Natural Theology," *Faith and Philosophy* 12, no. 2 (April 1995): 189-206.

Blackman, E. C. "Faith" in *The Interpreter's Dictionary of the Bible*. Edited by G. A. Buttrick, vol. 2, pp. 222-34. New York: Abingdon Press, 1962.

Blondel, Maurice. *Action* (1893). Translated by O. Blanchette. Notre Dame: University of Notre Dame Press, 1983.

———. *The Letter on Apologetics and History and Dogma*. Edited and translated by A. Dru and I. Trethowan. Grand Rapids: Eerdmans, 1994.

Bonner, Gerald. *St. Augustine of Hippo: Life and Controversies* (1963). Reissued Norwich, U.K.: The Canterbury Press, 1986.

BIBLIOGRAPHY

Bordo, Susan. *The Flight to Objectivity: Essays on Cartesianism and Culture.* Albany: State University of New York Press, 1987.

Borg, Marcus. *Meeting Jesus Again for the First Time: The Historical Jesus and the Heart of Contemporary Faith.* San Francisco: HarperCollins, 1994.

Bouwsma, William J. *John Calvin: A Sixteenth Century Portrait.* New York: Oxford University Press, 1988.

Braaten, Carl E., and Robert W. Jenson, eds. *Union with Christ: The New Finnish Interpretation of Luther.* Grand Rapids: Eerdmans, 1998.

Brandt, Richard. *Facts, Values, and Morality.* Cambridge: Cambridge University Press, 1997.

Broglie, G. de. "La vrai notion thomiste des 'praembula fidei,'" *Gregorianum* 34 (1953): 341-89.

Brown, David, ed. *Newman: A Man for Our Time.* Harrisburg, Pa.: Morehouse Publishing, 1990.

Brueggeman, Walter. *Texts Under Negotiation: The Bible and the Postmodern Imagination.* Minneapolis: Fortress Press, 1993.

Bryant, David. *Faith and the Play of Imagination.* Macon, Ga.: Mercer University Press, 1989.

Buber, Martin. *Two Types of Faith.* London: Routledge & Kegan Paul, 1951.

Buckley, Michael J. *At the Origins of Modern Atheism.* New Haven: Yale University Press, 1987.

Bultmann, Rudolph. *Kerygma and Myth.* New York: Charles Scribner's Sons, 1958.

———. *Theology of the New Testament.* Translated by K. Grobel. 2 vols. New York: Charles Scribner's Sons, 1951, 1955.

Bultmann, Rudolph, and A. Weiser. "Pisteuo, pistis, etc." Article in *The Theological Dictionary of the New Testament.* Translated by G. Bromiley. Edited by G. Kittel and G. Friedrich, vol. 6, pp. 174-228. Grand Rapids: Eerdmans, 1968.

Burrell, David. *Aquinas, God, and Action.* Notre Dame: University of Notre Dame Press, 1979.

Burtt, E. A. *The Metaphysical Foundations of Modern Science.* Atlantic Highlands: Humanities Press, 1952.

Calvin, John. *The Institutes of the Christian Religion.* 2 vols. Translated by F. L. Battles. Philadelphia: Westminster Press, 1960.

Castelli, Enrico. *Mythe et Foi.* Paris: Aubier, 1966.

Charry, Ellen. *By the Renewing of Your Minds: The Pastoral Function of Christian Doctrine.* New York: Oxford University Press, 1997.

Chenu, M.-D. *Toward Understanding Saint Thomas.* Chicago: Henry Regnery, 1964.

Clark, Mary T. "Augustine on Person: Divine and Human." In *Augustine: Presbyter Factus Sum.* Edited by Lienhard, Muller, and Teske, pp. 99-120. New York: Peter Lang, 1993.

Clark, Stephen R. L. *A Parliament of Souls.* Oxford: Oxford University Press, 1990.

Clifford, W. K. "The Ethics of Belief." In *Lectures and Essays* (1879). Reprinted in *Readings in the Philosophy of Religion: An Analytic Approach.* Edited by B. Brody. Englewood Cliffs, N.J.: Prentice Hall, 1974.

Creel, Richard. "Faith, Hope and Faithfulness," *Faith and Philosophy* 10, no. 3 (July 1993): 330-44.

Cristman, J., ed. *The Inner Citadel.* New York: Oxford University Press, 1989.

D'Arcy, Martin C., S.J. *The Nature of Belief.* New edition of 1931 original. St. Louis: B. Herder, 1958.

Davies, Brian. *The Thought of Thomas Aquinas.* Oxford: Oxford University Press, 1992.

Dihle, Albrecht. *The Theory of the Will in Classical Antiquity.* Berkeley: University of California Press, 1982.

Dowey, Edward A. *The Knowledge of God in Calvin's Theology.* Expanded edition. Grand Rapids: Eerdmans, 1994. Original edition, New York: Columbia University Press, 1952.

Dulles, Avery. *The Assurance of Things Hoped For: A Theology of Christian Faith.* New York: Oxford University Press, 1994.

Dunne, Joseph. *Back to the Rough Ground: 'Phronesis' and 'Techne' in Modern Philosophy and in Aristotle.* Notre Dame: University of Notre Dame Press, 1993.

Dunning, Stephen N. "Love Is Not Enough: A Kierkegaardian Phenomenology of Religious Experience," *Faith and Philosophy* 12, no. 1 (January 1995): 22-39.

Dupré, Louis. *Passage to Modernity: An Essay in the Hermeneutics of Nature and Culture.* New Haven: Yale University Press, 1993.

———. *Religious Mystery and Rational Reflection.* Grand Rapids: Eerdmans, 1998.

Eaton, Jeffrey. *The Logic of Theism.* Lanham, Md.: University Press of America, 1980.

Ebeling, Gerhard. *The Nature of Faith.* Philadelphia: Fortress Press, 1967.

Evans, C. Stephen. "The Epistemological Significance of Transformative Religious Experience: A Kierkegaardian Exploration," *Faith and Philosophy* 8, no. 2 (April 1991): 180-92.

———. *Faith Beyond Reason.* Grand Rapids: Eerdmans, 1998.

———. "Kierkegaard and Plantinga on Belief in God: Subjectivity as the Ground of Properly Basic Beliefs," *Faith and Philosophy* 5, no. 1 (January 1988): 25-39.

———. *Kierkegaard's "Fragments" and "Postscript":* The Religious Philosophy of Johannes Climacus. Atlantic Highlands: Humanities Press, 1983.

Evans, Donald D. *The Logic of Self-Involvement: A Philosophical Study of Everyday Language with Special Reference to the Christian Use of Language about God as Creator.* London: SCM Press, 1963.

Farrer, Austin. *Faith and Speculation.* New York: New York University Press, 1964.

———. *Saving Belief.* New York: Morehouse-Barlow, 1964.

BIBLIOGRAPHY

Ferreira, M. Jamie. *Doubt and Religious Commitment: The Role of the Will in Newman's Thought.* Oxford: Clarendon Press, 1980.

———. "Leaps and Circles: Kierkegaard and Newman on Faith and Reason," *Religious Studies* 30, no. 4 (December 1994).

———. *Transforming Vision: Imagination and Will in Kierkegaardian Faith.* Oxford: Clarendon Press, 1991.

Fitzgerald, Allan D. *Augustine through the Ages: An Encyclopedia.* Grand Rapids: Eerdmans, 1999.

Fowler, James. *The Stages of Faith: The Psychology of Human Development and the Quest for Meaning.* New York: HarperCollins, 1981.

Frei, Hans. *The Eclipse of Biblical Narrative: A Study in Eighteenth and Nineteenth Century Hermeneutics.* New Haven: Yale University Press, 1974.

Gadamer, Hans-Georg. *Truth and Method.* New York: Crossroad, 1986.

Gauchet, Henri. *The Disenchantment of the World: A Political History of Religion.* Translated by O. Burge. Princeton: Princeton University Press, 1997.

Gilson, Etienne. *The Christian Philosophy of St. Augustine.* New York: Random House, 1960.

Green, Garrett. *Imagining God: Theology and the Religious Imagination.* San Francisco: Harper and Row, 1989.

Gouwens, David J. *Kierkegaard as Religious Thinker.* Cambridge: Cambridge University Press, 1996.

Hadot, Pierre. *Philosophy as a Way of Life.* Edited by A. Davidson. Oxford: Blackwell, 1995.

———. *Qu'est-ce que la philosophie antique?* Paris: Gallimard, 1995.

Harrison, Carol. *Beauty and Revelation in the Thought of Saint Augustine.* Oxford: Oxford University Press, 1992.

Hauerwas, Stanley. *A Community of Character.* Notre Dame: University of Notre Dame Press, 1981.

Healey, J. P., D. Lührmann, and G. Howard. "Faith." In *The Anchor Bible Dictionary.* Edited by David N. Freedman, vol. 2, pp. 744-60. New York: Doubleday, 1992.

Heidegger, Martin. "Letter on Humanism." In *Martin Heidegger: Basic Writings.* New York: Harper and Row, 1977.

Heller, T. C., M. Sosna, and D. E Wellbery. *Reconstructing Individuals: Autonomy, Individuality, and the Self in Western Thought.* Stanford, Calif.: Stanford University Press, 1986.

Helm, Paul. *Faith and Understanding.* Grand Rapids: Eerdmans, 1997.

Henry, Paul, S.J. *Saint Augustine on Personality.* New York: Macmillan, 1960.

Hermisson, H.-J., and E. Lohse. *Faith.* Translated by D. Stott. Nashville: Abingdon, 1981.

Hick, John. *Evil and the God of Love.* London: Macmillan, 1966.

———. *Faith and Knowledge*. Ithaca: Cornell University Press, 1966.

Hill, Edmund, O.P. "Unless You Believe, You Shall Not Understand," *Augustinian Studies* 25 (1994): 51-64.

Hobbes, Thomas. *Leviathan Parts I and II* (1651). Indianapolis: Bobbs-Merrill, 1958.

Hoitenga, Dewey. *Faith and Reason from Plato to Plantinga: An Introduction to Reformed Epistemology*. Albany: State University of New York Press, 1991.

Hume, David. *Dialogues Concerning Natural Religion* (1779). London: Penguin Books, 1990.

———. *Enquiry Concerning Human Understanding (1748)*. Edited by A. Flew. Chicago: Open Court, 1988.

———. *A Treatise of Human Nature*. Edited by L. A. Selby-Bigge. Oxford: Oxford University Press, 1888.

Jaki, Stanley. *Newman's Challenge*. Grand Rapids: Eerdmans, 2000.

James, William. *The Will to Believe and Other Essays in Popular Philosophy*. New York: Longmans, Green, 1898.

Jeffreys, D. "How Reformed Is Reformed Epistemology? Alvin Plantinga and Calvin's 'Sensus Divinitatis.'" *Religious Studies* 33, no. 4 (1997): 419-32.

Jenkins, John I. *Knowledge and Faith in Thomas Aquinas*. Cambridge: Cambridge University Press, 1997.

Jordan, Mark. "Philosophy and Theology." In *The Cambridge Companion to Aquinas*. Edited by N. Kretzmann and E. Stump, pp. 232-51. Cambridge: Cambridge University Press, 1993.

Kant, Immanuel. *The Philosophy of Kant: Immanual Kant's Moral and Political Writings*. New York: Random House, 1949.

Kenney, Anthony. *What Is Faith?* Oxford: Oxford University Press, 1992.

Ker, Ian. *The Achievement of John Henry Newman*. Notre Dame: University of Notre Dame Press, 1990.

Kerr, Fergus. *Immortal Longings: Versions of Transcending Humanity*. Notre Dame: University of Notre Dame Press, 1998.

Kierkegaard, Søren. *Concluding Unscientific Postscript to "Philosophical Fragments."* 2 volumes. Translated by H. and E. Hong. Princeton: Princeton University Press, 1992.

———. *Fear and Trembling*. Translated by H. and E. Hong. Princeton: Princeton University Press, 1983.

———. *Philosophical Fragments*. Translated by H. and E. Hong. Princeton: Princeton University Press, 1985.

Kirwan, Christopher. *Augustine*. London: Routledge & Kegan Paul, 1989.

Koester, Craig. "Hearing, Seeing, and Believing in the Gospel of John," *Biblica* 70, no. 3 (1989): 327-48.

Kolakowski, Leszek. *God Owes Us Nothing: A Brief Remark on Pascal's Religion and on the Spirit of Jansenism.* Chicago: University of Chicago Press, 1995.

Konyndyk, Kenneth J. "Aquinas on Faith and Science," *Faith and Philosophy* 12, no. 1 (January 1995): 3-21.

Kretzmann, Norman. "Faith Seeks, Understanding Finds: Augustine's Charter for Christian Philosophy." In *Christian Philosophy.* Edited by T. Flint. Notre Dame: University of Notre Dame Press, 1990.

Kuhn, Thomas. *The Structure of Scientific Revolutions.* Chicago: University of Chicago Press, 1962.

Lee, James M., ed. *Handbook of Faith.* Birmingham: Religious Education Press, 1990.

Leith, John. *Creeds of the Churches.* Atlanta: John Knox Press, 1973.

Levinas, Emmanuel. *The Levinas Reader.* Edited by Seán Hand. Oxford: Blackwell, 1989.

Lindars, Barnabas, SSF. *The Theology of the Letter to the Hebrews.* Cambridge: Cambridge University Press, 1991.

Lindbeck, George A. *The Nature of Doctrine: Religion and Theology in a Postliberal Age.* Philadelphia: Westminster Press, 1984.

Lloyd, A. C. "On Augustine's Concept of the Person." In *Augustine: A Collection of Critical Essays.* Edited by R. A. Markus. New York: Anchor Books, 1972.

Locke, John. *An Essay Concerning Human Understanding* (1690). Abridged and edited by A. S. Pringle-Pattison. Atlantic Highlands: Humanities Press, 1978.

———. *A Letter Concerning Toleration* (1689). Edited by J. Tully. Indianapolis: Hackett, 1983.

———. *The Reasonableness of Christianity* (1695). Edited by I. T. Ramsay. Stanford, Calif.: Stanford University Press, 1958.

———. *Second Treatise of Government* (1690). Edited by C. B. Macpherson. Indianapolis: Hackett, 1980.

Louth, Andrew. *Discerning the Mystery: An Essay on the Nature of Theology.* Oxford: Oxford University Press, 1983.

Lubac, Henri de. *The Discovery of God.* Translated by A. Dru. Grand Rapids: Eerdmans, 1996.

———. *The Mystery of the Supernatural.* Translated by R. Sheed. New York: Crossroad, 1998.

Luther, Martin. *Martin Luther: Selections from His Writings.* Edited by J. Dillenberger. Garden City, N.Y.: Doubleday, 1961.

MacIntyre, Alasdair. *After Virtue.* Notre Dame: University of Notre Dame Press, 1981.

Malcolm, Norman. "The Groundlessness of Belief." In *Reason and Religion.* Edited by S. Brown. Ithaca: Cornell University Press, 1977.

Marion, Jean-Luc. *God Without Being.* Translated by T. A. Carlson. Chicago: University of Chicago Press, 1991.

Marshall, Bruce. "Aquinas as Postliberal Theologian," *Thomist* 53 (1989): 353–402.

Martyn, J. Louis. *Theological Issues in the Letters of Paul.* Nashville: Abingdon Press, 1997.

Matthews, Gareth, ed. *The Augustinian Tradition.* Berkeley: University of California Press, 1999.

———. "The Inner Man." In *Augustine: A Collection of Critical Essays.* Edited by R. A. Markus. New York: Anchor Books, 1972.

Means, Stewart. *Faith: An Historical Study.* New York: Macmillan, 1933.

Milbank, John. *Theology and Social Theory: Beyond Secular Reason.* Oxford: Basil Blackwell, 1990.

Mirandola, Pico della. *Oration on the Dignity of Man.* Translated by C. G. Wallis. Indianapolis: Bobbs-Merrill, 1965.

Mitchell, Basil. *Faith and Criticism.* Oxford: Oxford University Press, 1994.

Mooney, Edward F. *Selves in Discord and Resolve: Kierkegaard's Moral-Religious Psychology from "Either/Or" to "Sickness unto Death."* New York: Routledge, 1996.

Moore, Gareth. *Believing in God.* Edinburgh: T. & T. Clark, 1988.

Murdoch, Iris. *The Sovereignty of the Good.* New York: Schocken Books, 1971.

Muyskens, James. *The Sufficiency of Hope: The Conceptual Foundations of Religion.* Philadelphia: Temple University Press, 1979.

Newman, John Henry. *Conscience, Consensus, and the Development of Doctrine.* Edited by J. Gaffney. New York, Doubleday, 1992. Including: *The Theory of Developments in Religious Doctrine; An Essay on the Development of Christian Doctrine; On Consulting the Faithful in Matters of Doctrine; A Letter Addressed to His Grace, the Duke of Norfolk.*

———. *An Essay in Aid of a Grammar of Assent.* Westminster, Md.: Christian Classics, 1973.

———. *Fifteen Sermons Preached before the University of Oxford between* A.D. *1826 and 1843.* Reprint of the 1872 edition. Notre Dame: University of Notre Dame Press, 1997.

———. *Plain and Parochial Sermons.* San Francisco: Ignatius Press, 1997.

———. *The Theological Papers of John Henry Newman on Faith and Certainty.* Edited by J. D. Holmes. Oxford: Oxford University Press, 1976.

Niebuhr, H. Richard. *Faith on Earth: An Inquiry into the Structure of Human Faith.* New Haven: Yale University Press, 1989.

Nietzsche, Friedrich. *On the Genealogy of Morals and Ecce Homo.* Edited by W. Kaufmann. New York: Vintage Books, 1989.

Nussbaum, Martha C. *Love's Knowledge.* New York: Oxford University Press, 1990.

———. *For Love of Country: Debating the Limits of Patriotism.* Boston: Beacon Press, 1996.

———. *Poetic Justice: The Literary Imagination and the Public Life.* Boston: Beacon Press, 1995.

———. *The Therapy of Desire: Theory and Practice in Hellenistic Ethics.* Princeton: Princeton University Press, 1994.

O'Connor, Edward D., C.S.C. *Faith in the Synoptic Gospels.* Notre Dame: University of Notre Dame Press, 1961.

O'Connor, William R. "The Concept of the Person in St. Augustine's *De Trinitate*," *Augustinian Studies* 13 (1982): 133-44.

O'Leary-Hawthorne, John, and Daniel Howard-Snyder. "Are Beliefs About God Theoretical Beliefs? Reflections on Aquinas and Kant," *Religious Studies* 32, no. 2 (June 1996): 233-58.

Pascal, Blaise. *Pensées.* Translated by A. J. Krailsheimer. London: Penguin Books, 1966, 1995.

Pannenberg, Wolfhart. *Theology and the Philosophy of Science.* Philadelphia: Westminster Press, 1976.

Penelhum, Terence. "The Analysis of Faith in St. Thomas Aquinas," *Religious Studies* 13, no. 2 (1977): 133-54. Reprinted in Penelhum, *Faith.*

———. *Reason and Religious Faith.* Boulder, Colo.: Westview Press, 1996.

———, ed. *Faith.* New York: Macmillan, 1989.

Phillips, D. Z. *Religion Without Explanation.* Oxford: Basil Blackwell, 1976.

Pieper, Joseph. *Belief and Faith: A Philosophical Tract.* London: Faber and Faber, 1963.

Pitkin, Barbara. *What Pure Eyes Could See: Calvin's Doctrine of Faith in Its Exegetical Context.* New York: Oxford University Press, 1999.

Placher, William. *The Domestication of Transcendence: How Modern Thinking about God Went Wrong.* Louisville: Westminster/John Knox Press, 1996.

Plantinga, Alvin. "Reason and Belief in God." In *Faith and Rationality.* Edited by A. Plantinga and N. Wolsterstorff, pp. 16-91. Notre Dame: University of Notre Dame Press, 1983.

Pojman, Louis. "Faith without Belief?" *Faith and Philosophy* 3, no. 2 (April 1986): 157-76.

———. *The Logic of Subjectivity: Kierkegaard's Philosophy of Religion.* Birmingham: University of Alabama Press, 1984.

———. *Religious Belief and the Will.* London: Routledge & Kegan Paul, 1986.

Price, H. H. *Belief.* London: George Allen and Unwin, 1969.

Putnam, Hilary. *Reason, Truth, and History.* Cambridge: Cambridge University Press, 1981.

Quine, W. V. O. "Two Dogmas of Empiricism." In *From a Logical Point of View.* New York: Harper and Row, 1963.

Rawls, John. *Political Liberalism.* New York: Columbia University Press, 1993.

———. *A Theory of Justice.* Cambridge, Mass.: Harvard University Press, 1971.

Redondi, Pietro. *Galileo Heretic.* Princeton: Princeton University Press, 1987.

Rengstorf, K. H. "Semeion, etc." Article in *Theological Dictionary of the New Testament.* Translated by G. Bromiley. Edited by G. Kittel and G. Friedrich, vol. 7, pp. 200-269. Grand Rapids: Eerdmans, 1968.

Reumann, J. "Faith, faithfulness in the NT." In *The Interpreter's Dictionary of the Bible,* Supplementary Volume. Edited by K. Crim, pp. 329-35. Nashville: Abingdon Press, 1962.

Ricoeur, Paul. *Oneself as Another.* Translated by K. Blamey. Chicago: University of Chicago Press, 1992.

Rogers, Eugene. "Thomas and Barth in Convergence on Romans 1?" *Modern Theology* 12, no. 1: 53-74.

Rorty, Richard. *Philosophy and the Mirror of Nature.* Princeton: Princeton University Press, 1979.

Ross, James. "Cognitive Finality." In *Rational Faith: Catholic Responses to Reformed Epistemology.* Edited by L. Zagzebski. Notre Dame: University of Notre Dame Press, 1993.

———. "Rational Reliance," *JAAR* 62, no. 3 (Fall 1994).

Rowe, William. "Two Criticisms of the Cosmological Argument," *The Monist* 54 (July 1970).

Roy, Olivier du. *L'intelligence de la foi en la Trinité selon S. Augustin.* Paris: Etudes Augustiniennes, 1966.

Ryle, Gilbert. *The Concept of Mind.* London: Hutchinson, 1949.

Salaquarda, Jörg. "Nietzsche and the Judaeo-Christian Tradition." In *The Cambridge Companion to Nietzsche.* Edited by B. Magnus and K. Higgins. Cambridge: Cambridge University Press, 1996.

Sandel, Michael. *Liberalism and the Limits of Justice.* Cambridge: Cambridge University Press, 1982.

Sanders, E. P. *Paul and Palestinian Judaism.* Minneapolis: Fortress Press, 1977.

Schnackenburg, Rudolf. *The Gospel According to St. John,* vol. 1. New York: Crossroad, 1982.

Schweitzer, Albert. *The Mysticism of Paul the Apostle.* New York: H. Holt & Co., 1931.

Scott, T. Kermit. *Augustine: His Thought in Context.* Mahwah, N.J.: Paulist Press, 1995.

Sellars, Wilfred. *Science, Perception, and Reality.* London: Routledge & Kegan Paul, 1963.

Sessions, William Lad. *The Concept of Faith: A Philosophical Investigation.* Ithaca: Cornell University Press, 1994.

BIBLIOGRAPHY

Shepherd, Victor A. *The Nature and Function of Faith in the Theology of John Calvin.* Macon, Ga.: Mercer University Press, 1983.

Smith, Wilfred Cantwell. *Belief and History.* Charlottesville: University of Virginia Press, 1977.

———. *Faith and Belief.* Princeton: Princeton University Press, 1979.

Springsted, Eric O. "Faith, Belief and Perspective." In *The Philosophy of Peter Winch* (forthcoming).

———. "'Thou Hast Given Me Room': Simone Weil's Retheologization of the Political," *Cahiers Simone Weil* 20, no. 2 (1997): 87-98.

———, ed. *Spirituality and Theology.* Louisville: Westminster/John Knox Press, 1998.

Stock, Brian. *Augustine the Reader: Meditation, Self Knowledge, and the Ethics of Interpretation.* Cambridge, Mass.: Harvard University Press, 1996.

Strauss, Leo. *Natural Right and History.* Chicago: University of Chicago Press, 1953.

Stump, Eleonore. "Faith and Goodness." In *The Philosophy of Christianity.* Edited by G. Vesey, pp. 167-91. Cambridge: Cambridge University Press, 1989.

Surlis, P., ed. *Faith: Its Nature and Meaning.* Dublin: Gill and Macmillan, 1972.

Swinburne, R. *Faith and Reason.* Oxford: Oxford University Press, 1981.

Tamburello, Dennis E. *Union with Christ: John Calvin and the Mysticism of St. Bernard.* Louisville: Westminster/John Knox Press, 1994.

Taylor, Charles. *Sources of the Self: The Making of the Modern Identity.* Cambridge, Mass.: Harvard University Press, 1989.

Thomas, Emyr Vaughn. "Wittgensteinian Perspectives (Sub Specie Aeternatatis)," *Religious Studies* 31, no. 3 (September 1995): 329-40.

Tillich, Paul. *Dynamics of Faith.* New York: Harper and Row, 1957.

Toulmin, Stephen. *Cosmopolis: The Hidden Agenda of Modernity.* Chicago: University of Chicago Press, 1992.

Vos, Arvin. *Aquinas, Calvin, and Contemporary Protestant Thought: A Critique of Protestant Views on the Thought of Thomas Aquinas.* Washington: Christian University Press, 1985.

Walker, Ian. *Faith and Belief: A Philosophical Approach.* Atlanta: Scholars Press, 1994.

Wallace, Ronald S. *Calvin's Doctrine of the Christian Life.* Edinburgh: Oliver and Boyd, 1959.

Walzer, Michael. *The Spheres of Justice.* New York: Basic Books, 1983.

Ward, J. M. "Faith, Faithfulness in the OT." In *The Interpreter's Dictionary of the Bible,* Supplementary Volume. Edited by K. Crim, pp. 329-35. Nashville: Abingdon Press, 1962.

Warnock, Mary. *Imagination.* Berkeley: University of California Press, 1976.

Weil, Simone. *The Need for Roots.* Translated by A. Wills. London: Routledge & Kegan Paul, 1952.
———. *Selected Essays: 1934-43.* Oxford: Oxford University Press, 1962.
———. *Simone Weil.* Edited by E. O. Springsted. Maryknoll, N.Y.: Orbis Books, 1998.
———. *Waiting for God.* New York: Harper and Row, 1973.
Welch, Claude. *Protestant Thought in the Nineteenth Century.* New Haven: Yale University Press, 1972.
Williams, A. N. "Mystical Theology Redux: The Pattern of Aquinas' *Summa Theologiae*," *Modern Theology* 13, no. 1 (1997): 57-84.
Wilson, A. N. *God's Funeral.* New York: W. W. Norton and Co., 1999.
Winch, Peter. "The Expression of Belief," *Proceedings and Addresses of the American Philosophical Association* 70, no. 2: 7-23.
———. "Lessing and the Resurrection." Unpublished essay.
———. *Simone Weil: The Just Balance.* Cambridge: Cambridge University Press, 1989.
Wisdo, David. *The Life of Irony and the Ethics of Belief.* Albany: State University of New York Press, 1993.
Wittgenstein, Ludwig. *Culture and Value.* Translated by Peter Winch. Edited by G. H. von Wright. Chicago: University of Chicago Press, 1980.
———. *Philosophical Investigations.* New York: Macmillan, 1958.
———. *Philosophical Remarks.* Edited by R. Rhees. Chicago: University of Chicago Press, 1975.
———. *Tractatus Logico-Philosophicus.* Edited by Pears and McGuiness. London: Routledge & Kegan Paul, 1961.
Wolterstorff, Nicholas. *John Locke and the Ethics of Belief.* Cambridge, 1996: Cambridge University Press.
———. "John Locke's Epistemological Piety: Reason Is the Candle of the Lord," *Faith and Philosophy* 11, no. 4 (October 1994).
Zachman, Randall. *The Assurance of Faith: Conscience in the Theology of Martin Luther and John Calvin.* Minneapolis: Fortress Press, 1993.

INDEX

Abraham, 73-76, 84, 234
actions, 45, 48
Allen, D., 18, 229, 230
Ambrose, St., 126
Anselm, St., 243
anthropocentrism, 48, 49, 52, 66, 115
apocalyptic, 80, 86, 88
apologetics, 157
apprenticeship, 171, 188, 230
Aquinas, St. Thomas, xi, xiii, 3, 9, 12, 14, 19-21, 47, 51, 53, 128, 149, 152, 154-75, 178, 184, 186, 187, 239, 252
arguments for the existence of God, 1, 19, 44, 114, 153, 160, 161, 239, 243
Aristotle, 9, 30, 48, 126, 199-201, 229
assent, 118, 119, 124, 133, 151, 159, 169, 170, 187, 227, 231-33, 240. *See also* consent; faith: as thinking with assent
assurance, 150
Athanasius, St., 52
attention, 194, 196, 203-6, 208, 213, 218, 240.
Aubert, R., 151, 153
Augustine, St., xi-xiii, 3-5, 12-15, 25, 43-44, 47, 50, 53, 66, 79, 105-51, 171, 172, 179, 182, 184, 187, 189, 190, 214, 215, 231, 233, 250, 252
authority, 14, 124, 126, 129, 151, 152, 157, 158, 181, 187, 214
autonomy, 50, 189-91, 209, 253
Ayer, A. J., 34

Balthasar, H. U. von, 21, 73, 247
Barbour, I., 249
Barth, K., 161, 162
Baudelaire, C., 65
beauty, 117, 129, 130, 133
Becker, J., 87
Beker, J. C., 80
belief, 3, 5, 69, 164
Bellah, R., 42
Bentham, J., 56, 200
Berlin, I., 64, 65, 67
Bernstein, R., 35
Beversluis, J., 180
Bible, 69, 70, 119, 146. *See also* Scripture
Blake, W., 64
Blondel, M., 29, 33
Bordo, S., 26
Bouwsma, W. J., 188-89
Brandt, R., 57-59

Index

Broglie, G. de, 22, 152
Brueggemann, W., 46
Bryant, D., 46
Buber, M., 78, 217
Buckley, M., 21, 22, 25, 26
Bultmann, R., 88-91, 94, 99
Burtt, E. A., 23

Calvin, J., x-xi, xiii, 3, 15, 47, 79, 149-52, 156-60, 174-90, 214, 252
Catholicism, 149-56
causality, 48
certainty, 168, 189, 227
certitude, 30, 32, 154, 227, 228, 230, 234, 248
character, xi, 109, 110, 229
Charry, E., 93, 139
Chenu, M.-D., 163
choice, 44, 109, 191, 227, 228
Church. *See* community, ecclesial
Clark, M., 143, 145
Clarke, S., 22-23
Clifford, W. K., 2, 3, 5, 6, 10
Coleridge, S., 29, 33, 228
community, 66, 209-11, 221, 230, 245; ecclesial, xii, 25, 26, 81, 82, 87, 93, 97-100, 103, 104, 127, 132, 214, 248-49, 253
conscience, xi, 31, 57-59, 180, 185, 216, 219-32, 234, 236, 239, 240, 244, 246, 251
consent, 106, 109, 206-11, 219, 241. *See also* assent
Copernicus, 48, 50
Council of Trent, 150, 151, 184
Crates, 201-2
credere Deum, . . . Deo, . . . in Deum, 12, 136, 171

D'Arcy, M., 155
demonstration of God, 11, 15, 22, 158, 160, 163. *See also* arguments for the existence of God

Descartes, R., 14, 21, 22, 26, 33, 41, 48, 50, 54
desire, xiii, 227-30, 241, 242
depositum fidei, 21, 151, 155
Dickens, C., 196
Dilthey, W., 26
dissociation of sensibility, 27, 39
doctrine, 25, 79, 191, 245
Dowey, E. A., 159, 180, 185
Dulles, A., 12, 99
Dunne, J., 143
Dupré, L., 92, 155, 185, 189

Eaton, J., 239
Eliot, G., 197
empiricism, 35
Enlightenment, 20, 22, 42-43, 52, 151, 152, 155-57, 188
Epictetus, 108
ethics of belief, 10, 14
Euclid, 155
Evans, C. S., 12
Evans, D. D., 6
evidence, 10, 11, 13, 17, 18, 30, 152, 153, 158, 179, 236-38
evidentialism, 10, 160, 175
evil, 107, 110-12, 115
explanation and God, 18, 19, 24, 232, 235
expressivism, 65-66, 202
Ezekiel, 248

fact/value distinction, 35, 37-39
Faith: as an act of intellect, 151-54, 158, 164, 166, 168, 174; and authority, 120, 124-28, 214; and belief, 5-6, 10-11, 72, 73, 129, 162, 151-54, 158, 164, 166, 168, 174; in Christ, 70, 78-79, 94, 95, 100; and confession, 97, 100, 101, 103, 104, 172, 173, 244, 248; as discernment, 31, 76-77, 81; divine faith *(fides divina),* xi, 164, 243-44; as *ex auditu,* 90, 183; fecundity of, 242; historical, 13, 151; historical nature

267

INDEX

of, 25-27, 234-36; human *(fides humana)*, xi, 164, 165, 243, 244; in God, 243-49; implicit, 159; as knowledge, 99, 150, 152, 159, 160, 181; life of, 24, 81, 86, 186, 187, 238, 246-49; as openness *(disponibilité)*, xi, 68, 186, 215, 220-21; and opinion, 142, 166-68; personal nature of, 14, 25-33, 182, 232-42; and reason, 7, 8, 10, 13-16, 19, 20, 125-28, 187; as a spiritual concept, 231-42; as "thinking with assent," 12, 147, 167-72, 231-42, 245, 251; as trust *(fiducia)*, 72-76, 79, 81, 126, 150-51, 187, 242; unformed, 157, 159-60, 174, 178; as waiting, xi, 76-77, 81, 102, 103, 241; vs. works, 85, 151
Farrer, A., 236-39
Ferreira, J., 227
first and third person perspectives, 27-33, 59, 182, 205, 209, 210, 222
foundations, foundationalism, 33, 55, 175-77, 180, 187
friendship, 50, 219
Freud, S., 24, 226

Gadamer, H.-G., 28
Galileo, 20, 47
God, 4, 24, 44, 106, 117-18, 120, 121, 128, 135, 136, 143, 158, 166, 169, 172, 175, 187, 191, 207, 216, 220-23, 232, 237, 238, 240, 243, 245, 252
good, 61, 67, 68, 92, 115, 121, 128, 168-70, 173, 191, 193, 213, 220-22, 225, 229-32, 238-42.
grace, 83-85, 154, 155, 165
Green, G., 46

Hadot, P., 122, 252
Harrison, C., 129, 131
heart, 1-6, 187, 189
Hebrews, Letter to, xi, 78, 94, 100-104, 126, 173
Hegel, G. W. F., 28

Helm, P., 177, 178
Henry, P., 145
heteronomy, 65, 220
Hick, J., 115
Hill, E., 12
Hipparchia, 201-2
history, 47, 56, 222
Hobbes, T., 41, 54-56, 64
Hoitenga, D., 177
Holy Spirit, 81, 93, 160, 165, 183, 184
hope, 88, 102, 104, 160
Hume, D., 7-8, 11, 15-21, 27, 32-34, 52, 107-9, 116, 119, 216, 227, 232, 235

identity, 45, 87, 92, 93, 98-100, 103, 120, 116, 117, 223, 253
ideological argument, 114
illative sense, 31-32, 225
image of God, 106, 123, 137, 139, 143
imagination, xi, 46-47
"in Christ," 86-88
indifference of reason, 6, 14-16, 24, 189, 225
individualism, 52, 61, 63-66, 106
inner word, 130, 133, 137-47
interaction, 53, 61, 62, 175, 185, 186, 189, 231, 243, 245, 247
Isaiah, 4, 76-77, 106
itinerarium mentis ad Deum, 114, 122

Jaki, S., 251
James, H., 197, 202
James, W., 29
Jeffreys, D., 180
Jenkins, J., 163, 165, 171
Jesus Christ, xii, 15, 46, 77-103, 106, 130-32, 135, 137, 144, 182, 184-87, 218, 220, 234, 244, 246, 248
John, St., xi, xii, 70, 71, 77, 78, 94-100, 106, 120, 182, 190
Johnson, S., 251
Jones, J. R., 228-29
Jordan, M. D., 162
judgment, 30-32, 140, 227-30, 234

268

justice, 52, 131, 141, 142, 195-210
justification. *See* righteousness

Kant, I., 28, 42, 50, 63, 64, 191, 200-202, 205, 206, 214, 222
Kaufman, G., 180
Kenny, A., 226
Kerr, F., 202, 212
Kierkegaard, S. K., xiii, 3, 29, 33, 75, 160-61, 193
Klima, I., 158
knowledge, 120, 121, 127-28, 130, 145, 146, 150, 168, 176, 181, 182, 239, 251; Augustine on, 139-41; Calvin on, 181-82; of God, 3-5, 113, 114, 122, 124, 127, 127, 159, 160, 163, 164, 176, 179, 180, 182-87, 246-48, 253; Locke on, 9-10, 21, 33
Koester, H., 96
Kuhn, T., 35, 36

Laplace, S. P., 23
Law (divine), 80-83, 86, 186, 218
Leibniz, G. W., 22, 27, 115
Levinas, E., 217
liberalism, 52, 67, 68, 195-200, 202, 205
Lindars, B., 100
literature, 194-95, 200, 202
Lloyd, A. C., 145
Locke, J., x, 8-16, 18-19, 21, 22, 41, 52, 59, 60, 61, 67, 69, 106, 141, 216, 245, 252
Lockean-Humean picture, 7-24, 27, 30, 47
Louth, A., 27, 48
love, 12-13, 98, 122, 123, 129-32, 160, 171-72, 174, 198, 203, 207, 213
Lubac, H. de, 20, 44, 163
Luther, M., 79, 149-51, 185, 190-91

Machiavelli, N., 50
Manicheanism, 111, 125-27, 132, 142
Marcel, G., 154
Marion, J.-L., 15

Marshall, B., 163
Martyn, L., 80
Matthews, G., 116
mediation, 97, 100, 101
Melanchthon, P., 150
memory, 123, 139-41
metaphysics, 27, 109, 116
Milbank, J., 24, 46
miracles, 11, 12, 15, 16, 95-97
Mirandola, P. della, 49-50
mirror of nature, 33, 36, 38
Mooney, C., 75
moral frameworks, 39-40, 55, 59, 62, 211-12
moral reasoning, 53-56, 203, 234
Moses, 104
Murdoch, I., 42, 193-96, 202, 203, 223, 224, 230
mysticism, mystical, 92, 185, 186, 246

naturalism, 176
natural law, 60-61
natural theology, 155, 160-61, 175, 180
nature, 15, 20, 44, 65, 155, 163-65
neutrality of reason, 14-16
Newman, J. H., xi, xiii, 3, 30-33, 38, 128, 143, 164, 215-20, 222, 223, 225-31, 234-36, 241, 243, 245, 251
Newton, I., 22, 23, 28, 48, 64
Nicholas of Cusa, 191
Nietzsche, F., 24, 63, 207
Nussbaum, M., 195-203, 208, 211-13

obedience, 102, 186, 207
objectivity, 21, 38, 55
obligations, 205, 210, 216-19, 221-23, 226, 228
O'Connor, E. D., 77
O'Connor, W., 145
Old Testament, 71-77, 100, 102, 171
order, 50-51, 53, 66, 108, 112-18, 128
ordinary life, 51, 213
opinion, 166-68

269

INDEX

Paley, W., 27, 31
Pannenberg, W., 249
participation, xii, 86-94, 97, 98, 101, 102, 127, 146, 147, 165, 172, 173, 175, 184, 186, 187, 190, 195, 196, 213, 217, 225, 245, 246, 253
passions, xi, 2, 33, 230
Paul, St., xi, xii, 3, 42, 71, 77-95, 100, 106, 120, 126, 174, 190, 239
Penelhum, T., 157, 158
"perception of particulars," 194, 195, 197-200, 203, 208
Pelagians, Pelagianism, 185, 233
Phillips, D. Z., 16-18
philosophy, 34, 105, 199, 156, 157, 162, 178, 253; moral, 53, 56, 207; natural, 22-24, 28; political, 41, 53-56; of religion, 7, 11, 119
phronesis, 30, 46, 195, 199, 201, 229
physics, 21, 23
Pinsky, R., 202
Pitkin, B., 185
Placher, W., 24
Plantinga, A., 157, 158, 160, 175-80
Plato, xii, 50, 143, 203
Platonism, xii, 66, 101, 102, 106, 120, 121, 143, 146
Plotinus, 115, 142
Pojman, L., 10, 167
politics, 50, 195, 196, 199
positivism, 33-36, 39
practices of faith, 245
prayer, 27, 93, 204, 246, 247, 250
Price, H. H., 6
Protestantism, 149-52, 155-57
pseudo-Dionysius, 173
Putnam, H., 35, 37-39, 198, 202

Quine, W. V. O., 35

rationalism, 28, 64, 154, 212
Rawls, J., 61-62
reason, rationality, 2, 13, 31, 33, 39, 41, 53-55; criterial rationality, 33-37

Redondi, P., 48
Reformation, 150
Rengstorf, K., 95
ressentiment, 63, 207
resurrection, 78-81, 85-87, 92-93
revelation, xi, 95, 129-32, 143, 144, 153, 226, 251
righteousness, 82, 83, 86, 91, 138, 150, 183, 184, 191
rights, 205, 209-10, 218
Rogers, E., 163
Romanticism, 64-67
Rorty, R., 35, 200
Ross, J., 168, 176, 178
Rousseau, J. J., 63
Rowe, W., 18
Roy, O. du, 134, 143

sacraments, sacramental, 91, 97, 130, 187, 245-48
sanctification, 159
Sandel, M., 62
Sanders, E. P., 83, 86, 90
sapientia, 142. See also wisdom
Schiller, F., 64-65
Schliermacher, F., 28, 156
Scholasticism, scholastics, 23, 158, 188
Schnackenburg, R., 99
Schweitzer, A., 88
science, 20, 34, 36, 38, 39, 64, 155, 249, 250
scientia, 142, 143, 171
Scripture, 82, 131, 132, 180-82, 190, 243, 245. See also Bible
self, 41-43, 55, 63, 106, 107, 117, 120, 121, 141, 145, 215-17; inner self, 65, 66, 136, 193, 194, 216; moral self, x, 40-42, 93-95, 219-23, 230, 251
Sellars, W., 35
sensus divinitatis, 176-81, 183
Shelly, P. B., 49
Shepherd, V., 184, 186
sin, 80, 81
Smith, W. C., 56-57

social contract, 59-62
soul, 120, 132, 138, 142, 215-16, 220-23, 226
space: logical, 25, 161, 176; moral, 40-43, 45-48, 51, 52, 56, 63, 176, 213, 231; "Newtonian," 45-46, 59, 114
spectator's view, 24-25, 37, 39, 47
Stoics, Stoicism, 53, 108, 109, 191, 200, 201, 203, 205, 206
Strauss, L., 61
Stump, E., 168, 170
subjectivity, subjectivism, 29, 66, 155, 187, 234
suffering, 51, 112, 115
supernature, 20, 163-65

Tamburello, D., 185
Taylor, C., 39-41, 50, 51, 65, 66, 113, 114, 252
teleology, 23
theology, 21, 22, 25-26, 39, 156, 161, 162, 178, 249-51
Tillich, P., ix, x
Toulmin, S., 53
tradition, 210-11
tragedy, 213
transformation — moral and spiritual, 29, 32, 88, 124, 135, 138, 159, 160, 175, 182, 183, 213
Trinity, 139, 156, 161
Trollope, A., 224
truth, 6, 142, 151, 166, 167, 173

ultimate concern, ix-x
understanding, 4-5, 123, 135-41, 160, 168, 169
union with Christ, 183, 184, 186, 190
utilitarianism, 56-59

Vatican Council I, 154-55
Vatican Council II, 156
verification principle, 34-37
virtue, 121, 128, 142, 143, 146, 165, 166, 172-74
Vos, A., 156, 158, 177, 182

Walker, I., 78
Wallace, R. S., 185, 186
Walzer, M., 62
Warnock, M., 46
Weil, S., xiii, 117, 137, 203-13, 217, 218, 230, 232, 239-42, 245, 248, 250
will, 106-19, 122, 129, 139-41, 144, 166-71, 185, 227
Williams, A. N., 163
Winch, P., 62
Wisdo, D., 10, 15
wisdom, 90, 114, 130, 131, 142, 179. *See also sapientia*
Wittgenstein, L., 34-37, 69-71, 221, 232
Wolterstorff, N., 9, 10, 13, 177
Word (of God), 5, 95, 97, 106, 130, 133-38, 146, 147, 182-84, 214, 226